Hybrid Humour

Comedy
in Transcultural Perspectives

Edited by
Graeme Dunphy and Rainer Emig

Rodopi

Amsterdam - New York, NY 2010

Cover image: Morguefile.com

Cover design: Pier Post

Le papier sur lequel le présent ouvrage est imprimé remplit les prescriptions de "ISO 9706:1994, Information et documentation - Papier pour documents - Prescriptions pour la permanence".

The paper on which this book is printed meets the requirements of " ISO 9706:1994, Information and documentation - Paper for documents - Requirements for permanence".

Die Reihe „Internationale Forschungen zur Allgemeinen und Vergleichenden Literaturwissenschaft" wird ab dem Jahr 2005 gemeinsam von Editions Rodopi, Amsterdam – New York und dem Weidler Buchverlag, Berlin herausgegeben. Die Veröffentlichungen in deutscher Sprache erscheinen im Weidler Buchverlag, alle anderen bei Editions Rodopi.

From 2005 onward, the series „Internationale Forschungen zur Allgemeinen und Vergleichenden Literaturwissenschaft" will appear as a joint publication by Editions Rodopi, Amsterdam – New York and Weidler Buchverlag, Berlin. The German editions will be published by Weidler Buchverlag, all other publications by Editions Rodopi.

ISBN: 978-90-420-2823-4
E-Book ISBN: 978-90-420-2824-1
© Editions Rodopi B.V., Amsterdam - New York, NY 2010
Printed in The Netherlands

130

Internationale Forschungen zur
Allgemeinen und
Vergleichenden Literaturwissenschaft

In Verbindung mit

Norbert Bachleitner (Universität Wien), Dietrich Briesemeister (Friedrich Schiller-Universität Jena), Francis Claudon (Université Paris XII), Joachim Knape (Universität Tübingen), Klaus Ley (Johannes Gutenberg-Universität Mainz), John A. McCarthy (Vanderbilt University), Alfred Noe (Universität Wien), Manfred Pfister (Freie Universität Berlin), Sven H. Rossel (Universität Wien)

herausgegeben von

Alberto Martino
(Universität Wien)

Redaktion: Paul Ferstl und Rudolf Pölzer

Anschrift der Redaktion:
Institut für Vergleichende Literaturwissenschaft, Berggasse 11/5, A-1090 Wien

Table of Contents

Graeme Dunphy and Rainer Emig
Introduction   7

Alexander Wöll
Hybridity and Humour in Modern Polish Literature   37

Delia Chiaro
Laughing At or Laughing With? Italian Comic Stereotypes
Viewed From Within the Peripheral Group   65

Michiel van Kempen
Dutch Tulips in Unexpected Colours:
Humour in Dutch Migrant Writing: Kader Abdolah,
Sevtap Baycılı, Khalid Boudou, Edgar Cairo   85

Hédi Abdel-Jaouad
Beur Hybrid Humour   113

Graeme Dunphy
Cold Turkey: Domesticating and Demythologising
the Exotic in the German Satires of Şinasi Dikmen,
Muhsin Omurca and Django Asül   139

Rainer Emig
The Empire Tickles Back: Hybrid Humour (and Its Problems)
in Contemporary Asian-British Comedy   169

Notes on Contributors   191

Introduction

Graeme Dunphy and Rainer Emig

If laughter is the best medicine, it follows that painful experience often begets an incisive wit. The experience of exile and migration in twentieth-century Europe has been marked by feelings of displacement and insecurity not unlike those caused by more traditional, internal forms of alienation, by conflicts of interests and identities, by the often difficult co-existence of communities and the struggle for equality and recognition, and later also by a generation gap exacerbated by divergent cultural expectations. Among the many forms of expression which speak to and out of this situation, humour has become increasingly significant.

The aim of this collection of essays is to study diverse forms of "hybrid" humour, by cultural dissidents, migrants, and subsequent generations of ethnic minorities (the so-called second and third-generation migrants), in oral and written texts of various types. "Texts" may be taken to mean literature, oral performance, communicative art, film, the broadcasting media, and the internet. Comedy, a form which in itself embodies transgression, lends itself to the study of the culturally hybrid. In this context, hybridization (a process) or hybridity (a state) are to be understood as they are perceived in postcolonial theory. They are not simply amalgamations of existing cultural positions into homogenised new ones, but represent continuing exchanges and challenges, which substantially modify the positions from which they originate.

The European Union, which incorporates a diversity of historical experiences within a single framework, provides a useful geographical parameter for cross-border comparisons, allowing, as it does, a wealth of cultural contrast, yet with the common feature that economically dominant nations become hosts to migrants from cultures they have traditionally felt superior to. This volume will therefore focus mainly on the principal channels of mass immigration into Western European countries since the Second World War.

Migrant situations

Broadly speaking, recent large-scale immigration and the formation of new ethnic minorities in European countries have mostly resulted from two sociohistorical dynamics.[1] On the one hand there is the colonial displacement which arises when an imperial power -- Britain, France or the Netherlands -- maintains (or relinquishes) political control of the migrants' country of origin. Migration to the "imperial centre" can be analysed in terms of postcolonial discourse. On the other hand, there is the "guest worker" phenomenon in Germany, the Netherlands or Denmark, to which the categories of postcolonialism only very awkwardly apply. These two types of displacement context are historically quite distinct, but may nevertheless produce very similar kinds of migrant experience, and indeed, parallel kinds of humour. Alongside these there are a number of other significant classes of migrants. Refugees and asylum-seekers are at present possibly the most controversial. Others have a more privileged social status and a higher level of acceptability, such as employees placed in an overseas branch of their company or students taking advantage of educational opportunities in more distant parts of the "global village".

The term "economic migrant" is generally used in opposition to "asylum seeker" to indicate those who are not forced into emigration but leave home in the hope of improving their fortunes elsewhere. It is of course a loaded term, since for example an ambitious American promoted to a better position in the British branch of her company is unlikely to be described in such terms. Economic migrants come from poorer countries to take advantage of the easier access to wealth in western nations. Generally speaking, both colonial migrants and guest workers fall into this category. A typical pattern of economic migration involves the main earner of a family migrating in search of work and dependant relatives following, often several years later. Here we distinguish "primary immigration", that of the original migrant worker, from the "secondary immigration" of the family. Often primary immigration is intended by the migrants themselves as a short-term solution to economic pressures, and secondary migration becomes necessary when the period of residence becomes longer than anticipated. Even secondary immigration is frequently not envisaged as permanent, and many migrant families have found that it is only when the children have established themselves as adult

---

[1]   For recent literature on ethnic minorities and migration in Western Europe, see for example Peter Stalker, *The Work of Strangers: A Survey of International Labour Migration* (Geneva: International Labour Office, 1994); *Europe: A New Immigration Continent: Policies and Politics in Comparative Perspective*, ed. by Dietrich Thränhardt, 2nd edn (Münster: Lit Verlag, 1996); Emmanuel Todd, *Le destin des immigrés: Assimilation et ségrégation dans les démocraties occidentales* (Paris: Éditions du Seuil, 1994); Peter Stalker, *Workers without Frontiers: The Impact of Globalization on International Migration* (London and Boulder: Lynne Rienner Publishers, 2000).

members of the host community that the parents come to terms with the idea that they will possibly never return to their countries of origin.

Migrant communities differ from such indigenous ethnic groups as the speakers of Celtic languages in Britain, ethnic Germans in Alsace-Lorraine or the Danish population of Schleswig-Holstein, who were resident long before the boundaries of nation states defined them as minorities. Like these, migrants form structurally identifiable ethnic communities, but as newcomers their position is more precarious. When they first arrive they are seen as guests who should behave as such, and may be under pressure to integrate (put down roots in the host community) if not assimilate (become culturally invisible). Assimilation can involve a painful rejection of roots, but failure to assimilate carries the potential for conflict with the surrounding majority, particularly when religion or colour make the migrant group constantly conspicuous. The result is almost inevitably a hyphenated culture (Turkish-German, Arab-French, Black-British) which may privilege one part of the hybrid identity over the other (is it British-Asian or Asian-British?) and must justify its right to exist. The process of hybridisation may result in a confusion of identity or a personal rejection of one of the two cultural spheres, but it is also possible for migrants to merge their cultures into a personal cultural mélange and celebrate hybridity as their actual identity. The strategies for dealing with this are manifold, but there do seem to be certain constants. A comparison of the migrant situation in Britain, France, Germany and the Netherlands shows considerable variations in historical context, yet a number of underlying similarities.

Britain

Census data provides the best overview of the British situation.[2] The 1991 census was the first in Britain to ask questions about ethnicity, allowing a far clearer understanding of ethnic demographics than had hitherto been possible. The 2001 census refined this, for example by including a category "mixed ethnicity". The particular value of these figures is that they reflect how British residents themselves regard their own ethnicity. In 2001, 85% of

---

[2]   On ethnic minorities in the UK, see: *Culture, Identity and Politics: Ethnic Minorities in Britain*, ed. by Terence Ranger and others (Aldershot: Avebury, 1996); Onyekachi Wambu, *Empire Windrush: Fifty Years of Writing about Black Britain* (London: Gollancz, 1998); Heather Booth, *The Migration Process in Britain and West Germany: Two Demographic Studies of Migrant Populations* (Aldershot: Avebury, 1992); Nicola Piper, *Racism, Nationalism and Citizenship: Ethnic Minorities in Britain and Germany* (Aldershot: Ashgate, 1998); Catherine Lynette Innes, *A History of Black and Asian Writing in Britain* (Cambridge: Cambridge University Press, 2002). Also the publications of the Commission for Racial Equality.

the population of England and Wales gave their ethnic group as "White: British", which may be regarded as the traditional indigenous population. The ethnicity question in the census also included the categories "White: Irish" and "White: Other" (that is, white but neither British nor Irish). "White: Other" includes the significant and well-established Italian community as well as other EU citizens settled in the country as a result of the Union's open-borders policy ("free movement of labour, goods and services"). Some 4.63 million people in Britain, around 7.9% of the population, identified themselves as non-white, including those who described their ethnicity as "mixed". The majority of these are colonial migrants belonging to the three largest groups: Asians, Blacks and Chinese.

The largest ethnic minority in Britain, representing some 2.38 million people or about 4% of the British population, is the Asian community, that is, migrants who arrived mainly in the 1950s and 60s from India, Pakistan and Bangladesh. About two thirds of these are second-generation. In the British context, the word "Asians" specifically does not include migrants from either the "Middle East" (the Arab-Islamic world as far as Iran) or the "Far East" (China, Japan, South-East Asia). Some Indians lived in Britain during the period of the British Raj -- Gandhi is a notable example -- but large-scale migration from the subcontinent really began around the time of the British withdrawal from India (1947), triggered in part by the displacement of communities which resulted from the partition of the country, and it continued until primary immigration was inhibited by the 1962 Commonwealth Immigrants Act and the 1971 Immigration Act. A majority of British Asians are either Muslims or Sikhs.

There are about 1.19 million Black-British people (2% of the population); the census distinguished between "Black: African", "Black: Caribbean" and "Black: Other", and found that a little over half of Britain's blacks trace their origins from the Caribbean and the rest mostly from Africa. Unlike in the United States, there is no serious attempt in Britain to avoid the word "Black", nor any term equivalent to "African American". The Chinese population of Britain amounts to 0.24 million people, about 0.4% of the population. The majority trace their origins to Hong Kong or Singapore.

Most members of British ethnic minorities live in England: non-whites account for 9.1% of the English, 2.1% of the Welsh, 2.0% of the Scottish and only 0.7% of the Northern Irish population. The Asian community is concentrated particularly in London (especially Tower Hamlets, Newham, Brent and Southall), and in Birmingham, Bradford, Glasgow, Leicester and Manchester. Whereas Indians and Bangladeshis are more numerous in the Metropolitan area, with the Bangladeshis concentrated particularly in Inner London, Pakistanis are more likely to live in Northern and West Midland conurbations:

around 40% of Indians and 50% of Bangladeshis live in Greater London compared with less than 20% of the Pakistani community and around 12% of the overall British population. The concentration of the Black population in London is even greater: over 80% of the total Black-African population and nearly 60% of the Black-Caribbean population live in Greater London.

The census showed that the age profile in most ethnic minority communities is much younger than the profile for Britain as a whole, which means that they can be expected to grow both proportionately and absolutely over the coming decades. This tallies with data from the Department for Education and Skills, which reported in 2003 that 12.5% of all pupils in English schools are black or Asian. The Department expects the proportion to rise to 20% by 2010. In particular, people of mixed ethnicity are mostly young -- half of them are aged 15 or under -- reflecting perhaps the relatively recent upturn in the social acceptability of mixed marriages. According to the census 2% of all marriages in Britain today are interethnic.

France

France has the fastest-growing population of any country in the European Union today, and in part this is because it has known some of the most intensive and sustained immigration.[3] Like Britain, France has experienced inward migration above all in the context of the closing phase of its colonial history. The First French Colonial Empire, which was largely lost during the Napoleonic wars, focussed mainly on India, Quebec, Louisiana and the Caribbean; the Second French Colonial Empire, which was at its peak in the years between the two World Wars, included three North African possessions, Morocco, Algeria and Tunisia (collectively known as the Maghreb), large stretches of Sub-Saharan Africa -- perhaps most importantly Senegal and Niger -- and also Cambodia, Vietnam and parts of China, Lebanon and Syria, Madagascar, and many small islands around the world. All of these territories have to some extent left their mark on the ethnic mixture of modern France. There are Black-French populations connected to France's former West African and Caribbean possessions, and also a large Oriental community. However the colonial immigration in the twentieth century has been dominated above all by North Africans, particularly in the context of the French occupation and ultimate loss of Algeria. When Algerian independence was declared in 1962, roughly a tenth of the Algerian population were forced to flee to

---

[3]   On immigration in France, see: Klaus Manfrass, *Türken in der Bundesrepublik, Nordafrikaner in Frankreich: Ausländerproblematik im deutsch-französischen Vergleich* (Bonn and Berlin: Bouvier, 1991); M. Silverman, *Deconstructing the Nation: Immigration, Race and Citizenship in Modern France* (London: Routledge, 1992).

Metropolitan France, both Algerians of European or Jewish descent (*pieds-noirs*) and Muslim Algerians who had supported a French administration (*harkis*). Migration from the Maghreb continued throughout the subsequent decades, making people of Arab origin the largest of the new population groups in France today. Arab-French people are often called *Beurs*, originally a term of youth slang which has become almost standard -- to the extent that, while it was once italicised in newspapers, it is now no longer even emphasised.

The French census, unlike that in Britain, asks no question about ethnicity. However, the *Institut National de la Statistique et des Études Économiques* (INSEE), which organises the French census (since 2004 organised as a continuous rolling survey with annual reports) records the place of birth of all those resident in France, and extrapolating from this it is possible to discover that there are currently four million immigrants in France, of whom about a third have acquired French nationality. Perhaps a further ten million are children or grandchildren of immigrants, including *pieds-noirs* and other white migrant communities such as the significant groups of Italian and Portuguese migrants. This means that almost a quarter of the French population has some international migration experience in their family history in the course of the most recent three generations. Obviously, not all of these *français d'origine étrangère* are ethnic minorities in the British sense, but filtering out results for particular cultural communities can be difficult. While a statistical analysis of country of origin can easily be drawn from the census results in the case of foreign nationals (*étrangers*), the refusal of the establishment to deal with ethnicity as a demographic category means that naturalised minorities are for the most part invisible in French statistics, and the very high rate of naturalisation makes this a far greater problem for researchers than it is for example in Germany. However, some idea of the strength of the Arab-French population can be ascertained from statistics concerning religious affiliation. In 2003 it was estimated that between five and six million Muslims lived in France, of whom over a third trace their origins to Algeria, a quarter to Morocco and a tenth to Tunisia. This suggests that a North African Arab-Islamic cultural background is shared by over 3.5 million French residents, that is, at least 5.7% of the population.

Germany

The history of immigration into Germany in the second half of the twentieth century is dominated by the guest-worker programme, in German *Gastar-*

beiter.[4] Though this term has taken on a slightly negative connotation since the 1990s, it being perceived as disparaging to refer to a now permanently resident population of thirty years' standing as "guests", the word can still be used neutrally as a description of the historical context of migration. The post-war rebuilding of West Germany, which has been celebrated as an "economic miracle", required a greater labour force than the indigenous population could muster, so the Federal government actively advertised for foreign workers for labour-intensive manual jobs from Turkey, Italy, Yugoslavia, Greece and elsewhere, establishing a structured and official *Gastarbeiterprogramm* on the basis of inter-governmental contracts. The first such contract was signed with Italy in 1955, and by the early 1960s Turkish labourers had established themselves as the largest immigrant group. In September 1964 the millionth guest worker, a Portuguese carpenter, was solemnly presented with a moped when he arrived at the station in Cologne. However, unemployment problems in Germany resulting from an economic downturn in 1966 coincided with increased criticism of the policy of state-sponsored immigration, which led ultimately to the discontinuing of the scheme, and thus of large-scale primary migration, in 1973.

As the term "guest worker" implies, the foreign labourers who came to Germany on this scheme were intended by the authorities to be temporary visitors, and for the most part they understood themselves as such. Initially they were accommodated in spartan barracks and kept separate as far as possible from the German population. Many did indeed fulfil their plan to earn a tidy sum of money (by Turkish if not by German standards) and return home to set themselves up on the proceeds. However, as others became more settled, they were joined by their families, and so the guest communities gradually became permanent ethnic minorities. By the millennium, secondary migration had brought the number of foreigners resident in Germany as a result of the scheme to well over three million.

For Germany, we do not have the luxury of census results; in both Germany and the Netherlands, the regular census was discontinued in the 1980s because of a popular campaign of civil disobedience and criticism by the constitutional court of the data protection arrangements. However, the *Statistisches Bundesamt* (federal statistic office) processes information gathered by the local *Einwohnermeldeämter* (residency offices), which record every

---

[4]   On migration and the German guest worker situation, see: Booth; Manfrass; Piper; Elisabeth Lichtenberger, *Gastarbeiter: Leben in zwei Gesellschaften* (Vienna et al. Böhlau, 1984); *Ethnische Minderheiten in der Bundesrepublik Deutschland: Ein Lexikon*, ed. by Cornelia Schmalz-Jacobsen and Georg Hansen (Munich: Beck, 1995); Statistisches Bundesamt, *Strukturdaten und Integrationsindikatoren über die ausländische Bevölkerung in Deutschland* (Wiesbaden: Publications of the Statistisches Bundesamt, 2005).

change of address, and by the *Standesämter* (registry offices), which record births, deaths and marriages, and all of this information includes citizenship data. Thus a good picture of the population of resident aliens can be adduced. It should be noted, however, that as in France this data relates purely to nationality, not to ethnicity, and thus does not provide discrete information on immigrants who have adopted German citizenship. Figures for successful applications for naturalisation allow projections to be made, but data collected after naturalisation is no longer classified by country of origin, and thus estimates of the size of ethnic groups become progressively less accurate the more they become integrated.

In 2003 there were 7.3 million resident aliens in Germany, that is, 8.8% of the population. These break down into four roughly equal groups:

EU-citizens	1.8 million
Turks	1.8 million
Rest of Europe	2.2 million
Rest of world	1.5 million

Thus Turks are the largest single foreign nationality in Germany, followed by Italians and Greeks at 0.6 and 0.3 million respectively -- between them representing half of the total number of *EU-Ausländer*. Converting these figures into ethnicities, we may note that from 1992, the year in which the number of successful Turkish applications for German citizenship first rose above 5000, until 2003, some 0.6 million Turkish-Germans were naturalised. Allowing for the fact that their children will be born with German nationality, we may therefore assume that the number of German residents with Turkish ethnicity in 2003 was a little over 2.5 million, about 3% of the total population. We see then that traditional guest-worker countries are the source of about one half of all foreigners in Germany, but also that their overall numbers are not high in comparison with minorities in other European countries.

The Turks are by far the most visible ethnic minority in Germany. Not only do they form the largest single community, but they differ from the other guest-worker groups in that they are overwhelmingly Muslim and, particularly when they come from Southern Anatolia, they may look non-European. Thus even when they are well integrated they may attract hostility to the degree that, for example, a culturally acclimatised Italian would not. Other European minorities tend to attract less attention, though public irritation is occasionally heard at temporary visitors from Poland and Czechia conducting manual labour without official sanction. Refugees and asylum seekers, in total 1.1 million of them in 2003, are the subject of more controversial scrutiny especially from the political right, and a number of vicious attacks on asylum hostels in the early 1990s provoked international attention. Finally, one might mention that British, American and French forces are still stationed in Germany. While military personnel at these bases are not themselves included in German statistics, others associated with them may well be. It is interesting to note that, taking all categories of foreigners together, there is evidence that the alien population is becoming more settled: in 1992, 40% of foreigners living in Germany had been in the country for less than five years; by 2003 this figure had fallen to 26%, indicating a general stabilization.

A further complexity of recent German migration history is the *Aussiedler* (resettler) phenomenon. German policies of eastward expansion from early modern times onwards resulted in the presence of large German colonies throughout the Slavonic world. Under the *Bundesvertriebenengesetz* (federal exile law) of 1953, ethnic Germans resident in Eastern European countries have the right of abode in Germany and the right to German citizenship. During the Cold War years, however, emigration from Eastern Europe was difficult, and it was only with the introduction of the Soviet policy of *glasnost* in 1985 that significant numbers were able to take advantage of this right. What followed was a sudden wave of migration in the years 1987-92, over a third of a million people in 1989 alone. Those who came after 1992 are technically known as *Spätaussiedler*. Over the five decades to 2000, some 4.8 million *Aussiedler* were integrated into German society, the overwhelming majority of them -- 98% in the years 1997-2000 -- coming from the former Soviet Union. Many of these migrants came from Kazakhstan and other Caucasian CIS republics. German minorities in Poland and Rumania (Transylvania) also benefited from the scheme. Although in terms of both ethnicity and citizenship they are Germans and thus are not included in the statistics of foreign residents, these population groups are culturally quite distinct, do not necessarily speak German (only in 1997 was a basic language test made a qualification for *Aussiedler* status) and are often perceived by the German population as "Russians". A certain amount of ethnic humour can be drawn from the fact that this group of Germans may be less well integrated in Germany than the average Turk.

The Netherlands

The Netherlands are interesting as the only country under consideration here which has experienced both postcolonial immigration and the guest-worker programme.[5] Dutch imperial power was never as extensive as that of Britain or France, but in the Dutch Golden Age (the seventeenth century) a series of possessions were acquired, most importantly Indonesia, but also Sri Lanka, the Netherlands Antilles, Surinam, Guyana, parts of Malaysia, a coastal strip of Eastern Brazil and New Amsterdam (now New York). Imperial control of Indonesia continued until 1945, Surinam was Dutch until 1975, and the Antilles remain Dutch dependencies, though their status is subject to on-going renegotiation. Some 85% of the population of the Antilles are black. Like Britain, the Netherlands experienced an upsurge in immigration from colonies and former colonies in the immediate post-war years. Meanwhile the guest-worker programme was established parallel to that in Germany, but on a somewhat smaller scale: the term *gastarbeider* is a calque of the German word.

The *Centraal Bureau voor de Statistiek* defines an *allochtoon* (the official term often translated as "foreigner") as "a person living in the Netherlands of whom at least one parent was born abroad." One might note that by this definition the largest part of the Dutch royal family are *allochtonen*. The Bureau reports 3.1 million such people of foreign extraction living in the country in 2005 (19% of the population), of whom slightly over half belong to the first generation (themselves born outside the Netherlands), the rest to the second (one or both parents are immigrants). About a quarter of these originate in EU countries, mainly from Germany or Belgium; the largest groups from outwith the EU are, not surprisingly, either from the three major former Dutch colonies -- Indonesia, Surinam and the Dutch Antilles -- or from the two countries with which the Netherlands had the most productive guest-worker arrangements: Turkey and Morocco.

Indonesia	0.39 million
Surinam	0.33 million
Dutch Antilles	0.13 million
Turkey	0.39 million
Morocco	0.32 million

---

[5]   On ethnic minorities in the Netherlands, see: Saskia Voets, *Allochtonen in Nederland: De demografische ontwikkeling en samenstelling naar nationaliteit, geboorteland en geboorteland van de ouders* (The Hague: Stichting Nederlands Interdisciplinair Demografisch Instituut, 1989); *Integrating Immigrants in the Netherlands: Cultural versus Socio-Economic Integration*, ed. by Louk Hagendoorn, Justus Veenman and Wilma Vollebergh (Aldershot: Ashgate, 2003); Wasif Sadid, *Moslims in Nederland: Minderheden en religie in een multiculturele samenleving* (Alphen aan den Rijn : Samsom Stafleu, 1990); G. Blomsma, *Allochtonen en buitenlanders in de bouw* (Amsterdam: Economisch Instituut voor de Bouwnijverheid, 2003).

This definition of *allochtoon*, based as it is on family origins rather than citizenship, comes close to our concept of ethnic minorities. We may say, then, that ethnic minorities resulting from colonial migration represent about 5.2% of the Netherlands' population, those resulting from guest-worker contacts about 4.4%. The Bureau also provides figures on population according to nationality which show that two thirds of the people classed here as Turks and Moroccans are in fact Dutch citizens, while over 97% of those of Indonesian and Surinamese extraction have been naturalised.

Ethnic minorities in European comparison

One thing to emerge clearly from this brief survey of the migrant situations in the four countries is that the question of nationality figures very differently in each case. If we were to rank the four countries according to total immigration of all kinds expressed as a percentage of the total population, France would appear to have experienced the highest rates, followed by the Netherlands and Britain, with Germany having experienced the lowest rates, even if we include *Aussiedler* in the figures. The size of the non-white minorities is proportionately highest in the Netherlands, followed by Britain and France, with Germany again showing by far the smallest population of ethnic minorities. Yet if we look at the number of foreign nationals permanently resident, Germany has the highest figures, followed by Britain and France, with the Netherlands showing the lowest figures -- and this despite the fact that *Aussiedler* are listed as German citizens. This disparity is to be explained by the fact that Britain, France and the Netherlands have all been keen to naturalise their colonial or postcolonial migrants, while Germany has tended to make applications for citizenship difficult, especially for guest workers, whose naturalisation was until the mid-1980s seen as quite undesirable. Germany also has some of the most restrictive laws on dual citizenship, which for many immigrants is a stepping-stone to naturalisation. These distinctions become even more apparent in the second generation. France automatically grants citizenship to children born in the country, *les jeunes issus de l'immigration*, irrespective of the status of their parents. The principle of *ius soli*, or *le droit du sol*, is deeply entrenched in French constitutional thinking, despite the plaidoyers of the Le Pen party for a *droit du sang*. In Germany on the other hand, the incidence of children born to migrant families retaining their parents' citizenship is strikingly high, even when these second-generation migrants have established themselves in adult life as permanent residents who may be competent in no language other than German.

The relationship of majority to minority, the mechanisms by which they negotiate their relations, and hence the language which we use to describe this, are obviously conditioned in part by the prevailing political philosophy of the land of arrival, and this varies dramatically between countries under discussion here. The British and Dutch models, which are in many ways similar, result from an initial willingness at the point when colonies were being relinquished to "bring home" those colonials who did not wish to remain in the newly independent daughter states, including members of the indigenous populations who felt an attachment to the colonial centre. Thus both immigration and naturalisation were made very easy. As an apparent flood of "coloured people" (as they were called in politically-correct circles in the sixties) began to change the ethnic balance of inner cities, provoking for example Enoch Powell's remarks about repatriating "Commonwealth immigrants", the rules were tightened, but for smaller numbers migration remained a possibility, and British and Dutch citizenship were on offer after a relatively short period of legal residence. Moreover, official recognition of cultural diversity was given from the start, and today both the UK and the Netherlands boast of their pluralism. Public polity is to counter racism, which despite generally harmonious co-existence is still present in both countries at all levels of society, by the celebration of differences. Thus the terminology of "ethnic minorities" (Dutch: *etnische minderheden*) lies at the forefront of public discourse, ethnicity being understood as a subjective quality, as the choice a person would make when describing themselves in the census form. In Britain, inter-ethnic frictions are typically discussed under the label "race relations" (one thinks of the Brixton "race riots" of the early 1980s), though generally the term "ethnicity" has replaced "race" as the more acceptable term. One may see a distinction whereby "race" focuses on supposedly biological features and "ethnicity" on cultural distinctions, but in Britain, "Black" is both an ethnic and a racial signifier. The word "foreigner" and its Dutch equivalent *buitenlander* are reserved in correct usage for foreign nationals, though colloquially a person may be referred to loosely as "foreign" long after the paper-work is complete. As we have seen, however, Dutch does use the term *allochtoon*, which in colloquial speech is an intellectual-sounding synonym for *buitenlander*, as a technical term for a person of foreign extraction, and as such it is more an ethnic than a legal designation.

In France and Germany, on the other hand, there is a broad reluctance to speak of ethnicity in official contexts, though the reasons for this are quite different in the French and German situations. Academics and policy-makers in France conceptualize immigration quite differently from observers in Britain; the concept of an ethnic minority is seen as inherently Anglo-centric and incompatible with the Jacobin (French Republican) tradition, based as it is on the concept of the assimilation of diversity into a relatively homogenous notion of Frenchness. This goes back to the ideals of the French Revolution, which sought to overcome socio-cultural barriers, and is clearly related to the fact that there has also been less of a tradition of class-based analysis in France. Thus, postcolonial immigration has been welcomed, but in return a full assimilation was expected, with any elements of foreign culture being relegated to the private sphere. The terminology of *ethnie* is widely regarded as patronising, as though to acknowledge a person as Arab-French would be to belittle his Frenchness. Consequently, there is no institutional recognition of ethnic origin. Immigrants can be naturalised or they can remain *étrangers*, but there can be no institutional categories to differentiate ethnicity within the national community. Public polity therefore seeks to encourage immigrants to take French citizenship as quickly as possible, and expects from them a rapid adoption of a sense of French identity. This does not of course mean that all debate in France is marked a simplistic binary: *français* v. *étrangers*. It does mean that French thinking tends to be basically open to immigration, but has some difficulties with the idea of multiculturalism.

Germany differs from the other countries here in that post-war immigration was never connected to out-dated concepts of empire, and so there was never a nostalgic-affectionate sense of historical bonds between the migrants and the imperial centre. Guest workers were guests, and there was initially no desire to integrate them at all. Consequently, as in France, the official focus is on the passport question, but unlike in France, naturalisation is not made easy, and it is only since the mid-1990s that German Turks have begun to find access to citizenship in any numbers. In Germany, officialdom seldom speaks of *ethnische Minderheiten*, though academics are comfortable with this as a sociological term. The German word *Rasse* (like French *race*) is almost unusable because of its National Socialist connotations, and indeed the reaction against NS racial policies may go some way to explaining why the German discourse is concentrated on the question of nationality. Thus, the most usual terminology is *Ausländer* ("foreigners"), sometimes softened in left-wing parlance to *ausländische Mitbürger* ("foreign co-citizens"), which strictly speaking is an oxymoron. A near-synonym to *Ausländer* is *Fremde*, though semantically closer to "strangers, others, the unknown"; *Fremdenfeindlichkeit* is the usual German word for xenophobia.

In different ways, all four countries are involved in long-running debates about the implications of multi-culturalism. In Britain and the Netherlands, politicians of all the main parties accept the concept in principle, and it is left to controversial outsiders to question the equal status of minority cultures. The main focus of the debate lies in trying to identify what the British or Dutch identity now is, and what kind of unity can now be found in diversity. In France, by contrast, all major parties seem uneasy about the pluralist threat to French identity, and the debate revolves around the strategies for encouraging assimilation and thus a resolution of the problem. Only in Germany do we see a clear polarisation of politics on the specific question of pluralism: while the left wish to encourage the naturalisation of *ausländische Mitbürger* without pressing for assimilation, the right complains of the division of German society into *Parallelgesellschaften*, "parallel societies", and insists on the centrality of a German *Leitkultur*. The term *Leitkultur* was first coined by the Syrian-German political scientist Bassam Tibi in 1996 to mean the consensus of values shared by the different communities in Europe, the tolerant foundation on which a multicultural society could be built; in this original context it might be translated "cultural basis". However, in October 2000 the then CDU/CSU party chairman Friedrich Merz used the word in a sense almost antithetical to that of Tibi, referring to traditional German culture as the *deutsche Leitkultur* -- the "leading culture" of Germany -- to which foreigners must assimilate. This was an argument *against* multiculturalism.

The nature of multi-culturalism is a key question here. Often it is reduced to a culinary interchange, and indeed, there is no denying the degree to which Indian and Chinese food have come to dominate British popular culture, Indonesian restaurants almost monopolise the gastronomic scene in Amsterdam, while couscous and the *Döner kebab* have won the hearts even of the militant right-wing youth in France and Germany. On one level, these may indeed be, as Şinasi Dikmen jokingly suggested, a bridge.[6] Pop music has a similar potential. Meera Syal recently remarked that the most positive thing she had seen in recent years was a group of white teenagers dancing down the street singing "Young, Gifted and Black".[7] In the case of high-profile events like the Notting Hill Carnival, cultural diversity is unanimously acclaimed as an enrichment for the entire population. On such levels, pluralism is almost a commodity, it is non-threatening and it is a useful tool for conflict resolution. However, pluralism was more problematic when Arab girls wished to wear a traditional head-scarf in a French school, resulting in a vitriolic national debate which latterly has spilled over into Germany too, though there the ban on headwear only affects Turkish teachers. In Britain, the Blair government's policy of encouraging separate Muslim schooling was a source of acute controversy.

As racial prejudice has become socially more and more unacceptable, religious aspects of pluralism have increasingly become the focus of ethnic frictions, very much exacerbated by such occurrences as the London bombings of June 2005. The Netherlands have often been cited as the European role model for multi-culturalism, a society in which diversity is celebrated

---

6   See Graeme Dunphy's essay in the present volume.
7   Meera Syal speaking on BBC Radio 4's *Desert Island Discs* programme in June 2003.

and communities live harmoniously together. In particular, Amsterdam is famed for the degree to which different ethnic groups successfully co-exist. Under the surface, of course, the Netherlands too have their experience with racial intolerance and misunderstanding, but until 2004 this was seldom visible to outsiders. The murder of Theo Van Gogh in that year brought national and international attention to the potential which exists even in the Low Countries for interethnic conflict. Projections that some Dutch cities may soon have Islamic majorities may possibly test Dutch tolerance to an extent which has not yet been seen. For many whites, religion -- and in particular Islam -- is the point at which the celebration of cultural diversity becomes untenable. This may partly be because after the fall of Communism, western society found it convenient to paint Islam as the new oriental danger, not the first time that Middle Eastern religion has served such a function in the history of European mentality. Partly it reflects realistic concerns about fundamentalism and the status of women in some sections of the Muslim community. It is evident that many of the tensions currently being felt in all four countries can be seen as echoes of wider international disruptions caused by the post-9/11 conflict with fundamentalist Islam, though their reflex in the local press was certainly indicative of deeper strains within those particular societies.

In the search for models by which cultural diversity can be grasped, the tendency is frequently to reduce questions to simple binaries. We often speak of the majority and the minorities; in postcolonial theory favourite tags are dominating and dominated cultures, or, taking up the terminology of the guest worker affirmatively, we may use Rafik Schami's categories of guest and host cultures. This is where postcolonial theory has models to offer that may effectively be able to transcend the limitations of a thinking in binaries, but also enable us to understand critical articulations by migrant groups -- especially when they are made in the form of humour.

Hybridity

The term "hybridity", when used in a cultural context, owes its formulation to the postcolonial theorist Homi K. Bhabha. He developed it in order to critique earlier postcolonial concepts, especially that of "Orientalism", which was coined by Edward Said. Said's "Orientalism" is an extension of established theories of cultural self-images and ideas of Otherness and alterity that, ultimately, go back as far as sociological concepts of auto- and heterostereotypes, clichéd images of oneself or one's group and equally reified ideas of others. "Orientalism", in Said's formulation, described the totality of the

Western world's conceptualisation of "the Orient" as its Other -- and the concomitant ascriptions of certain character traits to "the Oriental".[8]

Bhabha did not wish to discredit this theory, but rather to release it from certain restrictive implications. These, for instance, suggested that the process of definition was a one-sided one in which the West defined the East, with the consequence that Said, perhaps against his intentions, assigned Europe an active role and relegated its Other(s) to a passive one. This, of course, continued the colonialist narrative of the West as explorer, discoverer, and creator in world history, and its Other(s), here the East, as the passive object of discovery, mapping, naming, definition, education, and exploitation.

Informed by poststructuralist theories and the deconstructive thinking developed by Jacques Derrida and others, Bhabha refused to invest in monolineal and monological concepts that unproblematically accept ontologies, that is histories of origins, and essences, which imply fixed and unchangeable positions. In line with deconstructive ideas, he moreover criticised the (according to Derrida) typically Western thinking in hierarchical binary oppositions, poles of opposites in which one occupies a position of inferiority in terms of value and/or power. In Said's formulation of "Orientalism", these would be East and West, with the West coming up trumps vis-à-vis the supposedly poorer, less developed, less mature East, a thinking that one can still trace in the problematic term "developing countries", which implies the idea of an inevitable teleological development whose goal can only be the standards and values of the West.

In Bhabha's more complex alternative model, identities are not inherent, and neither are they so stable as to simply impose identities on Others. On the contrary, they only emerge in the process of negation (this is one of the tenets of deconstructive thinking, that the negative, "not I", precedes any positive formulation of identity). Heterostereotypes are thus inseparable from autostereotypes and do not merely follow on from them. Identity enters a relation with others and thus ceases to be given, stable, and monolithic. Instead it becomes a process, a negotiation, and frequently suspended and even threatened. In relation to colonial encounters this means that the supposed colonisers might impose their political, educational, moral, and religious norms on the colonised. Yet the colonised's multiple "Othernesses" inevitably affect the norms and identities of the colonisers from the moment that Otherness is recognised (or even imagined) as such.

---

[8]   Bhabha's most condensed definition of hybridity is in Homi K. Bhabha, 'Signs Taken for Wonders: Questions of Ambivalence and Authority under a Tree outside Delhi, May 1817', in *The Location of Culture*, by Homi K. Bhabha, Routledge Classics, new edn (London and New York: Routledge, 2004), pp.145-174. Edward Said's seminal study is *Orientalism* (London: Routledge & Kegan Paul, 1978).

Britain is an excellent example of such an identity as negotiation. It only achieved its formulation as a world power through its Empire. Despite earlier acts of union, first with Wales, later with Scotland, it hardly makes sense to talk of a "Britain" before it had established its possessions overseas.[9] Contact with these exotic locations, their inhabitants, foods, customs and so forth proved decisive for a formulation of Britishness that, then, often conveniently suppressed any awareness that it owed its identity to an exchange rather than any essentially given qualities. Even dreams about an original "Englishness", such as the one frequently dreamed in the nineteenth century concerning supposed Anglo-Saxon roots that were tainted by the Normans after 1066, only worked by strategically ignoring complexity. It denied, for example, the fact that the Anglo-Saxons had themselves only entered the British Isles as settlers and invaders a few hundred years before the Normans, and had met a Celtic population there. These so-called Celts had in turn only arrived a few centuries before, displacing or assimilating even earlier inhabitants.

Identity, here cultural and national identity, is thus not merely based on interchange, but also on strategies of denial and fictionalisation. It is furthermore directly informed by desires that have very little to do with the search for any authentic or original "truth" about oneself, and much more with current needs.[10] Thus, Britain in the nineteenth century required an ideology to distance itself from the threat of a Napoleonic and post-Napoleonic France, and found it in the re-evaluation of now suddenly alien Normans (who had little to do with the French anyway, but were themselves descended from Scandinavian Vikings) versus now equally suddenly prototypically "English" Anglo-Saxons (who were in fact pagan Germanic invaders). Similar structures apply to France and the Netherlands, who were equally dependent on their overseas colonies for their developments into world powers from the seventeenth century onwards. To a lesser extent, it also applies to Italy. And even centralised France has had to work on a definition of *"la grande nation"* as a supposedly monolithic entity, something that was neither historically guaranteed -- as the multiple Medieval kingdoms within its present-day borders or joint-rule of parts of France and Britain by one king demonstrate. The case is a slightly different one for Germany, whose colonial ambitions hardly got off the ground before they were stopped by the First World War. Nonetheless, it might be correct to attribute colonial impetus even to Germany -- which replaced a political empire with ambitions to rule a cultural and intel-

---

[9] Cf. Linda Colley, *Britons: Forging the Nation, 1707-1837* (New Haven and London: Yale University Press, 1992).
[10] Cf. Rainer Emig, 'Introduction: Contemporary Anglo-German Relations', in *Stereotypes in Contemporary Anglo-German Relations*, ed. by Rainer Emig, Anglo-German Foundation Series (Basingstoke: Macmillan, 2000), pp.1-12.

lectual one through its philosophy, literature, music, education system, and engineering. The slogan *Vorsprung durch Technik*, advantage through technology, is still used in Britain to advertise German cars.

Colonial and (after the slow demise of empires in the twentieth century) postcolonial Europe, one could argue, needed much more elaborate means of dealing with internal ruptures and problems of origins and identities than its emergent nation states. On the one hand, the differences between individual European regions and even countries were significantly smaller than, for example, those between European, African, and Asian cultures. At the same time, the impact of these "exotic" cultures on Europe happened at a time when Europe was itself in the process of so-called "nation-building" with its attendant problems of forging identities. The relatedness of the two processes of colonial (dis-)identification and the emergence of national identities has only recently begun to be investigated.

But, to return to Bhabha, the process was by no means a unilateral one in which Britain, France, the Netherlands, Germany and other European countries dealt with the impact of their respective empires on their newly formulated cultural identities. The colonies quickly started asking about identities, too, and not only about their own, but also about the identity of the countries that had supposedly brought them culture, religion, and their political and education systems. What the novelist Salman Rushdie called "The Empire Writes Back" in fact started as soon as empires came into being. And it did not only write back from afar. As soon as colonies were established, not only its products were imported to the newly created "motherlands" (a paradoxical term -- especially for the colonised, but adopted by large numbers of them). Already in Elizabeth I's England, there were a significant number of black faces in London for instance, to the extent that public policy measures appeared to be called for. The first Indian restaurants opened in Britain in the second half of the nineteenth century. Colonial products became staples of the "motherland's" lifestyle, as the case of tea in British and sugar, coffee and cotton in all European cultures shows.

Yet people have more intricate ways of questioning cultural assumptions than tea and coffee (even though there were debates about the respective dangers of either of these substances, too). These can range from the supposedly docile and passive embodiment of colonial stereotypes -- in the shape of exotic exhibits at fun fairs or representations of stereotypical colonials in literature, on stage and later in films and on television. That this engagement with stereotypes of the Other is by no means over is shown in a number of essays in this volume. Yet even the stereotype can contain its own ruptures and complexities, as is shown, famously, in E.M. Forster's novel *A Passage to India*, where the supposed exotic and uncivilized "rapist" appears remarkably rational, civilized, and cultured compared to the hysterical representatives of the colonising power that accuses him. The supposed "take-over" by the colonised of characteristics that the hegemonic colonising power attributes (only) to itself is one of the aspects that particularly interested Homi Bhabha. He calls this process "mimicry" and insists that it is double edged in, on the one hand, confirming what is taken over as culturally potent, but, on the other hand, simultaneously challenging its power by the very fact that it can be successfully imitated -- imitated by those who are not supposed to have "natural" access to it.[11] In the case of the examples discussed in the essays of the present book, this mimicry extends from authorial and narrative positions via characters to genres of literature and the media. In the interplay of mimicry and stereotyping, in the adaptation to expectations all the way to assimilation, and in the contrary effects of transgression and parody, the location of the cultural products is analysed in the essays of this volume. All of them employ humour to do their work. This calls for a brief exploration of the structural similarities between hybridity and the comic.

Humour

Like hybridity, humour also rests on an exchange, usually between two positions, sometimes between three: the maker of a joke, its recipient, and its object. The object of the joke can be identical with the joke's producer and/or its recipient. Humour thus also functions in a precarious way as far as relationships and communities are concerned. It rests on difference (of positions, assumptions, and expectations), yet also on similarity. Otherwise jokes would not be understood as jokes and would end up as misunderstandings. In these respects, humour resembles hybridity structurally in its modification and transfer of positions.

Sigmund Freud is the first modern theorist of the joke. He views joking as the utterance of something otherwise repressed, that is as a symptom and an outlet of otherwise tabooed impulses. He thus puts joking on the same plane as slips of the tongue, dreams, but also lies (the famous "no" of the analysand).[12] His psychoanalytic interpretation of humour is undoubtedly intriguing, yet it ultimately fails to take into consideration the active production and the conscious use and interpretation of humour. All of the examples of a

[11] Homi K. Bhabha, 'Of Mimicry and Man: The Ambivalence of Colonial Discourse', in *The Location of Culture*, by Homi K. Bhabha, Routledge Classics, new edn (London and New York: Routledge, 2004), pp.121-131.

[12] Sigmund Freud, *Jokes and Their Relation to the Unconscious. The Standard Edition of the Complete Psychological Works*, trans. and ed. by James Strachey, 23 vols (1905; London: Hogarth Press, 1953), VIII, 3-236.

humorous engagement with hybridity analysed in the present volume use humour consciously and in controlled ways. Yet Freud's concept of the joke is in striking agreement with an influential position toward postcolonial utterances, Gayatri Spivak's influential essay 'Can the Subaltern Speak?', which questions the very possibility of making dialogic statements from a postcolonial position.[13] Her argument assumes that in order even to gain a position from which one can make such an utterance and on which it would be comprehensible, a subscription to the dominant hegemonic power of the coloniser is already required. This power manifests itself, for example, in the structures of the colonising language. It further encompasses ideological assumptions, such as the hierarchy of dominant colonising culture and subaltern colonised culture.

Any utterance, including the humorous one, would thus ultimately be condemned to impotence. It would in fact be a mere masquerade, along the lines of Freud's symptom, merely disguising existing power structures rather than questioning, subverting and unsettling them. This does not disqualify Spivak's model altogether, but it makes it pessimistic and disabling in its final consequences. What it downgrades is exactly that which is upheld by humorous postcolonial interventions: the power of language (or signs in their widest sense) to establish within existing narratives (such as "identities" or "histories") intermediate spaces for the articulation of something new. "Articulation" is indeed what ideological theory calls this process, and it posits it in a dynamic and potentially subversive relation with "representation" -- which can and does frequently happen from the outside and/or in hegemonic ways, as auto- and heterostereotypes, clichés and prejudices.[14]

Spivak's critical model of subaltern utterances is also not very different from another classic of humour theory, that proposed by the Russian formalist Mikhail Bakhtin. In his seminal study *Rabelais and His World*, he uses the late Medieval French writer François Rabelais as the starting point of a theory of the carnivalesque, which is both a theory of the function of humour in Western cultures and an assessment of the mechanisms of ideological dominance and dissidence. For Bakhtin, carnival is a temporary reversal of power structures, a kind of safety valve that permits cultural taboos a transient manifestation -- without however thereby undoing underlying structures of power permanently. In this respect, Bakhtin's concept of humour is analogous to Freud's notion of the joke as a temporary eruption of the unconscious into the

[13]   Gayatri Chakravorty Spivak, 'Can the Subaltern Speak?', in *Colonial Discourse and Postcolonial Theory: A Reader*, ed. by Patrick Williams and Laura Chrisman (Brighton: Harvester Wheatsheaf, 1994), pp.66-111.
[14]   Cf. Stuart Hall, 'Signification, Representation, Ideology: Althusser and the Poststructuralist Debates', *Critical Studies in Mass Communication*, 2 (1985), 91-114.

conscious and similar to Spivak's question of the possibility of subaltern utterances.

Yet Bakhtin also stresses an effect of the carnivalesque that exceeds the merely transient:

> This temporary suspension, both ideal and real, of hierarchical rank created during carnival time a special type of communication impossible in everyday life. This led to the creation of special forms of marketplace speech and gesture, frank and free, permitting no distance between those who came in contact with each other and liberating from norms of etiquette and decency imposed at other times.[15]

A little later, Bakhtin starts to differentiate what he initially (and somewhat misleadingly) calls "marketplace speech and gesture" into forms in which we can recognize the special communicative patterns of humour, also in its hybrid shape:

> A new type of communication always creates new forms of speech or a new meaning given to the old forms. For instance, when two persons establish friendly relations, the form of their verbal intercourse also changes abruptly; they address each other informally, abusive words are used affectionately, and mutual mockery is permitted.[16]

What makes Bakhtin's description useful for postcolonial material is not the problematic claim concerning new forms of speech, but the more complex variation of "new meaning given to old forms" in conjunction with its effect of establishing a bond between hitherto distant individuals, a bond that is acknowledged and cemented by mutual mockery.

Here we approach the communicative and ultimately cultural function of humour, something that is strategically ignored by Freud but highlighted by linguistic approaches to jokes.[17] For them, jokes are first and foremost linguistic performances that require the recognition of an existing code and then its variation all the way to the transgression and violation of existing rules and norms. At the same time, however, they also demand the flexibility of the recipient to comprehend the transgression and violation as merely playful, in fact as the shift or switch to yet another set of norms and rules. If this were not the case, a joke would misfire and simply end up as a misunderstanding or as meaningless. We all know how easily this can happen. In order to make

---

[15] Mikhail M. Bakhtin, *Rabelais and His World*, trans. by Hélène Iswolsky (Bloomington and Indianapolis: Indiana University Press, 1984), p.10.

[16] Ibid., p.16.

[17] For a comprehensive overview, see Salvatore Attardo, *Linguistic Theories of Humour* (New York: Mouton, 1994). See also Diana Boxer and Florencia Cortés-Conde, 'From Bonding to Biting: Conversational Joking and Identity Display', *Journal of Pragmatics*, 23 (1997), 275-295.

its jokes work, humorous material needs to master existing conventions passively (i.e. identify the potential for a joke, understand how the cliché works) and actively (i.e. be able to make a joke that is identifiable as one). Yet Spivak's question remains pertinent: is "mastery" not merely a form of submission to the dominance of the hegemonic model, a model that is already given both linguistically and ideologically?

Perhaps it makes sense to approach this tricky question from the other side of Bakhtin's equation. In his model (which is hierarchical as far as class structure is concerned, but surprisingly non-hierarchical in postulating an exceptional space for the joking encounter), there suddenly is "no distance between those who came in contact with each other", and, moreover, the effect of this sudden change is "liberating from norms of etiquette and decency imposed at other times." What happens to the supposedly hegemonic readership that enjoys hybrid humour? What happens to existing cultural structures, such as those of the media industry and their viewers, listeners, buyers, and advertisers, when they successfully appropriate hybrid material? Do they really remain unchanged, while the appropriated material becomes assimilated? What is at stake is a further instance of hybridisation, one that can be compared to translation, if translation is taken in its widest possible sense. In *Constructing Cultures: Essays on Literary Translation*, Susan Bassnett states that "by pretending that we know what translation is, namely an operation that involves transfer across a binary divide, we tie ourselves up with problems of originality and authenticity, of power and ownership, of dominance and subservience".[18] In his essay 'The Postcolonial and the Postmodern', Homi Bhabha goes one step further and argues:

> Culture as a strategy of survival is both transnational and translational. It is transnational because contemporary postcolonial discourses are rooted in specific histories of cultural displacement, whether they are the "middle passage" of slavery and indenture, the "voyage out" of the civilizing mission, the fraught accommodation of the Third World migration to the West after the Second World War, or the traffic of economic and political refugees within and outside the Third World. Culture is translational because such spatial histories of displacement -- now accompanied by the territorial ambitions of 'global' media technologies -- make the question of how culture signifies, or what is signified by *culture*, a rather complex issue.[19]

---

[18]   Susan Bassnett, *Constructing Cultures: Essays on Literary Translation* (Clevedon: Multilingual Matters, 1998), p.27.

[19]   Homi K. Bhabha, 'The Postcolonial and the Postmodern: The Question of Agency', in *The Location of Culture*, by Homi K. Bhabha, Routledge Classics, new edn (London and New York: Routledge, 2004), pp.245-282 (p.247).

Yet when does translation become travesty? In order to address this tricky issue, it helps to consult Homi Bhabha once again, this time his ideas on stereotypes and mimicry. On the structure of the stereotype, when viewed from a position which is structural, psychoanalytic, and postcolonial, he writes:

> The stereotype, then, as the primary point of subjectification in colonial discourse, for both colonizer and colonized, is the scene of a similar fantasy and defence -- the desire of an originality which is again threatened by the differences of race, colour and culture. [...] The stereotype is not a simplification because it is a false representation of a given reality. It is a simplification because it is an arrested, fixated form of representation that, in defying the play of difference (which the negation through the Other permits), constitutes a problem for the *representation* of the subject in significations of psychic and social relations.[20]

In other words, the stereotype results from a refusal to enter the simultaneously constructive and deconstructive process that is the translation of positions, in other words hybridity -- or perhaps more correctly hybridisation.

Hybrid humour -- and its problems: the perspectives of the essays in this volume

In the opening essay of this volume, Alexander Wöll takes us back to the origins of hybridity in the subversive mixing of supposedly "high" and "low" cultures. In his example of the modern Polish poet Miron Białoszewski he outlines how a strong cultural norm, here Polish Catholicism, can -- through humour -- enter a productive interchange with cultural and political ideas that actually counter its supposed monolithic power. The surrealism and comedy of many of Białoszewski's texts open up the possibility of hybridity *within* one culture and prove that diversity and change are inherent in every culture and not necessarily the product of cultural encounters. Yet they also inversely demonstrate that even the humorous violation of norms leads to outsider status -- here culturally and linguistically.

That, despite examples like Białoszewski's experimental poetry, entering a process of translation and hybridisation is rarely a free choice, that it is generally governed and restricted by individual and communal conditions, such as those of wealth, education, and primarily linguistic ability, is clear. Indeed, bilingualism, both when it is successful and when it fails, may be far more important as an element in migrant identity than postcolonial theorists

---

[20]   Homi K. Bhabha, 'The Other Question: Stereotype, Discrimination and the Discourse of Colonialism', in *The Location of Culture*, by Homi K. Bhabha, Routledge Classics, new edn (London and New York: Routledge, 2004), pp.94-120 (p.107).

have hitherto appreciated. What is also difficult, if not impossible to assess, are the individual subjective and personal elements in entering -- or refusing to enter -- the cultural translation processes that can lead to monolithic identities or pluralistic identities and societies. A great deal has been written about the migrant "crisis of identity", to the point where this can easily become a cliché itself. The psychology of human identity is extremely complex and it would be absurd to suggest that in the case of migrants it can be reduced to the simple dualism of two competing cultures.

Nevertheless, every migrant must make cultural choices, and this means either standing aloof from the host culture or assimilating to it, or more usually finding a middle way, a personal mix-and-match culture. This can be a very happy solution: some migrants indeed speak of their two cultures as overlapping circles, and describe how the two communities can meet in the intersection, but only the hybrid can move easily throughout the full diameter of both. For other people, the experience can be less happy: some find that the circles do not intersect, and describe how their attempt to locate themselves within both cultures results in a failure which leaves them belonging to neither group, the experience of "between". Interestingly enough, both success and failure can be expressed through humour.

The problems of hybridity continue in the second generation, which we might call the post-migrant generation. In some ways they are even more intense there. In the second essay in this volume, Delia Chiaro looks at the depiction of Italians in international advertising campaigns -- both by Italian and by multinational companies -- and especially at the reaction of Italian migrants in Britain and America to the depiction of stereotyped "Italianness". She starts by outlining the long history of Italian stereotypes (as noisy and disorganised cowards, Latin lovers who are eternally attached to their mother's apron strings, obsessed with food, or members of criminal organizations) and places them within established sociological paradigms such as in- and out-group stereotyping. She also points out critical reactions to such stereotyping. Her project continues with an empirical assessment based on a questionnaire distributed among members of (first- and second-generation) Italian migrants to the United States. These were confronted with television adverts featuring Italian stereotypes, commercials that are also broadcast in Europe: a commercial for Walls Cornetto, two versions of commercials for Goodfella's Pizza, and a further two for Bertolli Oil. The Italian migrant audience was then ask to rate the commercials according to the criteria "sad" or "funny", "entertaining" or "dull", "clever" or "stupid", "appealing" or "irritating", and "flattering" or "insulting". The results were surprising. They are used by Chiaro for a reassessment of preconceptions about active and passive, friendly and hostile positions of first- and second-generation migrants towards humorous and not so humorous depictions of themselves.

Michiel van Kempen shifts the focus to literature as a traditional form of expressing identities in his essay on humour in Dutch migrant writing. He assesses the works of Kader Abdolah, Sevtap Baycılı, Khalid Boudou, and Edgar Cairo through the lens of postcolonial theory for their engagement with the often problematic norms and values of liberalism and tolerance prevalent in the Netherlands at least until the 11 September acts of terrorism. Van Kempen shows how attitudes towards ethnic identities and positions concerning assimilation and adaptation change with successive generations of migrant Dutch writers, starting from the generation of the seventies and eighties, who came predominantly from the Dutch Caribbean, such as the Surinamese Leo H. Ferrier, Bea Vianen, Edgar Cairo, and Astrid Roemer and the Antilleans Frank Martinus Arion, Tip Marugg and Boeli van Leeuwen. In the eighties, they were joined by the Turkish writer Halil Gür who won several literary prizes.

Yet it was the generation of the nineties who managed to enter the literary mainstream. Books by Abdelkader Benali, Hafid Bouazza and others showed a new way of appropriating the Dutch language at a time when nearly all Dutch cities were transformed into multicultural locations and the art world also experienced similar changes. Writers like Kader Abdolah, Cynthia McLeod, Clark Accord, Mozes Isegawa, and Lulu Wang then found their place in Dutch literary circles, even when -- like the last two -- they did not even write in Dutch. Van Kempen's detailed assessments of the often grotesque black humour expressed in the works of especially Abdolah, Boudou, and Cairo shows in detail how attitudes towards linguistic and cultural positions change, and how this change is expressed through humour.

Hédi Abdel-Jaouad investigates Beur humour, starting from the term "Beur" itself. He finds that "Beur" is rooted not only in racial but also in linguistic hybridisation, a self-designation, often purposefully self-deprecating, that is an invention of necessity if not adversity. In an essay that encompasses "rock'n Raï" singer Karim and bands such as Carte de Séjour and Zebda, rap artist Ridan, comedian Rachida Khalil and her male counterpart Jamel Debbouze, he shows how stereotypical self-depiction is often a way to pre-empt the passive acceptance of negative, media-generated immigrant stereotypes. The essay continues with Franco-Algerian filmmaker Merzak Allouache who, in his recent films, has dealt with issues related to Beurs and their interaction -- or lack thereof -- with the culture of their parents in a serious but also humorous way. It further covers Beur literature in the shape of the writings of Azouz Begag. Abdel-Jaouad's comprehensive essay concludes with a look at the use of the new medium of cyber space for the articulation of minorities within the immigrant minority: gays, lesbians, and Judeo-Maghrebians.

Graeme Dunphy investigates the bourgeoning Turkish comedy scene in Germany, which manifests itself in a wide variety of media, from traditional literature via cartoons to stand-up comedy both in theatres and on television. In a discussion located in a wider ongoing debate on self-exoticism in German migrant literature, this essay looks at ways in which elements of the exotic can take life in humorous discourse.

Rainer Emig analyses the success of the recent British television comedy programme *Goodness Gracious Me*, the first successful attempt at television comedy with Asian themes, scriptwriters, and actors. He places it in the context of the increasing cultural visibility and impact of British citizens of Asian descent, but also in the framework of globalised media formats. In several detailed analyses of sketches from *Goodness Gracious Me*, he asks about the presentation and possible subversion of clichés, yet he also questions if the creation of a new "third space", as advocated in Bhabha's theories, is really possible in a programme relying heavily on stereotypes -- both of "Asianness" and "Britishness".

It would be more than arrogant to suggest that the spotlights thrown on the rich and continually evolving manifestations of dissident, migrant and post-migrant humour in Europe by the diverse approaches to hybrid humour in the present volume represent anything like a complete or even comprehensive view. The essays gathered here attempt to approach this dynamic cultural mode of expression from new angles. Questions we set out to ask included: How do hybridity and hybridization, cross-, inter-, bi-, and multiculturality manifest themselves in humour? What do dissidents and migrants laugh at? Are there fundamental features which are not culture-specific? Is the humour of the colonial migrant parallel to that of the guest worker? How does humour operate as a form of protest? Of passive resistance? Of self-assertion? Of reconciliation? As a safety-valve? As a means of accepting a situation or as a spur to change it? When laughter is against the "others", is there a clear distinction between "laughing at" and "laughing with"? Is this racism? ("Inverted" racism?) How does self-irony relate to this? Does laughing both at the minority (self) and the majority (the others) create a balance? Is migrant humour different in the first, second and third generation?

The present volume offers tentative answers to some of these questions and suggests directions for exploration of others. The field calls for further and continual research, and any position established will need to be reassessed, criticised and probably revised -- in line with the underlying concept of hybridisation. Recent tragic events, such as the first European suicide bombings in London, show us that concepts such as integration and assimilation continue to remain problematic and that ideals such as multiculturalism might be fictions rather than represent viable realities. Yet such tragic expressions of ethnic and religious plurality at odds with democratic notions of modern societies only heighten the urgency of investigating which models might be viable -- or at least more viable than what we have experienced so far. This is all the more pressing since migrant existences are unlikely to be restricted to people from so-called "developing countries" outside Europe. Globalisation and the challenges of shifting market- and workplaces are likely to turn even the supposedly settled "white" Europeans into migrants in the near future. The scenarios and challenges analysed in the essays in this volume might then come to resemble the realities of life for most people. Homi Bhabha's generalising statement that "all forms of culture are continually in a process of hybridity"[21] can thus be read as a kind of reassurance as well as a call for continual awareness, reflection and action.

Bibliography

Attardo, Salvatore, *Linguistic Theories of Humour* (New York: Mouton, 1994)

Bakhtin, Mikhail M., *Rabelais and His World*, trans. Hélène Iswolsky (Bloomington and Indianapolis: Indiana University Press, 1984)

Bassnett, Susan, *Constructing Cultures: Essays on Literary Translation* (Clevedon: Multilingual Matters, 1998)

Bhabha, Homi K., *The Location of Culture*, Routledge Classics, new edn, (London and New York: Routledge, 2004)

——., 'Of Mimicry and Man: The Ambivalence of Colonial Discourse', in *The Location of Culture*, by Homi K. Bhabha, Routledge Classics, new edn (London and New York: Routledge, 2004), pp.121-131.

——., 'Signs Taken for Wonders: Questions of Ambivalence and Authority under a Tree outside Delhi, May 1817', in *The Location of Culture*, by Homi K. Bhabha, Routledge Classics, new edn (London and New York: Routledge, 2004), pp.145-174.

——., 'The Other Question: Stereotype, Discrimination and the Discourse of Colonialism', in *The Location of Culture*, by Homi K. Bhabha, Routledge Classics, new edn (London and New York: Routledge, 2004), pp.94-120.

---

[21]   Jonathan Rutherford, 'The Third Space: Interview with Homi Bhabha', in *Identity: Community, Culture, Difference*, ed. by Jonathan Rutherford (London: Lawrence and Wishart, 1990), pp.207-221 (p.211).

Bhabha, Homi K., 'The Postcolonial and the Postmodern: The Question of Agency', in *The Location of Culture*, by Homi K. Bhabha, Routledge Classics, new edn (London and New York: Routledge, 2004), pp.245-282.

Blomsma, G., *Allochtonen en buitenlanders in de bouw* (Amsterdam: Economisch Instituut voor de Bouwnijverheid, 2003)

Booth, Heather, *The Migration Process in Britain and West Germany: Two Demographic Studies of Migrant Populations* (Avebury: Aldershot, 1992)

Boxer, Diana, and Florencia Cortés-Conde, 'From Bonding to Biting: Conversational Joking and Identity Display', *Journal of Pragmatics*, 23 (1997), 275-295.

Colley, Linda, *Britons: Forging the Nation, 1707-1837* (New Haven and London: Yale University Press, 1992)

Emig, Rainer, 'Introduction: Contemporary Anglo-German Relations', in *Stereotypes in Contemporary Anglo-German Relations*, ed. Rainer Emig, Anglo-German Foundation Series (Basingstoke: Macmillan, 2000) pp.1-12.

Freud, Sigmund, *Jokes and Their Relation to the Unconscious. The Standard Edition of the Complete Psychological Works*, trans. and ed. by James Strachey, 23 vols (1905; London: Hogarth Press, 1953), VIII, 3-236.

Hagendoorn, Louk and Justus Veenman and Wilma Vollebergh, eds, *Integrating Immigrants in the Netherlands: Cultural versus Socio-Economic Integration* (Aldershot: Ashgate, 2003)

Hall, Stuart, 'Signification, Representation, Ideology: Althusser and the Poststructuralist Debates', *Critical Studies in Mass Communication*, 2 (1985), 91-114.

Innes, Catherine Lynette, *A History of Black and Asian Writing in Britain* (Cambridge: Cambridge University Press, 2002)

Lichtenberger, Elisabeth, *Gastarbeiter: Leben in zwei Gesellschaften* (Vienna et al.: Böhlau, 1984)

Manfrass, Klaus, *Türken in der Bundesrepublik, Nordafrikaner in Frankreich: Ausländerproblematik im deutsch-französischen Vergleich* (Bonn and Berlin: Bouvier, 1991)

'Meera Syal', *Desert Island Discs*, BBC Radio 4, June 2003.

Piper, Nicola, *Racism, Nationalism and Citizenship: Ethnic Minorities in Britain and Germany* (Aldershot: Ashgate, 1998)

Ranger, Terence, and others, eds, *Culture, Identity and Politics: Ethnic Minorities in Britain* (Aldershot: Avebury, 1996)

Rutherford, Jonathan, 'The Third Space: Interview with Homi Bhabha', in *Identity: Community, Culture, Difference*, ed. by Jonathan Rutherford (London: Lawrence and Wishart, 1990), pp.207-221.

Sadid, Wasif, *Moslims in Nederland: Minderheden en religie in een multiculturele samenleving* (Alphen aan den Rijn: Samsom Stafleu, 1990)

Said, Edward, *Orientalism* (London: Routledge & Kegan Paul, 1978)

Schmalz-Jacobsen, Cornelia, and Georg Hansen, eds, *Ethnische Minderheiten in der Bundesrepublik Deutschland: Ein Lexikon* (Munich: Beck, 1995)

Silverman, M., *Deconstructing the Nation: Immigration, Race and Citizenship in Modern France* (London: Routledge, 1992)

Spivak, Gayatri Chakravorty, 'Can the Subaltern Speak?', in *Colonial Discourse and Postcolonial Theory: A Reader*, ed. by Patrick Williams and Laura Chrisman (Brighton: Harvester Wheatsheaf, 1994), pp.66-111.

Stalker, Peter, *The Work of Strangers: A Survey of International Labour Migration* (Geneva: International Labour Office, 1994)

———., *Workers without Frontiers: The Impact of Globalization on International Migration* (London and Boulder: Lynne Rienner Publishers, 2000)

Statistisches Bundesamt, *Strukturdaten und Integrationsindikatoren über die ausländische Bevölkerung in Deutschland* (Wiesbaden: Publications of the Statistisches Bundesamt, 2005)

Thränhardt, Dietrich, ed., *Europe: A New Immigration Continent: Policies and Politics in Comparative Perspective*, 2nd edn (Münster: Lit Verlag, 1996)

Todd, Emmanuel, *Le destin des immigrés : Assimilation et ségrégation dans les démocraties occidentales* (Paris: Éditions du Seuil, 1994)

Voets, Saskia, *Allochtonen in Nederland: De demografische ontwikkeling en samenstelling naar nationaliteit, geboorteland en geboorteland van de ouders* (The Hague: Stichting Nederlands Interdisciplinair Demografisch Instituut, 1989)

Wambu, Onyekachi, *Empire Windrush: Fifty Years of Writing about Black Britain* (London: Gollancz, 1998)

Hybridity and Humour in Modern Polish Literature

Alexander Wöll

The poetry of the Polish "New Wave" poet Miron Białoszewski represents a hybrid aesthetics that is close to Mikhail Bakhtin's original concept of an encounter of folk and official culture. This creates works that display ambivalence between seriousness, especially of religious references, and their subversion through imaginary and linguistic excess, which frequently leads to seemingly infantile or kitschy effects. By thus attacking important bases of Polish cultural identity through subversion, Białoszewski's hybrid humour can be interpreted as a critical reassessment of nationalism as well as a quasi-Formalist defamiliarisation of the expected role of poetry. The hierarchy of ordinary everyday objects and events and exceptional and "sacred" ones is strategically and critically reversed to unsettling effect.

The poetry of Miron Białoszewski is a unique phenomenon in Polish literature -- especially since in it humour and hybridity subvert national pathos. The author can best be consigned to the generation of the *Nowa Fala* (New Wave).[1] Many poems deriving from this movement from around 1970 onwards explored poetically the ways in which public language can influence and steer the people.[2] Białoszewski's poetry resembles that of Tadeusz Różewicz and the prose of Tadeusz Borowski, for all three of them are in search of a more authentic and poetic language.[3] If the term "hybrid", according to its Greek root, means something bundled, crossed-over or mixed, then this is an appropriate characterisation of the diverse stylistic elements and reference texts in this kind of poetry. Białoszewski himself is master of such hybrid phrases and word plays, although he sets great store by not following any particular literary direction. The only uncontroversial thing about him is the rather uninspiring division of his work into three phases: early (1956-

---

[1]   Its most important representatives are Ryszard Krynicki (*1943), Ewa Lipska (*1945), Julian Kornhauser (*1946), Adam Zagajewski (*1945) and Stanisław Barańczak (*1946). See Małgorzata Spychała, *Nowa fala* http://www.spychala.info/ar001/ms12.pdf (last accessed 23 August 2008).

[2]   The Polish avant-garde is most commonly divided into Futurism (Tytus Czyżewski, Bruno Jasieński, Stanisław Młodożeniec, Anatol Stern, Aleksander Wat), the Krakow Avant-garde (Tadeusz Peiper, Julian Przyboś, Jan Brzękowski, Jalu Kurek) and Late Modernism (Józef Czechowicz, Adam Ważyk). Białoszewski utilises elements from all of these groups, yet merges them in such a hybrid fashion that he cannot really be counted among any of them. See Bogdana Carpenter, *The Poetic Avant-garde in Poland, 1918-1939* (Seattle et al.: University of Washington Press, 1983).

[3]   See Madeline G. Levine, 'Fragments of Life: Miron Białoszewski's Poetic Vision', *The Slavic and East European Journal*, 20 (Spring 1976), 40-49.

1965), middle (1966-1977) and later work (1978-1983), even though he was known to Warsaw intellectuals even before his first publication in 1956 as an experimental playwright, director, actor and poet. Białoszewski's style hardly fits into the Polish literary tradition because his texts reject the pathos-laden patriotic co-option of literature in the service of national politics, breaking for example with the myth of Poland as a buffer for the West against the Asian hordes and replacing pathos with wit. In particular his book of reminiscences of the Warsaw uprising of 1944 (*Pamiętnik z powstania warszawskiego*, 1970) thus caused a scandal. He writes against the overwhelming romantic tradition of Polish literature with its military-messianic discourse.[4] He subversively undermines the harmonically and homogenously conceived Polish Catholic tradition of the sacrifice of Christ for the sins of the world by imbuing it with countless foreign words, idioms and images. Likewise, he introduces into high culture many elements of everyday culture, giving respectability to genres normally excluded from the literary canon, ranging from kitsch to children's prayers. At the same time he deliberately blurs generic boundaries, combining idiomatic phases to novel phrases and metaphors.

Białoszewski is thus in the strictest sense a hybrid author *par excellence*, although his themes are neither postcolonialism nor ethnic multiculturalism. There is probably no Polish writer of the 20th century who is more frank and comfortable about his own homosexuality; he plays with gender roles, slotting his hybrid third element into polarity of masculine and feminine. His characteristic way of playing with language mixes words and semantic fields, as the following programmatic short poem shows:[5]

mironczarnia
[Cykl: *Leżenia*/ Tomik: *Mylne wzruszenia*]

męczy się człowiek Miron męczy
znów jest zeń słów niepotraf
niepewny cozrobień
yeń

---

[4]   Maria Janion therefore places him in the tradition of Stanisław Brzozowski (and his critique of romantic visual art), of Tadeusz Peiper (and his critique of romantic rationalism) as well as of Witold Gombrowicz (and his critique of romantic collectivism). See Maria Janion, 'Wprowadzenie', in *Gorączka romantyczna* (Warsaw: PIW, 1975), p.19.

[5]   Miron Białoszewski, *Obroty rzeczy. Rachunek zaściankowy. Mylne wzruszenia. Było i było*, Utwory zebrane, 1 (Warsaw: Państwowy Instytut Wydawniczy, 1987), p.246. The translations of Białoszewski's poems in this article are by Rainer Emig and Graeme Dunphy.

(**Miron Torture**
[Cycle: *Lying down/* Volume: *Erroneous contact*]

This person Miron torments himself, torments
Yet again he cannot formulate his words
Unsure of what is to be done (or: what he has done)
Yen)

The first impression left by this poem is of a hybridization of word boundaries, semantic denotations and cultural levels. The title plays on Polish idioms: *czarna godzina* is for example the "hour (or time[s]) of crisis"; *czarny*
means "black, dark, gloomy"; a *męczarnia* is a pain, a torture or a torturer.
The neologism of the title, *mironczarnia*, thus smelts the "dark hour" and the
"torment" with the poet's forename, "Miron". This is developed in the first
line where, in the absence of punctuation, it is unclear whether the "person
Miron" torments himself or whether the "one" torments oneself (in a passive
sense) and also Miron (in an active sense) torments someone. The collocation
niepewny cozrobień ("unsure of what is to be done" or "what he has done")
links with the idiom *nie wiedzieć co zrobić* ("not knowing what one should
do") and is combined with *słów niepotraf* ("not finding words"). In Polish,
potrafić is an imperfective verb meaning "to be able, to understand, to
know", which is here negated in breach of the rules of orthography. The
Polish negative particle *nie* is always written separately from the verb, so that
niepotraf is actually a noun here (literally "yet again there is a non-
formulation of the words"). Thus the lyrical I is supposedly lacking in talent
and skill in combining words. Elżbieta Winkiecka regards this crucial strategy of linguistic hybridisation by the author in a metaphorical fashion (in
contrast to symbol, allegory, and irony) as "syllepsis" (Greek: "summary").
Its result is grammatically correct, though semantically nonsensical and as a
rule ironic, since an expression is used in which a literal and a metaphorical
meaning are made indistinguishable. Through this "contrary intertext" a specific form of linguistic joke is created by triggering at times the literal and at
others the non-literal interpretation, which as an end result merely permits an
illogical and therefore ironic meaning.[6] It is precisely these two distinct
frames that one can call the nucleus of Białoszewski's hybrid humour, since
there is an "idiotic" and usually religious inner frame that consists of firm
temporal, spatial and/or ethical boundaries. The little miracles (in the sense

---

[6]   Cf. Elżbieta Winiecka, *Białoszewski sylleptyczny* (Poznań: Wydawnictwo 'Poznańskie
     Studia Polonistyczne', 2006), pp.7ff. Compare also Michael Riffaterre, 'Syllepsis', *Critical
     Inquiry*, 6 (1980), 625-629; and Jacques Derrida, *La Dissémination* (Paris: Editions du Seuil,
     1972), p.249.

proposed by Todorov as "das Wunderbare/le merveilleux/the marvellous"[7]) that can happen inside such a secure frame make the educated reader smile, since he recognises the limitations as such and simply "knows better".[8]

The *yeń* at the end of the poem sounds like a gentle sigh underlining the message that someone does not know what he is doing. However, *yeń* rhymes with *leń* ("laziness"), suggesting also that for the moment someone cannot find the creative energy for his poetry. Also, the final word stands in an internal rhyme with the prepositional pronoun *zeń* (= *z niego* = "from him"). Ultimately the theme is literary creativity and inspiration, while both of these traditional topoi of poetry are also humorously challenged. What is characteristic of Białoszewski is the absence of a clear division between the lyrical subject and the physical author. The lyrical subject speaks of the author in the third person as "this person", but the title and the presence of the forename in the body lend this an autobiographical connotation.[9] This ironic distancing from himself as the author is consciously developed by Białoszewski into a characteristic feature of own work, marked more by the aesthetic beauty of the text than by semantic content, and more by playful punning than by reality. But it is not only the words and the levels of communication which are hybrid; so is the genre. Is the poem an epigram? A satire? A self-parody? Or an aphorism? Elements of all four mingle in a hybrid genre which defies categories. This hybridisation is programmatic for Białoszewski, and can be observed in the following central poem which implies a fundamental confession of the author's poetic creed:[10]

leżenia	(Lying down
[Cykl: *Leżenia*/ Tomik: *Mylne wzruszenia*]	[Cycle: *Lying down*/ Volume: *Erroneous contact*]
1	1
naprzeciw nocnych szpar	opposite nightly gaps
ciemno-ja	dark-me
mieszkanio-ja	dwelling-me
leżenio-ja	lying-me

[7]   Tsvetan Todorov, *The Fantastic: A Structural Approach to a Literary Genre* (Ithaca: Cornell University Press, 1975).

[8]   See Erving Goffman, *Frame Analysis: An Essay on the Organization of Experience* (New York: Harper & Row, 1974). See also Jacques Derrida, *The Truth in Painting*, trans. by Geoff Bennington and Ian McLeod (Chicago: University of Chicago Press, 1987).

[9]   See Richard Nycz, 'Tropy 'ja': Koncepcje podmiotowości w literaturze polskiej ostatniego stolecia', in Richard Nycz, *Język modernizmu: Prolegomena historycznoliterackie* (Wroclaw: Fundacja na Rzecz Nauki Polskiej, 1997), pp.85-116.

[10]   Białoszewski, *Obroty rzeczy*, pp.233-234.

2	2
leżenie	the Lying
w wydłużenie się	in the self-stretching
bez jednej poprzeczki złości która skraca	without a hurdle of irritation, which shortens
idzie się tylko na długość idzie się idzie	one only goes horizontally, goes and goes
puszcza się w dobrze sobie bycie	one sets out into well-being
nie kończy się	it never ends
3	3
kiedy leżę nie nadaję się do wstania	when I lie, I am not fit to stand up
leżenie zapuszcza korzenie	the lying sends down roots
nie wierzę w poruszenie się	I don't believe in moving
zawsze do wyrwania zielony	always green to getting up [setting off]
4	4
takie leżenie-myślenie jak ja lubię	such lying-thinking, the way I like it
to jest niedobre z natury	that is by nature not good
bo niech ja w naturze	for leave me in nature
tak sobie leżę-myślę	thus lying-thinking
to zaraz napadnie mnie coś i zje	and something will attack me and devour me at once
5	5
leżąc w łóżku chcę być dobrym	lying in bed I want to be good
przez sen rośnie dużo dobroci	in the dream much good grows
leżenie dobroć wygrzewa	lying warms the good
ale wstanie ją zawiewa	but getting up blows it away)

In this poem Białoszewski programmatically develops his entirely private *vita contemplativa* about a lyrical I which is endowed in all his texts with autobiographical references to the author.[11] Like this poem, which is shaped by a hypnotically repetitive rhythm and creates a "childlike" impression through its simple syntax, his entire oeuvre is for the most part stylised auto-biography and mystified diary, mixed with fictional elements.[12] In his micro-cosm of every-day in the bedroom the clear binaries of art and kitsch, of important and unimportant, of dream and reality are deliberately mixed, and thus superseded. For this reason, the author's texts have often been dismissed as "anti-poetics" and "anti-literature", when the conscious hybridity of this supposed anti-literaricity met with a lack of understanding on the part of the recipients.[13] The lyrical I in the poem perceives his own space as a kind of

---

[11]   See Julian Przyboś, 'Raj i śmierć' in *Zapiski bez daty* (Warsaw: PIW, 1979), p.307.
[12]   See Małgorzata Łukaszuk-Piekara, *'Niby ja': O poezji Białoszewskiego* (Lublin: Wydawnictwo Katolickiego Uniwersytetu Lubelskiego, 1997), p.22.
[13]   See the negative criticism quoted in Małgorzata Łukaszuk-Piekara, p.9.

theatre of objects,[14] a stage filled with things which cannot be understood and possessed by active movements but only passively in the muse of lying still. This passive contemplation with the naïve perspective of a child is celebrated liturgically by the lyrical I like a religious ritual almost to the point where the self is forgotten.[15] The self is lost completely in the peripheral existence of its surroundings. None of its experiences of the higher and lower spheres surrounding it are integrated systematically into any model; only the individual "nightly gaps" ("naprzeciw nocnych szpar") surround the self like four walls. The disconnected meditative experiments lead to no higher order, so that they seem random and of little importance. As the self does not distinguish the supposedly significant things from the useless, it dignifies all that is marginal.[16] The lying contemplation appears to be accumulative and intensifying, because the dreams link the concrete objects with memories. Separate memory spaces overlap and invade each other with no regularity, and become models of potential courses of action, so that in this hyperculturalisation of the lying daydream in the hyperspace of sign, form and image a defactification[17] takes place and existence is surrounded by arbitrary possibilities. The

---

[14]   Lyrical I and real author merge, for Białoszewski himself used to write lying down in his home and staged amateur performances for his friends there. See Anna Sobolewska, *Maksymalnie udana egzystencja: Szkice o życiu i twórczości Mirona Białoszewskiego* (Warsaw: Instytut Badań Literackich, 1997), pp.7ff.

[15]   Cf. Jerzy Wiśniewski, *Miron Białoszewski i muzyka* (Łódź: Wydawnictwo Uniwersytetu Łódzkiego, 2004), pp.36-39.

[16]   "*Ja* liryczne jego wierszy w zupełności bowiem sprowadza się do bytu peryferyjnego, to znaczy do przeżyć 'z niższych sfer', znajdujących się poza wzorami integracji. Białoszewski zapisuje doświadczenia byle jakie, nie włączających się w żaden wyższy porządek, rozproszone i mało znaczące. Nie usiłuje przy tym, co jest rzeczą bardzo znamienną, nobilitować owych marginaliów -- przez przypisywanie im jakichś 'oficjalnych' wartości lub przez chwyty poetyzacji. Przeciwnie: pozostawia je konsekwentnie we właściwym im rejestrze. [...] Autor 'leżeń' bowiem nie tylko ogranicza się do kręgu tematów peryferyjnych, ale -- co więcej -- usiłuje utrwalać je w specyficznym języku peryferyjnym. [...] Wypowiedziane w jakikolwiek inny sposób przestałyby po prostu być sobą. Wszelki przekaz odpowiadający wymaganiom jakiejś znormalizowanej konwencji porozumiewania się -- przenosiłby je automatycznie do 'wyższych sfer', klasyfikował i porządkował"; Janusz Sławiński, 'Czytamy wiersze: 'leżenia'. Interpretacje', *Tygodnik Kulturalny*, no. 21 (1967).

[17]   "Defactification" ought to be understood as a counter-term to Martin Heidegger's fundamentalist ontological terminology: "Bei Heidegger ist die 'Kultur' (wohlgemerkt ein Fremdwort) *als solche* negativ besetzt. Schon die Ausbreitung des Terminus 'Kultur' etwa in Form einer 'Kulturphilosophie', wäre ein Anzeichen des beginnenden Verfalls. Das Verstehen der fremdesten Kulturen und die "Synthese" dieser mit der eigenen' führt, so heißt es schon in 'Sein und Zeit', zur 'Entfremdung, in der sich ihm (sc. dem Dasein) das eigenste Seinkönnen verbirgt' (*Sein und Zeit*, S. 178). Die Hyperkultur, die das Dasein defaktifizierte, führte zu einer radikalen Entfremdung. Auch Heideggers Daseinsontologie ließe sich als der Versuch interpretieren, die Philosophie selbst zu re-faktifizieren, und zwar gegen jenes Denken, das 'ohne Mark, Knochen und Blut' (sic!) nur ein 'literarisches Dasein fristet' (see

expression "the lying sends down roots" ("leżenie zapuszcza korzenie") presumably comes close to what Gilles Deleuze and Félix Guattari have called rhizome, a root which has no selective memory and thus is diffuse:

> A rhizome, being the underground stem of a plant, is fundamentally different from large and small roots. Onions and bulbs are rhizomes. Plants with large or small roots can in quite a different sense be called rhizomorphic, and one might ask whether the rhizomatic is not precisely that which makes botany unique. [...] Every point on a rhizome can (and must) be connected with every other. This is quite different from a tree or a root, in which a point, an order, is laid down.[18]

In the contemplation of the lying self, transitions form between the margins (the "nightly gaps") and the centre (the awareness of the "lying-I"), between the moments of concentration and the renewed diffusion. The "standing up" at the end would draw the rational boundaries of the things and of the self (internality, memory) back into the consciousness and thus paradoxically let all the links and interconnections of the imaginary hyperspace "fall back".

Białoszewski develops similar images of active interference and passive "letting fall back" in other poems, such as the following "Water Ode":[19]

A oto garść mowy wiązanej prez BABĘ Z MOSTU z okresu zawichostu	(And here a handful of bound verse of the WOMAN FROM A BRIDGE from the Zawichost era
Oda do wody (Wodooda) [Cykl: *Rozkurz* / Tomik: *Kabaret Kici Koci*]	**Ode to the water (Water Ode)** [Cycle: Whirling up / Volume: *Kabaret Kici Koci*]
Co woda ujmie, to doda. Wody mi zawsze szkoda. Nie tej zawziętej, ujętej, Ale nasłanej, dodanej.	What the water takes away, it also adds. I always feel sad for the water. Not about the unyielding, the captured, But about the dispatched, the added.)

Martin Heidegger, *Die Grundbegriffe der Metaphysik: Welt-Endlichkeit-Einsamkeit*, Gesamtausgabe, vol. 29/30, Frankfurt am Main: Klostermann, 1983, p.16 and 121)." Quoted from Byung-Chul Han, *Hyperkulturalität: Kultur und Globalisierung* (Berlin: Merve, 2005), p.76. See also my analysis of foreign languages and cultures in other poems by Białoszewski (especially *Merry-go-round with Madonnas* [*Karuzela z Madonnami*]) in 'Myths and Democratic Attitudes in Poland and Russia: An Intermedial Comparison', in *Democracy and Myth in Russia and Eastern Europe*, ed. by Alexander Wöll and Harald Wydra (London: Routledge, 2007), pp.141-165 (pp.143-146).

[18] Gilles Deleuze and Félix Guattari, *Tausend Plateaus: Kapitalismus und Schizophrenie*, trans. by Gabriele Ricke and Ronald Voullie (Orig. 1980; Berlin: Merve, 1992), p.16.

[19] Miron Białoszewski, *Rozkurz*, Utwory zebrane, 8 (Warsaw: Państwowy Instytut Wydawniczy, 1998), p.268.

The city of Zawichost stands on the Weichsel between Kraków and Lublin. In the subtitle the poem is called an "ode". The genre requires a high linguistic register and a hymn to something splendid. Indeed a battle between the grand duke Roman Mstislawitsch, who had founded the dukedom of Halytsch-Wolodymyr and captured Kiev, and the Polish duke Leszek, to whom he owed the Dukedom of Halytsch, took place in Zawichost. Roman indeed died in this battle in 1205.[20] This "Zawichost episode" therefore offers scope for an ode, yet instead, a simple village woman on a bridge is depicted. The superscript also suggests that the poem is a florilegium, composed in "bound speech" (verse) like an aesthetic bunch of flowers. Rhythmically the text is a short four-liner (*czterowiersz*), while the ode is a long poem in stanzas. The expectations raised by the title are thus not fulfilled. What follows is no ode in elevated, pathos-laden language; instead the four-liner becomes a travesty of the genre. The poem also revolves around the Polish word *wodolejstwo* ("chatter"). The poem neither depicts a concrete object in nature nor a unique situation or occurrence. The "dispatched" water symbolises on an abstract level the historical changes in the world, which do not have any particularly tragic effects on the circulation of water. The water becomes an image for passive filling and active draining away. The reader might assume that the old woman perhaps scoops the water into a bucket and works with it; the space left in the river where the water was removed is immediately filled by other water. On a far more abstract level, however, the theme appears to be the eternal cycle of nature. Everything that suddenly is no longer there must be refilled, against its will. "Feeling sad" ("szkoda") thus expresses not the loss but the replenishment, the filling of the old space with new water. This is also the motto of the volume from which the poem has been taken. The Polish word *rozkurz* has associations of a swirling up and spreading of dust, which had been covering objects and thus obscured the ancient beauty. Here the replacement of old with new is connected with a refreshing of the perception, which in the last analysis remains hybrid through and through. Quite in the spirit of the Russian formalists, water and

---

[20]   In this respect the ode is linked with the secular medieval Polish tradition: "Reports about the medieval secular songs in Poland date back as far as the beginning of the 15th century. Jan Długosz († 1480, the chronist of the Jagiellonic epoche [sic!]) makes note about two historical songs that were sung by the people of his time: on the death of prince Roman at Zawichost (1205) and on Ludgarda, the wife of prince Przemysław who had been strangled upon the order of her husband (1283). From numerous synodes on which all customs in connection with heathen cultic actions were banned and from Latin homilies we know the incipits of the folksongs that had accompanied the then banned practices: 'Miły miłą miłuje' ('The lover loving his beloved', ca. 1390), Nie wybiraj junochu oczyma (ca. 1460), etc.'"; Monika Fahrnberger, 'On Homophonic Secular Music of the Middle Ages', http://www.completorium.republika.pl/e_homop2.htm (last accessed 12 August 2008).

paper, two conventionally irreconcilable elements for the writer, are also the images with which the following poetic "narrative" echoes the "Water Ode":[21]

Opowieść Lu. He. [Tomik: *Było i było*]	(A Tale of Lu[dvik] He[ring] [From the slim volume: *It used to be and it used to be*]
dawno, dawno, na Spokojnej zapchało się w ubikacji, zawołali rzeczoznawcę, zbadał, orzekł: -- za dużo papieru! za mało wody! za dużo papieru! za mało wody!	A long, long time ago, in Spokojna Street[22] the toilet was blocked, a specialist was called, examined it, and declared: -- too much paper! too little water too much paper too little water
-- a co robić?	-- and what can one do?
-- mniej papieru! więcej wody! mniej papieru! więcej wody!	-- less paper! more water! less paper! more water!)

The poem seems to present a short dramatic dialogue in the style of a burlesque and makes fun of the all-knowing expert, behind whose masquerade the literary critic can be discerned, while the occupant of the house spends his time with ink and paper as a writer. It is a crude caricature of the institutionalised literary business, a mixture of clowning and farce that is deliberately "anti-poetic" and childlike. While this second water poem tends towards nonsense, the first ode contains a statement that parallels the motto of the entire volume of poems from which the text derives. In the same way that water expands, replaces and refills, the Polish word *rozkurz*[23] is associated with whirling up or raising dust -- dust that has settled on things and hides their old beauty. Here the replacing of the old by the new is connected with a freshening of perception, yet one that remains hybrid through and through. Quite in the way proposed by the Russian Formalists, a new way of seeing in literature has filled the old space with new water, which thereby no longer remains the old space. The paradox of this poetics lies in the fact that its sources are in popular culture, yet it nonetheless requires an elite and edu-

---

[21] Białoszewski, *Obroty rzecz*, p.336.
[22] Literally, "Complacency Street" or, more liberally translated, "in the quiet street".
[23] Białoszewski, *Rozkurz*.

cated reader who understands its unusual transformations of folk culture and appreciates the humour of the texts.[24]

This new look of a historically educated reader at the tradition is also required for the interpretation of the following poem:[25]

Tryptyk pionowy
[Cykl: *Ballady peryferyjne* / Tomik: *Obroty rzeczy*]

Sny, moje sny!
Jak dzwon -- ten próg.
Patyki cienia wiszą.
Brązowo gładzi,
szaro kłuje,
a pod palcami
    rąk i nóg
tak samo --
    mnie
      czy im
kurzą się pnie
    piszczały
      krosna
    dziurami melodyjnymi:

1
W dole -- w dole -- z góry na dół
Cecylia gra na maglu,
kufry, klaty przesuwa,
drewniane zęby -- jej męczeństwo -- --

(The vertical Triptych
[Cycle: *Peripheral Ballads* / Volume: *Changing things*]

Dreams, my dreams!
Like a bell -- this threshold.
The branches of the shadow hang.
Brown smoothes,
Gray pricks,
and under the fingers
    of the hands and the toes of the feet
all the same --
    to me
      or them
the tree stumps dust
    squeaked
      the weaving loom
    through the melodic holes:

1
In the deep -- in the deep -- from top to bottom
Cecilia plays on the washing mangle,
She pushes suitcase-gadgets, cages,

---

[24] This corresponds to a wave of modern children's literature in the early Soviet Union. Authors like Korney Ivanovich Chukovsky, Samuil Yakovlevich Marshak, Daniil Kharms, Vladimir Vladimirovich Mayakovsky, Osip Emilyevich Mandelstam or Boris Leonidovich Pasternak followed the aim of writing literature for the non-aristocratic part of the population that would nonetheless uphold the demands of those educated enough to appreciate literature: "Chukovskii learned that small children tend to transform harsh sounds into more mellifluous ones, which at the same time are usually easier to pronounce; recall the phenomenon he labelled *èkikiki*. A great part of childish non-sense talk or trans-sense language (*zaum*), as distinct from adult *zaum*, is not intentional nonsense but simple sound reorganization with no semantic distortion intended. This is not to imply that meaningful content is invariably essential in children's poetry. Sometimes just the opposite is true. Pure sound can play an important role. [...] Many poems can be classified under the purely aesthetic function -- poems that do not preach, nor ostensibly teach, but exist for pure, simple pleasure. Into this category fall numerous rhymes of folk origin and the more recent nonsense verse of Edward Lear, Lewis Caroll, T.S. Eliot, Dr. Seuse, and of course Chukovskii, to name just a few of the most outstanding examples"; Elena Sokol, *Russian Poetry for Children* (Knoxville: The University of Tennessee Press 1984), pp.20, 22.

[25] Białoszewski, *Obroty rzeczy*, pp.52-53.

święta Cecylia w politurach,
koło -- manuał -- emmanuel
wał -- interwał -- fuga.

wooden teeth -- her martyrdom -- --
St. Cecilia in the French polish,
(Mangle)Wheel -- manual -- Emmanuel
(Metal)Roller -- interval -- fugue.

2
A ta Dorota -- nosicielka,
a kosze jak skóra chleba,
w koszach węgle, na węglach drzewa,
schody w pręgach,
        sęki na plecach -- --
wysoka droga omdlewa.

2
And this Dorothy -- a carrier,
and the baskets like bread crust,
coal in baskets, wood on the coal,
weals on the steps
        knotholes on her back -- --
the high path makes her faint.

3
U góry -- szare szare sznury,
u góry święta Weronika,
rozpięte ręce w strych -- i w strych -- --
w płachtach bielizny mokra twarz
wysycha i ucicha...

3
And up -- grey, grey strings,
and at the top St Veronica,
hands stretched towards the attic -- and into
    the attic -- --
in the washing cloths a wet face
dries out and becomes silent...

...Taki śnie mój! Stary sprzęcie,
w koronce korzenie masz i czub.
Na zawiasach dzwon się kręci
na zamknięcie
                snu.

...Thus my dream! Old device,
In the pattern of the roots you also have a
    tuft of hair
in the hinges a bell turns
to close
                the dream.)

By definition, a triptych (from Greek *triptychos*, "in three parts") is a work of art on three boards, one fixed and two attached to it with hinges allowing it to be closed. The form is typical of gothic altarpieces, and there is generally an inner, often encoded relationship between the three representations. Bia-łoszewski's tryptich is vertical, so that the hinged wings must be imagined folding out above and below. The semantic narration of an event opens at the beginning of the poem and closes at the end, like in a triptych. The author uses the words "open" and "close" ("na zamknięcie" in the second last line) in a transferred meaning: the unnumbered strophe at the beginning ends with a colon and thus opens the triptych; the last strophe, which begins with three dots, closes it. The three strophes in the middle section of the poem form the central picture of the triptych, which must be laid out graphically from top to bottom. It describes a large house in three parts from bottom to top. The first part depicts the basement or ground floor, the second the stairs, the third part the events in the attic beneath the roof, where traditionally in old houses the washing is hung out to dry. Squeaking doors form a framework for this visual image. The motif of the threshold, the hinges, and the doorway come from the unnumbered parts of the poem. The squeaking movements of threshold and hinges are linked to the musical movement of the bells.

The content of the triptych is the hard and painful daily physical work of the women: turning the mangle (Cecilia)[26], carrying wood and coal upstairs (Dorothy)[27] and hanging up the wet washing (Veronica).[28] This scenery is couched less in socialist concepts of a class struggle than in ironic humour. Instead of her familiar organ, Cecilia has to operate the mangle. Dorothy carries coal and wood in place of flowers and fruit. As well as holding the

---

[26] The reader must know the classical attributes of these three saints in order to understand the poem correctly: St Cecilia is the patron saint of music. In the Catholic tradition she was a martyr who was murdered in the Roman district of Trastevere (West of the Tiber, a few kilometres south of the Vatican). Legend has it that she converted many people to Christianity, for which reason the Roman prefect Almachius had her put in a bath of boiling water. However the hot water could not harm her. When the executioner then tried to behead her, he was unable to decapitate the "stubborn" saint. She lived another three days and distributed her riches among the poor. Cecilia was one of the most popular saints, and her name became a common girl's name. Cecilia is known as a helper in distress and as patron of church music. She owes this role to a translation error, according to which she is supposed to have played the organ at her own wedding. Another legend tells of the wedding feast: while music was played, she sang -- in her heart and only for God: "Lord, let my heart and body remain pure, so that I do not get harmed." She is addressed in the first prayer of the Eucharist. See http://www.heiligenlexikon.de/BiographienC/Caecilia.html (last accessed 5 June 2008).

[27] St Dorothy is the Catholic patron of gardeners, flower sellers and newlyweds. According to her legendary biography she was born around 290 in Caesarea as daughter of Christian parents, and was to marry the heathen governor Apricius. She rejected him, and for this she was tortured. The first sufferings with boiling oil could not harm her: she emerged from the cauldron "as if anointed with a rich balm". After renewed threats, she was locked for nine days and nights without food in a dark prison, from which however she came forth more beautiful than ever. Then she was condemned to beheading. On the way to the place of execution, Dorothy spoke repeatedly the name of her bridegroom Jesus. When the heathen lawyer Theophilus, who was standing by the road, heard this, he declared mockingly that he too would believe in Jesus if she brought him fruit and flowers from the garden of her fiancé. At this, an angel appeared with a basket full of flowers and fruit. Theophilus was converted and openly proclaimed Jesus Christ. This made the governor so angry that he had Theophilus beheaded along with Dorothy. See http://www.heiligenlexikon.de/BiographienD/Dorothea.html (last accessed 5 June 2008).

[28] The legend of St Veronica recalls how she told the messengers of the sick emperor Tiberius that Jesus had once asked her to keep his image on a cloth, because she could not follow him from place to place. She passed him the cloth and received it back with his countenance emblazoned upon it. (The legendary etymology derives her name from Latin *verus* and Greek *eikon*, "true image".) Tiberius was healed thanks to the cloth. The legend of Veronica took its final form in the 15th century. According to this version, she was one of the holy women who lamented Christ on his way to Golgotha. When she wiped the sweat from Jesus' brow, she found his features permanently marked on it. She is patron of priests' housekeepers, of washerwomen, seamstresses, and all who weave or trade in linen. See http://www.heiligenlexikon.de/BiographienV/Veronika.html (last accessed 5 June 2008).

veil of Christ, Veronica hangs countless bed-sheets and linen cloths in the attic.

Thus the text blends the lives of the working women into a hybrid with the histories of the martyrs. This is interwoven with associations from the passion of Christ: his fainting on the hill of Golgotha, the blows of the whip and the weals on the steps, the hands stretched out, and the wet faces of the women. Indirectly the text echoes Socialist Realism and its labour thematics: it could almost be read as a parody of the motifs of the ideal workers and collectivism. Białoszewski shows the everyday heavy work of the women. The triptych as a religious genre stands in contrast to the Socialist odes in which collective work is praised, and to the narratives of the heroes of labour. It also lives from intermedial dialogue, for example with Gothic paintings in the context of Polish Catholicism. In it we find the motifs of "dream", "shadow", and "dust" which are so characteristic of Białoszewski. The dream opens and closes the poem, analogously to the doors in the text. The motif of the threshold suggests that the action unfolds on the boundary between dream, imagination, memory, and reality. The time from dawn to dusk forms a space of consciousness. Shadows and dust stand symbolically for the great age of people and things; but it is precisely in shadows and dust that the "factual" and "realistic" view of the world is broken as in a prism, so that a new perception of reality becomes possible. Such a hybrid of dream and reality, and of old and new, combines with intertextual allusions in the next poem too:[29]

Stara pieśń na Binnarową
[Cykl: *Ballady rzeszowskie* / Tomik: *Obroty rzeczy*]

Prowadź nas, pszenico,
złota błyskawico,
przez fiolety owych wzgórz
między blaski kukuruz
z żółcielami pospołu,
słonecznikiem upału,
miodem rozlanym powietrza --
dywanami spod Biecza.

Wyjdźcie, stłoczone w kapliczce
świątki z dziwacznym licem,
pokażcie najbliższą drogę
fiołkowym i żółtym rękawem.

(The old song of Binnarowa
[Cycle: *Ballads from Rzeszów* / Volume: *Changing things*]

Lead us, wheat,
you golden lightning,
over the violet of these hills
between the splendour of the corn cobs,
together with the sow thistles,
with the heat of the sunflowers,
with the spilt honey of the air --
with the carpets from the region of Biecz.

Come out, you who are huddled in the chapel,
figures of saints with strange faces,
point the next way
with the violet blue and yellow sleeve.

---

29   Białoszewski, *Obroty rzecz*, pp.16-19.

Już woda z rowem zakręca.
Kończy się droga gorąca.
Wierzby zgromadzone
dmuchają w pnie spękane.
Widać czarne prawie
bożych ścian modrzewie.
A szparami zapachy się leją
od pajęczyn, kwiatów i drewien.

Already the water turns away, with the
   ditch.
The hot path ends.
The gathered willows
blow into their burst trunks.
One almost sees the black larchwood
of the nearly divine walls.
And through the cracks smells break out
   from the cobwebs, flowers and bits of
   wood.

O Anioły-Stróże,
o deski w różnym kolorze --
od kaplicy swojej wyjdźcie,
tęczę z drewna nam pokażcie,
w skrzyp cichuśki i lekkuśki
odemknijcie drzwi kościoła.

O guardian angels,
o boards in various colours --
come out of your chapel,
show us the wooden rainbow,
in the still and easy creaking
open the church door.

Otworzyły!

They have opened it!

O pajęczyno kolorów!!

O you cobweb of colours!!

Bogarodzica Dziewica,
złotem gotycka Maryja
nad ołtarzem płonąca
koralami u szyi,
u twego syna Gospodzina
cała Jerozolima:
na ścianie
po prawej stronie
w żółtościach,
w kolcach zieleni
skręcone -- głowa przy głowie
orszaki wielkopiątkowe
farbami i kurzem się trzęsą
na kusych nogach.
Kyrie elejson!
Adamie -- ty boży kmieciu,
Ewo -- z tej samej kłody,
we dwoje ołtarz dźwigacie,
aż pogrubiały wam łokcie.
Kyrie elejson!

The virgin Mother of God,
the golden gothic Mary
burning above the altar
with corals around her neck,
with your son, the Lord
all of Jerusalem:
on the wall
on the right side
in yellow tones
in the thorns of green
twisted -- one head beside the other
Good Friday followers
they tremble with colours and dust
on short legs.
Kyrie eleison! ["Lord have mercy"]
Adam -- you divine servant,
Eve -- of the same lineage,
together you bear the altar
until your elbows are swollen.
Kyrie eleison! ["Lord have mercy"]

A po prawej stronie
białe, zapylone
"trzy Maryje poszły,
drogie maści niosły...
Gdy na drodze były,
tak sobie mówiły:

And on the right side
the white, dusty
"three Marys went walking
carrying costly salves…
When they were on the way,
they spoke thus with one another:

Jest tam kamień niemały,
a któż go nam odwali?"

-- -- Grób święty
zarósł pajęczynami -- --
-- -- -- anioły siedzą
zakurzone, białe --
śpiewają:
"-- Nie trwóżcie się, Dziewice,
    ujrzycie Boga lice...
    Wstał z martwych, tu go
    nie,
    tylko jego odzienie...
    Alleluja!"

Gdy prowadzili ołtarz,
święty Michał stał na szczycie,
trzymał miecz zapylony
i wagę z przydrożnym kurzem.
Ale pułap kwiecisty
kościoła
był za niski
dla archanioła,
więc przefrunął ponad chór,
wziął miecz, wagę,
na niej -- kurz
i tak czuwa.

Drewniany Michale Archaniele,
ty na drewnianych aniołów czele,
Stróżu Stróżów malowanych
i
posiwiałych od śniegu
niecałych po zacieku...

Oto pomniejsze Stróże
o tęczowym kolorze
wśród kaplicy swojej
trzeszczą w cytry i wiole
rano, wieczór, we dnie, w nocy
ludzkim śpiewom do pomocy.

Śpiewy zostały
w kalinie, w jęczmieniu...
w makówkach --
pod ołtarzami...
Gdy potrącić je,
roznosi się pył po sumie:
"...Ty przez aniołów...

There is a stone, not small,
who will push it away for us?"

-- -- The holy sepulchre
is blocked by cobwebs -- --
-- -- -- the angels sit
dusty, white --
they sing:
"-- Fear not, you virgins,
    you will see the face of God
    He is arisen from the dead, here he is
    not
    only his cloak…
    Alleluja!"

When they carried the altar,
St. Michael stood at the front,
he held a dusty sword
and scales with the dust of the street.
But the flowery heavenly roof
of the church
was too low
for the archangel,
so he flew over the choir,
took the sword, the scales,
on it -- dust
and stands guard so.

You wooden archangel Michael,
You at the zenith of the wooden angels,
you patron of the painted patrons
and
of those greyed by snow,
of those damaged by traces of water…

See the little guards
in rainbow colours
in the middle of their chapel
squeaking in zithers and viols
in the early morning, the evening, day and
    night
to help the human songs.

The songs remained
in the snowball, in barley,
in poppy flowers --
below the altars…
When one touches them,
the dust spreads after the high mass:
"...you through the angels…

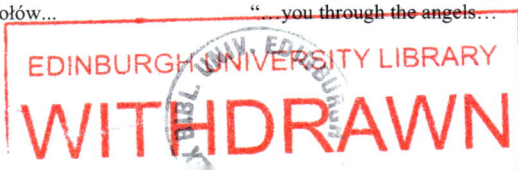

...ty przez aniołów...	...you through the angels...
...ty przez aniołów..."	...you through the angels..."
Cisza.	Silence.
W nawie	In the nave
na cieniach zastrzałów	on the shadow of the buttresses
ostatnia tajemnica:	the last secret:
po lewej ręce	behind the left hand
zbawieni,	the redeemed.
po prawej	behind the right hand
potępieni,	the damned,
a wszyscy	and all
przyprószeni...	covered with dust...
Amen.	Amen.)

Michal Głowiński calls this poetry about concrete Polish locations "little narratives" ("małe narracje"), since they hover between prose and poetry.[30] The title of the poem refers in the first instance to the second oldest wooden church in Małopolska, which bears the name of the archangel Michael. The little village of Binarowa, not far from Biecz, has boasted this church since around 1500. It was built exclusively of sweet-smelling pinewood, and has a single nave. A tower was erected above the entrance, as were a vestibule and a chapel dedicated to the guardian angel on the south side. The interior decoration is a hybrid of architectural styles: Gothic figures from the 14th and 15th centuries, among them a Madonna and child on the main altar, stand alongside Baroque pictures from the 17th century; likewise 17th century are the richly ornamented carved pews, the confessionals, the priest's chair and the chancel.[31] For the composition of this poem it certainly also played a role that Leszek Soliński, Białoszewski's long-standing friend, came from Żarnowiec near Binarowa. The region is in any case thoroughly hybrid: particularly in the "golden age" of the country (1506-72) the Poles here lived alongside Ruthenian Voivodes, Jews and Ukrainians.[32] The poem focuses on an old, wooden, dusty chapel in this peripheral provincial town, in which the kitsch of everyday culture meets with high culture. The altar appears to be made of carved wood, and biblical stories are presumably painted on wooden panels. Everything is covered with dust, symbolising the decay of the old folk cul-

---

[30]   Michał Głowiński, 'Małe narracje Mirona Białoszewskiego', in *Teksty: Teoria literatury, krytika, interpretacja*, ed. by Polska Akademia Nauk, Instytut Badań Literackich, 1:2 (Warsaw: Zakł. Narodowy Im. Ossolińskich, 1970), pp.10-28.

[31]   See   http://www.wrotamalopolski.pl/root_de_Visitenkarte+vom+Malpolska/Einzigartig/ UNESCO-Objekte/Binarowa+-+Hl_+Michael+Erzengel+Kirche/default.htm (last accessed 5 June 2008).

[32]   See Hanna Konicka, *La Sainteté du détail infime: L'œuvre de Miron Białoszewski (Varsovie 1922-1983)* (Paris: Presses de l'Université Paris-Sorbonne, 2005), pp.67ff.

ture, of which only a few remnants of an older religious culture shimmer through. The artwork brings to life a historical myth (the resurrection of Christ), and reflects also a ritual which is repeated and reflected as "history" (the Easter celebration).

Formally, the text imitates the genre of an Easter Play, i.e. a religious dramatic enactment of Christ's Resurrection that was staged as part of the Easter celebrations. The religious content of such plays was increasingly secularised during the Middle Ages, especially by integrating the non-biblical figure of the ointment seller (in charge of anointing Jesus' corpse), which shifted the performance towards a folk play.[33] That the poem refers to this old tradition is already implied in its title. It begins with a solemn apostrophe and ends with the invocation "amen". The rhythmic structure is also reminiscent of Medieval verses of folk poetry. The content and the artefact as such always remain ambiguous. The "guardian angels" are simultaneously "boards in various colours" ("deski w różnym kolorze"). Likewise Adam and Eve are wooden blocks ("kłody"). What is at stake is the ambivalence of art on the one hand and the materiality of painting and woodcarving that has gathered dust over the years on the other. Thus the poem connects with the triptych, in which the saints are also lowered onto the dusty ground of the quotidian -- from up high to down below. Citations from other texts produce a kind of collage, when for example the "Prayer to the Guardian Angel" ("Modlitwa do Andioła Stróża") is invoked: "Aniele Boży, Stróżu mój, ty zawsze przy mnie stój. Rano, wieczór, we dnie, w nocy bądź mi zawsze ku pomocy. Strzeż duszy, ciała mego i zaprowadź mnie do żywota wiecznego. Amen." ("My guardian angel, stay by my side. In the morning and in the evening, day and night, protect me always. Guard my soul, my body, and lead me to eternal life. Amen.") In the text only hybrid allusions to the prayer are recognisable: "trzeszczą w cytry i wiole/ rano, wieczór, we dnie, w nocy/ ludzkim śpiewom do pomocy" ("squeaking in zithers and violas/ in the early morning, the evening, day and night/ to help the human songs"). The famous Polish "Bogurodzica" ("God bearer", Cracow 1506), the oldest extant poem in Polish and an emblem of Catholicism, is similarly cited. No original is known,[34] yet its most popular version reads: "Bogurodzica dziewica, Bogiem sławiena Maryja,/ U twego syna Gospodzina matko zwolena, Maryja!/ Zyszczy nam, spuści nam./ Kyrie eleison". ("God bearer and virgin, Mary blessed of God,/ mother chosen by your son, the lord, Mary!/ Win blessing for us, pass it down into our world,/ Kyrie eleison"). In the text, the famous prayer to the mother of God is only echoed: "Bogarodzica Dziewica,/ złotem gotycka

---

[33]   See http://www.nd.edu/~gantho/anth354-532/Muri458-465.html (last accessed 7 June 2008).
[34]   See Hans-Peter Hoelscher-Obermaier, 'Zur Genese der 'Bogurodzica'', *Die Welt der Slaven*, 27, new series 6 (1982), 90-105.

Maryja/ nad ołtarzem płonąca/ koralami u szyi,/ u twego syna Gospodzina"
("The virgin Mother of God,/ the golden gothic Mary/ burning above the
altar/ with coral necklace,/ with your son, the Lord"). A fundamental difference between the two versions is Białoszewski's concern for the Gothic
statue only, not for the Mother of God as in the original poem. Thus the text
makes art and not religion its theme. All the citations from religious hymns,
prayers, statues, and rituals make the reader aware how our present day is a
hybrid of the past. Beneath the dust of the figures lies a centuries-old culture,
and intertextually the Catholic tradition, whose individual elements reappear,
bringing the old texts back to life for the present. In the last strophe, a "final
secret" is thematised: the scenery of the last judgment astonishes the ob-
server/reader because in contrast with the tradition, the damned appear at the
right hand of God and the redeemed on his left. Thus the poem takes the
perspective of the observer and not that of God within the artwork, resulting
in a mirror-image inversion of the sides. This distances the reader from the
metaphysical nothingness -- the dust from which we come and to which we
shall return, which covers everything more and more. The fear of the "final
secrets" is thus lessened and the idea of transcendence remains literally hanging in the balance, as the three dots at the end of the poem insist. Although
other citations are placed in inverted commas, the final "amen" is not.[35] The
lyrical I has assimilated the hybrid elements in a kind of poetic act of wor-
ship.
     All in all, Białoszewski's writing style demands a maximum of dedication
from the reader, because the hermetic passages of the poem are often only
interpretable through detailed intertextual knowledge and comprehensive
cultural competence. Despite his language experiments, the author differs
from the radicalism of the avant-garde. The lyrical I seeks a relationship to
the reader which mostly involves a direct address, and tries to maintain this
through confessions, explanations and invocations. The following poem can
be read as a kind of explicit, glowing and solemn vow to uphold humility and
not to rise above everyday things, or above the reader:[36]

O mojej pustelni z nawoływaniem	**(On my hermitage with invitation**
[Cykl: *Szare eminencje/* Tomik: *Obroty rzeczy*]	[Cycle: *Éminences grises* / Volume: *Changing things*]
1	1
Nie jestem godzien, ściano,	I am not worthy, o wall,
abyś mię ciągle syciła zdumieniem...	that you always fill me with

---

35   See Konicka, p.74.
36   Białoszewski, *Obroty rzecz*, pp.71-72.

to samo -- ty -- widelcze...
to samo -- wy -- kurze...

amazement...
the same -- you -- o fork...
the same -- you -- o accumulations of
    dust...

Jakże jednak tu nie ulec
twojej piramidzie mojego odosobnienia?
a twoim -- brzękom nazwy
        która nadziewa
        moje ciasto ucha?
a waszym szarym -- z was samych --
    drogom
        w które i mnie zabieracie?

How then not yield here
to your pyramid of my seclusion?
and to your -- clattering of the name
        which fills
        my earwax?
and to your gray paths -- from you
    alone --
        on which you also take me?

Tak
w mojej pustelni kusi:
samotność
pamięć świata
i to, że mam się za poetę.

Yes
luring in my hermitage:
loneliness
memory of the world
and the fact that I see myself as a poet.

Dziwię się
i dziwię siebie,
i komentuję wciąż żywoty otoczenia.

I wonder
and I wonder about myself
and I comment always on the lives of
    my environment.

Więc nocą
mija dni czterdzieści
albo cały anachoreta,
a owe pychy
        apetyty
        swawolne wole
robią ze mnie gniazdo.

So at night
forty days have passed
or the entire anchorite,
and this arrogance
        appetite
        playful will
they make a nest of me.

2

Kruk mi chleba nie przynosi,
a grota -- numerowana,
wisi drzewo ze sznurków,
kwitnie papierami,
kwitnie świecznik ze stołowych nóg
a drugi świecznik -- prawdziwy.

The raven brings me no bread,
and the grotto -- is numbered,
wood hangs from strings,
it blossoms with papers,
the candlestick blossoms, made of the
    legs of a kitchen table
and the second candlestick -- the real
    one.

Ostatecznie -- mówię z ludźmi.
Nie piszę dla samych szaf.
Wiec bądź -- o ja! -- garbaty
garbem pokory przed ziomkami
i garbem porozumienia.

Finally -- I speak with people.
I write not for my own wardrobes.
So -- o I! -- hunchback
with   hunched   humility   before
    compatriots
and with the hunch of communication.

Zrozumcie po ciemku:
brzęczy srebrna korona stołu,
słychać miasto w skrótach i ukosach.
Zapalcie światło:
czy nie zamiesza się
każdy z was -- w żółtej szklance,
dokoła której
      ociera się półtora wymiaru?
Zgaście światło:
oto magazyn kontemplacji,
cały jesteś pokryty sercem,
rozgrzesz mnie!
Włóż, włóżcie papierowe kwiaty do
   czajników,
pociągajcie za sznury od bielizny
i za dzwony butów
na odpust poezji
na nieustanne uroczyste zdziwienie...!

[styczeń 1955 r.]

Understand in the dark:
the silver table crown hums,
you can hear the town in abbreviations
   and slants.
Light the lamp:
whether each of you
won't mix -- in the yellow glass,
against which
      one and a half of the dimension
   rub?
Put out the light:
that is the pantry of contemplation,
you are all covered with heart,
absolve me!
Put the paper flowers into the kettles,
pull on the cords of the washing
and on the bellropes of the shoes
for poetry to be forgiven
for neverending solemn wonder...!

[January 1955])

The text is an anti-legend, or rather, a parody on the legend as a genre. The invocations, prayer formulae and echoes of odes and hymns are not ironic, however; they are cheerful. The poet expresses humorously his faith in the inestimable value of reality. The various objects like wall, fork and dust are laden with meaning, and in the first strophe they are treated like deities, which effects a sacralisation and ritualisation of the everyday world. The vocative of fork, wall and accumulations of dust follows the vocative of prayer in *ojcze* ("[our] father"). The poem celebrates a transformation of the dust analogous to the transubstantiation of the Eucharist: the objects all appear familiar, yet in their differentness they defy appropriation by the observer. As strange things, they are surrounded by a numinous secret. To accentuate this unfathomable quality of the objects of everyday life, a whole series of biblical allusions are woven into the text, as when the Centurion of Capernaum, whose servant lies at home on his death bed, sends a message to Jesus:

"Lord, don't trouble yourself, for I do not deserve to have you come under my roof. That is why I do not even consider myself worthy to come to you. But say the word, and my servant will be healed. For I myself am a man under authority, with soldiers under me. I tell this one, 'Go', and he goes; and that one, 'Come', and he comes. I say to my servant 'Do this', and he does it." When Jesus heard this, he was amazed at him, and turning to the crowd following him, he said, "I tell you, I have not found such great faith even in Israel." Then the men who had been sent returned to the house and found the servant well. (Luke 7,6ff.)

This Bible passage is reflected in the first two lines of the poem: "Nie jestem godzien, ściano/ abyś mię ciągle syciła zdumieniem..." ("I am not worthy, o wall, that you always satisfy me, in amazement"). In another passage from Luke's Gospel, John the Baptist says: "I baptise you with water. But one more powerful than I will come, the thongs of whose sandals I am not worthy to untie. He will baptise you with the Holy Spirit and with fire" (Luke 3,16). Meanwhile in Matthew 4,1-11, the temptation of Jesus in the wilderness, the Devil is active in the loneliness of the desert for 40 days and 40 nights.

A general aspiration of Białoszewski's, which separates him significantly from the rest of the contemporary literary landscape, is to be a poet without falling into the trap of arrogance. By means of humour, the poet's rejection of the world, over which his art raises him, is reconciled to his solidarity with the world, which he seeks to understand more fully and thus to improve. The concrete motifs of the grotto, the temptation, the fasting, the contemplation and the raven[37] are taken from the lives of the two anchorites and hermits Antonius "the Great" (251-356) and Paul (†341), the "Father of all hermits". The beginning of the second strophe makes clear that these motifs are being parodied: the raven brings no bread here, the grotto is numbered like an apartment, and the "temptation" is literary ambition. The "paper flowers" at the end of the poem and the "wood hanging from strings" ("drzewo ze sznurków") are unique props, which kit out the poet's space -- his desert -- like a funfair. Both objects could also have been made by craftsmen inspired by folklore, or by children, but all these knick-knacks and trinkets are here a great poetic passion. Has this "pyramid of my seclusion" ("piramidzie mojego odosobnienia") now become, in the imagery of the hybridity theories, more of a "bridge" (Heidegger), "steps" (Bhabha) or "circus" (Cage)? The humorous depiction of everyday things is far from Martin Heidegger's concept of the "bridge", which for him is a place which amasses and dimensionalises, permanently re-facticising objects; yet neither does it quite correspond

---

[37] Analogously God sent Elias to the rivulet Krith in order to punish him with loneliness during a draught. Ravens supplied him with bread and meat (1 Kings, 17, 2-6). The raven who supplies bread is a sign of God's mercy towards good people. Furthermore Noah opened the windows of the Ark after forty days and sent out a raven that "flew here and there until the water was dried up from the earth" (Genesis 8, 7). Two ravens also form the attribute of Meinrad (Meginrad) of Einsiedeln. Presents given to him from gratitude were instantly distributed by him among the poor. Such an attitude was certainly the reason why two robbers, whom he had just given bread and wine, killed him with a club. The two ravens that Meinrad had raised and fed pursued the murderers and led to their imprisonment.

to Homi Bhabha's concept of the "stairwell" as a "hither and thither" which only admits an ordering of objects as "upper and lower":

> Heidegger's bridge is ultimately a *theological* concept. It is exactly his theologising of the world that interrupts hybridisation. In doing so, it radically reduces plurality. It has a de-hybridising effect. Heidegger's "things" are also far from hybrid. One should never forget that Heidegger has always remained a philosopher of "self-sameness", of "authenticity", of "origin" and "essence". Bhabha still thinks too dialectically. Dialectic does not simply mean contradiction and reconciliation. Dialectic is first and foremost the countering tension of the distinguished. It is precisely this dialectic, i.e. present and agonistic tension that does not permit a playful form of plurality. The gap to which Bhabha transforms the border is dialectic in so far as it is governed by this countering drive. Thus Bhabha remains largely caught in the agonistic-dialectic tension between coloniser and colonised, between ruler and ruled, master and servant.[38]

Against this, Białoszewski's "pyramid" comes closest to a circus (an arena, a crossroads) as envisaged by John Cage, where heterogeneous sound events, which lack internalisation, centre and subjectivity, coexist harmoniously. Białoszewski specialises in such playful childlike blending.

In contrast to irony, which is seldom to be found in his texts, his humour permits such a juxtaposition of mutually antagonistic aspects (things, behaviours, situations, utterances), where points of importance uncover an absurd facet, the beautiful conceals a beauty flaw, or the banal is outweighed by the painful. These contrasts are not played against each other by a pun, although the humour initially highlights such oppositions. But in the texts the hybrid discords are existentially incorporated into being. The unachievable ideals intend to inspire humility and tolerance in the reader, as Białoszewski spells out in another poem:[39]

Podłogo, błogosław!
[Cykl: *Szare eminencje*/ Tomik: *Obroty rzeczy*]

Buraka burota
   i buraka
   bliskie profile skrojone,
   i jeszcze buraka starość, którą tak kochamy,

   i nic z tej nudnej fisharmonii
   biblijnych aptek
   o manierach
   i o fornierach w serca, w sęki

(O floor, bless!
[Cycle: *Éminences grises* / Volume: *Changing things*]

The grey-brown of the turnip
   and of the turnip
   more closely carved profiles,
   and still the age of the beetroot, which we so love,

   and nothing from this boring fisharmonium
   of biblical apothecaries
   about manners

---

[38]   Han, pp.28-29.
[39]   Białoszewski, *Obroty rzeczy*, pp.61-62.

homeopatii zbawienia...
tu nie fis
i nie harmonia,
ale dysonans

and about veneer in the hearts, in
the knotholes
about the homeopathy of salvation...
here no F#
and no harmony
but dissonance

ach! i flet zaczarowany
w kartofle -- flet
w kartofle rysunków i kształtów
zatartych!
    to stara podłoga
       podłoga
    leżąca strona
       boga naszego powszedniego
       zwyczajnych dni
    i takie słowo koncertujące
    w o-gamie
    w tonacji z dna
    naszej mowy...

ah! and the magic flute
into the potatoes -- a flute
into the potatoes of drawings and
smudged forms!
    this old floor
       floor
    the lying side
       of our everyday God
       our ordinary days
    and such a concerting word
    in o-gamie
    in tones from the depths
    of our speech...

Podłogo nasza,
błogosław nam pod nami
błogo, o łogo...

Our floor,
bless us below us
bless, o floor...

[Garwolin, 16 listopada 1954 r.]

[Garwolin, 16 November 1954])

Already the assonance of the first line "Buraka burota" ("The grey-brown of the turnip") sounds like a nursery rhyme. Białoszewski invokes the tonal universe of words in this poem in a kind of song. The visual and acoustic elements are combined: because of the knotholes where once the branches met the trunk, the old wooden floor is, to use a musical metaphor, not mono-tone, but dissonant. In contrast to a veneer, it is authentic, that is, not artificially combined. Nevertheless precisely this hybrid element of the branch holes is located in it analogously to a musical F#, an intermediate tone, not a pure F, nor a pure G, but something between them. But it is neither this "impure" F# nor the "pure" harmony which are praised in the poem, but the hybrid dissonance between them. The rhyme of *flet* ("flute") and *kartofle* ("potato") in the couplet "ach! i flet zaczarowany / w kartofle -- flet" ("ah! and the magic flute/ in the potato -- a flute") links Mozart's *Magic Flute* with an everyday potato. High culture and everyday culture are thus playfully mingled. It is not in the musical scale (Polish *gama*) that this song of the poet is codified, but in the *o-gamie*, the tones of which defy systems. Analogous to this, Białoszewski forms from the Polish *podłoga* ("floor") a hybrid word chain via *boga* (genitive of *bóg,* "God"), *błogo* ("blessedness"), *błogosław* (imperative singular of *błogosławić*, "to bless"), to *łogo* (a neologism on analogy with *łado*, the Refrain in Slavic wedding songs; at the same time, *łogo* is also "the floor" again, without its prefixed *pod*, "under"). With the help of this paronomasia with its dominant o-vowel and its syllable sequence *łoga -- oga -- łogo*, the following thought is suddenly pushed to the surface: that which is located right at the bottom, beneath the feet, this "old floor" ("to stara podłoga") is "the lying side/ of our everyday God", whose "blessing" alone guarantees our peace. These two lines of verse, and the expression "of ordinary days" ("zwyczajnych dni") are a variation on the "give us this day our daily bread" of the Lord's Prayer. The search for a specific tone is thus linked to the concern about the harmonisation of the discourse with its theme: the point is the aesthetic of the juxtaposed reality, which we have beneath our feet or in our hands.[40] On this, Białoszewski notes: "Popsongs/ song, cabaret,/ opera/ from speaking to/ song/ and back,/ where one merges with the other?/ Is there a threshold?/ The confusion of genres/ in a Polish plait;/ from this one can lie, dance,/ sing,/ as it was/ in the beginning (in a cave)/ spoken-sung/ [...] grey High Mass".[41] Białoszewski tries to breach the thresholds and to supersede them. He is a hybrid author in the fullest sense of the word. Whereas Heidegger saw the threshold as a middle space, where inside and outside meet, but which is entirely orientated towards the inside, Białoszewski's hybrid concept overcomes thresholds: "The human being of the future will probably not be a threshold-crosser, with pained expressions, but a tourist with cheerful smiles. Should we not greet him as *homo liber*? Or should we, with Heidegger or with Handke, remain a *homo doloris*, who turns to stone on the threshold? In *Phantasien der Wiederholung* (Fantasies of repetition), Handke writes 'If you feel the pain of the thresholds, you are not a tourist; there can be a transition'".[42]

To close with, let us include one of the shorter poems:[43]

---

[40]   See Konicka, pp.79-81.

[41]   "szlagierowość/ podśpiewywania, kabaret,/ operowość/ od mówienie do/ śpiewania/ i z powrotem,/ gdzie jedno przechodzi w drugie?/ I czy jest taki próg?/ Splątanie gatunków/ w jeden kołtun;/ od tego można leżeć, tańczyć,/ śpiewać,/ jak było/ na początku (w jaskini)/ mówienio-śpiewanie/ [...] szara msza." In: *Fragmenty: Dodatku materacowego zostały udostępnione przez Annę Sobolewską.* Here quoted from Wiśniewski, p.43.

[42]   Han, p.82.

[43]   Białoszewski, *Obroty rzeczy*, p.241.

namuzowywanie			(post-musungings
[Cykl: *Leżenia/*	Tomik:	*Mylne*	[Cycle: *Lying down/* Volume: *Erroneous*
wzruszenia]			*contact*]

Muzo	Muse
Natchniuzo	Inspirituse

tak	I
ci	Ending so
końcówkuję	I for you
z niepisaniowości	from unwrittenness

natreść	satisfy
mi	my
ości	ness
i	and
uzo	use)

(1961)	(1961)

The title of this ode, "namuzowywanie", emphasizes by its prefix *na-* the process by which the poet calls on the muse. The grammatical structure of this invocation is exciting. The artificial word is reminiscent of *nanizy-wanie*,[44] the stringing of one pearl after another on a string. This muse is not a metonymically contorted image of the poet himself, but rather a classically conceived authority external to the poet. The poetic muse, addressed in the vocative in the style of the Baroque, is intended to help to glean the miraculous from the otherworld and draw it into this world. The suffixing in the title and in other words in the poem is a conscious "endinging". *Końcówka* are the "grammatical endings", but also a "sharp point" or the "final struggle". The "tak ci końcówkuję" of the second strophe means: "kind of end(ing)ing a little bit." Hence the permanent death of the poet without an apocalyptic final point -- a poet's death which precisely does not happen. "z niepisaniowości" means that there is nothing here to write, that the Muse wants to make out of this impossibility a contrary materialisation: "natreść mi" -- "fill me with content." All that remains of this at the end, after the great poetic feasts and celebrations, is the bare bones, the "ości". And after the loss of the initial *M*, the vocative of the invoked poetic *Muzo* remains only as "uzo".

This poem belongs to the collection *Leżenia* (Lying down): the poet does not stand up to declaim his inspirational muse with pathos, but instead lies on the divan like in the *Symposium*, so that merely an "erroneous sentiment" (*Mylne wzruszenia*) -- thus the title of the volume -- is possible. At any rate,

---

[44] From *nanizać* = "to unlace, to untie".

Białoszewski's work never ends with a dead poet, but rather with the presumed dead who gets up again, as in a slapstick film. The cultural concept of the poetic muse breathing content into a work is combined with the linguistic-literary struggle of the poet, which he genuinely feels. For it is also the language itself, the dynamic *sdvig* [45] (and not the structure) which makes this poem alive and expressive. Białoszewski does not even begin to take the concrete death of a poet seriously. Let the poet die as he pleases. His linguistic wit, which makes the banalities of everyday life (and even death) bearable, has already overcome all terrors of a poet's death: death here has indeed lost its sting.

Bibliography

Białoszewski, Miron, *Obroty rzeczy. Rachunek zaściankowy. Mylne wzruszenia. Było i było*, Utwory zebrane, 1 (Warsaw: Państwowy Instytut Wydawniczy, 1987)

———., *Donosy rzeczywistos'ci*, Utwory zebrane, 4 (Warsaw: Pan'stwowy Instytut Wydawniczy, 1989)

———., *Rozkurz*, Utwory zebrane, 8 (Warsaw: Państwowy Instytut Wydawniczy, 1998)

Carpenter, Bogdana, *The Poetic Avant-garde in Poland, 1918-1939* (Seattle et al.: University of Washington Press, 1983)

Deleuze, Gilles and Félix Guattari, *Tausend Plateaus: Kapitalismus und Schizophrenie*, trans. by Gabriele Ricke and Ronald Voullie (Orig. 1980; Berlin: Merve, 1992)

Derrida, Jacques, *La Dissémination* (Paris: Editions du Seuil, 1972)

———., *The Truth in Painting*, trans. by Geoff Bennington and Ian McLeod (Chicago: University of Chicago Press, 1987).

Fahrnberger, Monika, 'On Homophonic Secular Music of the Middle Ages', http://www.completorium.republika.pl/e_homop2.htm (last accessed 12 August 2008)

---

[45] With *sdvig* the Russian Formalists mean in the broadest sense any shift of one or more structures against one another or into one another (for example the technique of enjambement of verse endings). In a narrower sense *sdvig* means the shifting of word boundaries. In contrast to this, *faktura* is that which is made, i.e. the tangible object quality of a work of art in space. See Aagen Hansen-Löve, *Der russische Formalismus: Methodologische Rekonstruktion seiner Entwicklung aus dem Prinzip der Verfremdung* (Vienna: Verlag der Österreichischen Akademie der Wissenschaften, 1978), pp.90-96. See also Wöll, pp.154ff.

Głowiński, Michał, 'Małe narracje Mirona Białoszewskiego', in *Teksty: Teoria literatury, krytyka, interpretacja,* ed. by Polska Akademia Nauk, Instytut Badań Literackich, 1:2 (Warsaw: Zakł. Narodowy Im. Ossolińskich, 1970), pp. 10-28. [also in: *Gry powieściowe: Szkice z teorii i historii form narracyjnych* (Warsaw: PWN, 1973)]

Goffman, Erving, *Frame Analysis: An Essay on the Organization of Experience* (New York: Harper & Row, 1974)

Han, Byung-Chul, *Hyperkulturalität: Kultur und Globalisierung* (Berlin: Merve, 2005)

Hansen-Löve, Aagen, *Der russische Formalismus: Methodologische Rekonstruktion seiner Entwicklung aus dem Prinzip der Verfremdung* (Vienna: Verlag der Österreichischen Akademie der Wissenschaften, 1978)

Hoelscher-Obermair, Hans-Peter, 'Zur Genese der 'Bogurodzica'', *Die Welt der Slaven,* 27, new series 6 (1982), 90-105.

http://www.heiligenlexikon.de/BiographienC/Caecilia.html (last accessed 5 June 2008)

http://www.nd.edu/~gantho/anth354-532/Muri458-465.html (last accessed 7 June 2008)

http://www.wrotamalopolski.pl/root_de_Visitenkarte+vom+Malpolska/Einzi gartig/UNESCO-Objekte/Binarowa+- +Hl_+Michael+Erzengel+Kirche/default.htm (last accessed 5 June 2008).

Janion, Maria, 'Wprowazenie', in *Gorączka romantyczna* (Warsaw: PIW, 1975)

Konicka, Hanna, *La Sainteté du détail infime: L'œuvre de Miron Białoszewski (Varsovie 1922-1983)* (Paris: Presses de l'Université Paris-Sorbonne, 2005)

Levine, Madeline G., 'Fragments of Life: Miron Białoszewski's Poetic Vision', *The Slavic and East European Journal,* 20 (Spring 1976), 40-49.

Łukaszuk-Piekara, Małgorzata, *'Niby ja': O poezji Białoszewskiego* (Lublin: Wydawnictwo Katolickiego Uniwersytetu Lubelskiego, 1997)

Nycz, Richard, 'Tropy 'ja': Koncepcje podmiotowości w literaturze polskiej ostatniego stolecia', in *Język modernizmu: Prolegomena historycznoliterackie* (Wroclaw: Fundacja na Rzecz Nauki Polskiej, 1997), pp.85-116.

Przyboś, Julian, 'Raj i śmierć' in *Zapiski bez daty* (Warsaw: PIW, 1979), p.307

Riffaterre, Michael, 'Syllepsis', *Critical Inquiry,* 6 (1980), 625-638.

Sławiński, Janusz 'Czytamy wierze: 'leżenia'. Interpretacje', *Tygodnik Kulturalny,* no. 21 (1967)

Sobolewska, Anna, *Maksymalnie udana egzystencja: Szkice o życiu i twórczości Mirona Białoszewskiego* (Warsaw: Instytut Badań Literackich, 1997)

Sokol, Elena, *Russian Poetry for Children* (Knoxville: The University of Tennessee Press, 1984)

Spychała, Małgorzata, *Nowa fala* http://www.spychala.info/ar001/ ms12.pdf (last accessed 23 August 2008)

Todorov, Tsvetan, *The Fantastic: A Structural Approach to a Literary Genre* (Ithaca: Cornell University Press, 1975)

Winiecka, Elżbieta, *Białoszewski sylleptyczny* (Poznań: Wydawnictwo 'Poznańskie Studia Polonistyczne', 2006)

Wiśniewski, Jerzy, *Miron Białoszewski i muzyka* (Łódź: Wydawnictwo Uniwersytetu Łódzkiego, 2004)

Wöll, Alexander, 'Myths and Democratic Attitudes in Poland and Russia: An Intermedial Comparison', in *Democracy and Myth in Russia and Eastern Europe*, ed. by Alexander Wöll and Harald Wydra (London: Routledge, 2007), pp.141-165.

Laughing At or Laughing With?
Italian Comic Stereotypes Viewed From Within
the Peripheral Group

Delia Chiaro

National and cultural stereotypes in popular jokes and in the mass media, here in TV series like *The Sopranos* and commercials for Italian food products, are often seen as simple and inflexible when it comes to their effect on the audience. That this is not the case is shown by the empirical study of the responses of Italian migrants to comic Italian stereotypes in English-language media. Different responses (such as amusement, indifference, or resentment) can be observed in relation to the cultural status of the issues addressed, which reflects the acceptance of certain ideas and the taboo-status of others. Yet there are also striking differences in the reactions to such humorous clichés between first- and later-generation migrants. This shows that hybridity in humour is not an essential quality of the humorous text or artefact, but generated to a considerable extent by the position and attitude of the audience of these jokes.

1. Introduction

English-speaking culture has a long tradition in which Italian stereotypes are exploited for comic purposes in a wide range of humorous discourse. From joke forms to films, television programmes and advertisements, Italians are widely depicted as cowards in World War II jokes; as noisy and disorganised in films such as *The Italian Job*[1] and *Blame it on the Bellboy*[2]; as Latin lovers like Joey (Kevin Kline) in *I Love You to Death*[3] or as the sexually active senior citizens in the Bertolli olive oils UK advertising campaign (2003); as eternally attached to their mother's apron strings and obsessed with food, as in the Dolmio tinned tomatoes advertising campaign or else as members of criminal, Mafia-style organizations as in the Renault Megane 2005 advertising campaigns.

Davies argues that certain types of ethnic humour, particularly those in which the outsider is in some way depicted as an "underdog" or "inferior" by the hegemonic majority, arise from feelings of economic or sexual fear in the minds of a consolidated and well established group directed against the new "peripheral" group entering their society.[4] Thus it is hardly surprising that migrants are the butt of stupidity jokes in many cultures (the Irish in England;

---

[1]   Dir. by Peter Collinson (1969).
[2]   Dir. by Marc Herman (1992).
[3]   Dir. by Lawrence Kasdan (1990).
[4]   Cf. Christie Davies, *Jokes and Their Relation to Society* (Berlin: De Gruyter, 1998).

Poles in the USA; Belgians in the Netherlands and France etc.). In Italy itself, which until recently had a strong tradition of outward migration but little or no internal flow of migrants, the *meridionali*, namely southerners who left the poor towns and villages of the South to seek employment in the affluent cities of the North, became the butt of such jokes. The trait of stupidity in Italian jokes is frequently pinned onto the *carabinieri*, one of the country's police forces, a profession which is traditionally heavily populated by southerners in search of easily available employment. Today, however, while *carabinieri* jokes continue to flourish, those about stupid southerners in general have been replaced by those regarding *extra-comunitari* (literally those "from outside the EC"); manual workers from Asia, Africa and Eastern Europe. Thus from peripheral migrants, Italians themselves have now shifted to inhabit the centre and consequently permit themselves the newly acquired privilege of becoming the perpetrators of jokes in which new arrivals become the butt. Nevertheless, outside Italy jokes in which Italians are the underdogs still survive, and stereotypes certainly die hard. Italians who inhabit collections of ethnic jokes are depicted as being dirty, greasy imbeciles with an obsession for spaghetti, while the women contentedly sport excessive body hair and engage in sex with their brothers. Again, a cursory glance at commercials from across Europe and the USA clearly reveals copywriters' distinct liking for negative Italian stereotypes, so much so that the Order of the Sons of Italy in the USA have felt the need to conduct a survey to demonstrate that the majority of Italians are neither criminals nor blue collar workers, arguing that the US Census Bureau reports that two-thirds of the Italian Americans in the workforce are employed in white-collar jobs as executives, physicians, teachers, attorneys and administrators.[5] Yet, at the time of writing (Spring 2005), the print campaign in the UK for the French Renault family Megane car, was advertised by means of a "family" photo of a group of Italo-American gangsters. One Megane TV ad shows a group of gangsters round a table at a summit meeting while in another, a Mafia-style boss jokingly threatens to blow up another thug's car against the musical background of Italian opera. In Italy, the same advertisements are aired with subtitles as in the original version, the hoodlums' speech is typecast by heavy Italo-American accents. Again, by simply surfing around the Internet, we find numerous less than positive Italian stereotypes. For example, the Mars corporation promote their Italian-style Dolmio pasta sauces by means of an Italian family of muppets headed by a moustachioed *Papa* and a house-proud *Mama*, the tablecloth is obligatorily red and white checked and all speak with

---

[5]   Results of the survey can be obtained from the association itself at www.osia.org.

a heavy pseudo-Italian accent. And it would seem that such kind of stereotyping is not at all unusual.

Thus, the research question we ask ourselves is, how do the actual objects of such humour, namely Italians living in the places where jokes in which Italians are depicted as being hairy, dirty and cowardly are prevalent and where such stereotyping exists, react to being the butt of comic discourse? How do Italian migrants feel about being represented as loud and dirty? And what of commercials in which they are being portrayed as criminals? Do they find them amusing? Our working hypothesis envisaged that the closer to the culture and the more Italian the informant, the more he or she would be irritated by such humorous discourse, in other words, that Italian migrants would not have the "measure of emotional distance from the subject matter of that humour"[6] which might allow them to laugh at themselves in view of the very nature of certain stereotypes displayed in humorous discourse concerning their culture, while their offspring were more likely to have acquired such distance. Thus, it was hypothesized that first-generation migrants would be more offended or irritated by negative stereotypes than their offspring, offspring would be less offended than their parents but more offended than their non-Italian spouses and so forth. This hypothesis would fit in well with what Mintz has described as the four developmental phases in ethnic humour.[7] In a first stage the central group tends to be critical of the peripheral group via ethnic jokes. During the second stage the peripheral group becomes critical of its own group through the telling of self-deprecating jokes. In the third stage, the group becomes realistic and able to laugh at itself. Finally, in the fourth stage, the peripheral group is able to make fun of the majority.

In order to test our hypothesis, a questionnaire was developed to explore the attitudes of Italian migrants towards both ethnic jokes in which Italians appear as underdogs and commercials which contain Italian stereotypes. The questionnaire was administered to a small, convenient, self-selected sample of Italian migrants and their offspring. Elaboration of raw data reveals that respondents have somewhat ambivalent feelings towards such humour.

2. Laughing at Italians and Italianness

Now, it could be argued that the way in which Italians are stereotyped and depicted in jokes is in good humour and rarely malevolent. In fact, if we contrast them with jokes about Germans or Jews, it would not be unfair to

---

[6]   Eliot Oring, *Jokes and their Relations* (Lexington: University Press of Kentucky, 1992), p.54.
[7]   Larry Mintz, *Humor in America: A Research Guide to Genres and Topics* (Westport, CT: Greenwood Press, 1998).

say that these can be quite vicious, in a way in which jokes about Italians are not. The same can be said about stereotyping. There is something far more malicious about comparing present-day Germans to members of the SS (for example the British press references to Pope Benedict XVI as "God's Rott-weiler") than alluding to Italian military cowardliness. Such comic benevolence towards Italians may well be due to the fact that they have rarely been powerful in modern times; since they have never been as oppressive as other powerful nations like the French, the Germans or the Russians, the varieties of humorous discourse tend to be affable rather than spiteful, when compared to joke forms about so many other ethnic groups. Although Italians are seen as bad soldiers, they are at the same time seen as good human beings who as immigrants tend to integrate well and not cause problems:

> They [Italians] realise that charm works better than arrogance. They sell meals and ice cream, which forces them to be friendly. The meals are good and the food has status. They are not so successful as to cause envy nor so useless as to be a burden. They are bad Catholics and do not irritate people of other religion. Therefore there are no political, economic or religious reasons to hate them.[8]

So while members of other ethnicities are regarded by the central majority as being lazy drunkards (e.g. the Irish in England) or canny misers (the Scots in England and the Genoese in Italy), the only remaining shortcomings attributed to Italians are personal hygiene, stupidity and sexuality. It is important to notice that, even though jokes are told in jest, in other words, in an "it's only a joke" fashion, they can, paradoxically, be considered both unimportant (note the need for the word "only" in "I was only joking") and yet at the same time extremely important ("I suppose you think that's funny?"). On balance, unlike forms of comedy produced for the stage or the screen in which jokes are polished by scriptwriters and comedians, ethnic jokes are extremely significant because they are one of the few forms of popular culture which are truly created by the people for the people. In fact, they may well be the only remaining narrative form linked to the traditional village storyteller[9] and even if today jokes are told and spread over the Internet by e-mail and websites, they are still invented and spread by the people, for the people. But jokes are simultaneously unimportant, as they can never have the consequences of political rhetoric, persuasive advertising or even malicious gossip. Yet comedians in the media can still cause public uproar if they joke about subjects which are "off limits" and entire groups of people can be offended by a video clip which pokes fun at them.

---

[8]   Christie Davies, personal communication.
[9]   Cf. Christie Davies, 'The Right to Joke', *Research Report* 37, The Social Affairs Unit, 2004, http://socialaffairsunit.org.uk/digipub.

2.1. Negative traits represented in stupidity jokes about Italians

Davies has discussed the issue of jokes on Italian militarism at length, claiming that the stories of Italian military ineffectiveness, retreat and defeat are not only perceived as humorous across Europe, but along with "stories about German militarism, organization, dedication, efficiency and atrocities are universally known, accepted and even seen as significant throughout Europe".[10] Such stories appear to be hundreds of years old and probably originated in France where they can be traced back to a medieval comic image of the Lombards, the gibes of Rabelais and the wit of Montaigne, a kind of French humour which survived in the nineteenth and early twentieth centuries and then emerged as a cycle of narrative jokes after the humiliating French defeat by the Axis powers followed by occupation in 1940, "such jokes are thus a statement of the self-image of the French as the warrior nation of Europe, an assertion of *la gloire de la France*."[11]. In an early attempt at political correctness, during World War II, the BBC even decreed a ban on jokes about unsoldierly Italians. Nevertheless, the following example was broadcast on the radio in 1941:

> What is it that has feathers on the head but isn't a bird -- has two legs but runs faster than a hare?
> I don't know, what is it?
> An Italian soldier. [12]

Interestingly, such jokes are not about real cowardice at all, but about a tendency to surrender, desert or run away in an organized war which can be explained in relation to the history of Italy and the way in which the country was unified into a nation. In fact, such jokes fit in with Davies' framework of "comically defective attributes" (stupid/canny; cowardly/militaristic; promiscuous/sexless and drunken/teetotal) displayed in opposed sets of ethnic jokes, claiming that they stem from four central concerns of modern society. These

---

[10]   Davies, *Jokes and Their Relation to Society*, p.148.
[11]   Christie Davies, *The Mirth of Nations* (New Brunswick, NJ: Transaction, 2004).
[12]   This joke is quoted by Davies vaguely as having been recounted in 1941: "During the Second World War there were even earnest discussions in committee in the B.B.C. about whether jokes about Marshal Goering's corpulence were allowable or unacceptably stoutist. Political correctness really does parody itself. In 1940 a ban on jokes about the Italians being unsoldierly, derived from their unsatisfactory performance in World War I, was decreed because the B.B.C. feared that a new-found ferocity on the part of the 'German-officered' Italians would lead to the jokes rebounding on the joke-tellers"; Christie Davies,. 'The Right to Joke.' *Research Report* 37. The Social Affairs Unit, 2004. http://socialaffairsunit.org.uk/ digipub.

defective attributes are simply pinned onto suitable groups.[13] In the case of
the cowardly/militaristic opposition, examples can be easily found in the
joked-about group's military history, and where there is no local group to be
found, it is always possible to borrow from a distant country. In Anglo-Saxon
countries (and not only there), Italy seems to lend itself perfectly to be joked
about in terms of militaristic under-achievement.

In other joke types, Italians are seen as dirty, "greasy dagoes" with excessive
hair growth in both males and females:

> What is the difference between an Italian and a monkey?
> A monkey has more fleas.

> Why don't Italians have acne?
> It slides off.[14]

Interestingly, while most European jokes about Italians, or indeed about any
nationalities subject to stupidity profiling, do not include dirtiness in the traits
they attribute these groups, US, Canadian and Swiss jokes do. Furthermore, it
is worth considering that if in serious discourse the word "dirty" has a
stronger connotation than the term "stupid", a believer in hostility theory of
humour should infer that Americans feel more hostile towards Italians (and
other peripheral groups) than most of their European counterparts. Once
more, according to Davies, it is the absence of the quality of dirtiness in
European jokes that strengthens the claim that the USA is a "country obsessed with rational hygiene and physical perfection"[15] rather than feelings of
anti-Italianness. Why it should be that Italians have been chosen as being
dirty is difficult to say. In Canada, it is the Newfoundlanders who are depicted in jokes as dirty, and in the USA, alongside unclean Italians, we find
jokes populated with unwashed Poles too, while in the UK and Italy, the Irish
and *carabinieri* are stupid but perfectly clean. However, cowardly or dirty, it
would be wrong to think that others truly see Italians as being spineless or
unclean. In fact, Davies is highly critical of the Freudian view that jokes are
tendentious and that they contain hidden forms of antagonism against a certain group, thus revealing attitudes and values of the group which actually
tells the jokes.[16] Again, in jokes, both male and female Italians tend to be

---

[13]   Cf. Davies, *The Mirth of Nations*, p.188.

[14]   Julius Alvin, *The New Treasury of Gross Jokes* (New York: Kensington Books, 2004),
p.119.

[15]   Davies, *Jokes and Their Relation to Society*, p.173.

[16]   Ibid., pp.172-173. This joke was retrieved from the BBC Written Archive in Caversham, file
R 34/275/1 and I am grateful to Christie Davies for generously supplying me with these
files.

portrayed as sporting excessive body hair despite the fact that today Italian women are, generally speaking, extremely well groomed:

> How do you recognize an Alitalia plane?
> From the hair beneath its wings.

> Why do Italian men grow moustaches?
> So they can resemble their mothers.

In Italian jokes, hairy women are certainly not an object of desire:

> Lei aveva tutto quanto un uomo può desiderare: muscoli, baffi e peli sul petto.

> (She had everything a man could want: muscles, a moustache and a hairy chest.)[17]

Thus, perhaps jokes about hairy women, like those about the lack of personal hygiene, simply reflect an American obsession with personal sanitation and total control of one's body. Presumably, Mediterranean people are darker and consequently more naturally hirsute than people from the North, but in a society which sees an attribute such as body hair in terms of "superfluous" and "unsightly", especially in females, its presence can only be considered a feature of negative Otherness.

2.2 Stereotypes

The HBO series *The Sopranos* caused outrage amongst Italo-American associations for the way in which it portrays Americans of Italian heritage. These organizations were quick to point out that according to the 2000 US Census, the total number of American Italians living in the USA was between 14 and 15 million of whom, according to FBI statistics, a mere 1,150 (0.0078%) are actually criminals. Nevertheless, out of a total of 1233 films distributed since 1928, 859 (69%) portray Italo-Americans in a negative light. In fact, 500 characters in these films represent Italian mobsters and while only 58 of these correspond to mob characters who really existed, the remaining 422 are invented criminal characters.[18]

Similarly, if we examine advertisements, it would appear that Mafia-style mobsters are indeed a popular theme. For example, the International Dairy Food TV commercials aired in the USA feature "Vinny" and a friend who

---

[17] My liberal translation from Ballanzone, *Le 331 migliori barzellette* (Milano: Omega, 1982), p.40.

[18] The source of this data is a survey carried out by the Order of the Sons of Italy with the assistance of the Commission for Social Justice and UNICO National, the Italian American One Voice Coalition and Italian American Pride, Summer 2003 (www.osia.org).

attempt to break the bones of a man who owes them money, but since the intended victim drinks milk, they can't hurt him. In another ad, four dark, heavy, hairy young men wearing gold chains menace a group of senior citizens in a diner. The elderly men triumph over the bullies because milk makes them strong. According to the National Italian American Foundation, a number of Italian American groups despise such stereotyping and argue that while society is rather adept at doling out offensive stereotypes: the lazy Mexican, the cheap Jew, the drunken Irishman, the dangerous African American, none are likely to be found in mainstream ads, yet Italian hoodlums are, thus proving Italian negative stereotypes to be an exception. Could it be that Italian comic stereotypes promote sales?

In a study of advertisements for Italian agro-food products both in print and on the Web, I have observed that, unlike "pretend-Italian" brands truly Italian agro-food producers tend not to promote their wares transnationally via the use of comic stereotypes.[19] As the name suggests, so called "pretend-Italian" brands are those which are not "made in Italy" at all, but rather are traditional Italian foods and drinks produced elsewhere yet promoted and sold as genuinely Italian. Dolmio pasta sauces are a good example of a "pretend-Italian" brand which in reality is produced by the gigantic Mars corporation. Furthermore, I have also noted that while "truly" Italian brands adopt sober stereotypical images of Italy (sunshine, Mediterranean images of olive groves, art etc.) once these companies merge with larger multinationals they tend to switch to a more comic style, presumably because humour is a successful marketing strategy transnationally. This can be seen in the ads of a company like Bertolli, (member of the multinational giant Unilever), which promotes its oils by means of comic stereotypes.[20] Drawing on Hofstede's dimensions of culture,[21] De Mooij maps out different advertising styles across cultures, dividing styles in terms of a "Direct and Explicit" dimension (e.g. Germany, Austria, Scandinavia and the UK and the USA) and an "Indirect and Implicit" dimension (e.g. Italy, France and Spain, the Arab World, Japan, China, India and Brazil).[22] Furthermore, she observes a marked preference for humour in commercials in the UK and the USA (along with Hol-

[19]   Cf. Delia Chiaro, 'Translational and Marketing Communication: A Comparison of Print and Web Advertising of Italian Agro-food Products', in *Key Debates in the Translation of Advertising Material*, ed. by Beverly Adab and Cristina Valdés, *The Translator* (Special Issue), 10 (2004), 313-328.

[20]   Ibid., 'Translational and Marketing Communication', pp.322-323.

[21]   Cf. Geert Hofstede, *Cultures and Organizations: Software of the Mind* (London: McGraw Hill, 1991).

[22]   Marieke De Mooij, 'Translating Advertisements: Painting the Tip of an Iceberg', *Key Debates in the Translation of Advertising Material*, ed. by Beverly Adab and Cristina Valdés, *The Translator* (Special Issue) 10 (2004), 179-198.

land, Norway, Sweden and Denmark), while the humour factor is not prominent in cultures which lean towards the Indirect and Implicit Dimension axis.[23] Thus medium to small Italian companies which merge into larger multinationals that are aware of culture-specific styles and tastes in advertising are likely to accommodate to humorous styles once cognisant of them.

However, despite the outrage of Americans of Italian heritage, not all stereotyping is unpleasant in nature. Presumably, the cliché of the food-loving extended family and the cool, fashionable Latin Lover can be received more or less positively by Italo-Americans. The same is probably true of what can be considered the most persistent, yet possibly the most endearing Italian stereotypes of all; that of inefficiency and disorganization. In the European "hell" scenario the Italians are portrayed as the organizers:

> Heaven is where the police are British, the chefs are French, the mechanics German, the lovers Italian and it's all organized by the Swiss.
> Hell is where the police are German, the chefs are British, the mechanics French, the lovers Swiss and it's all organized by the Italians.

3. The field study

In order to explore the attitudes of migrants towards humorous discourse in which Italians are clearly used as the butt, a questionnaire was designed and administered to a small sample of both first and second-generation Italian migrants.

3.1 The questionnaire

The questionnaire was divided into three sections. The first section served to record respondents' socio-demographic details such as gender, age and level of education. As our hypothesis supposed that the closer a person was to Italian culture the more irritated the person would be by the derision of Italians and Italianness, respondents were asked to state their connection to Italy, that is, whether they were born there and subsequently migrated, whether they had migrated and then returned or whether they were tied to Italy by parentage, by marriage, and so forth. In other words, our working assumption was that people who actually migrated would be more emotionally involved in such humour than an offspring for example, or a person who had simply married into an Italian family and that this closer involvement would cause them to react more negatively towards Italian ethnic humour.

---

[23] De Mooij, p.195.

The second section contained questions which set out to investigate firstly respondents' attitudes towards politically incorrect jokes in general (i.e. those based on demeaning women, homosexuals, disabled persons etc.), and secondly their attitudes towards jokes which specifically put down Italians. Respondents were also asked to report on how openly they reacted to being told Italian jokes in a number of different situations; in other words whether they laughed openly or displayed irritation towards them in a variety of social contexts which went from private environments to work and social frameworks.

In the final section of the questionnaire, respondents were asked to watch six short video clips each containing an advertisement which played on Italian stereotypes. Subsequently, they were asked to express their reaction to each one by means of a series of Differential Semantic Scales which elicited reactions in terms of extremes. In other words each respondent had to judge each clip in terms of being either "Sad" or "Funny"; "Entertaining" or "Dull"; "Clever" or "Stupid"; "Appealing" or "Irritating" and "Flattering" or "Insulting" with "Indifferent" as a central point on each scale.

3.2 The sample

For reasons of practicality and convenience, respondents were contacted via personal networking both amongst the Italian community in Youngstown (Ohio, USA) and amongst migrants who had returned to Italy after having lived as immigrants in the USA. Respondents were chosen randomly according to the provison that they had some sort of family tie with Italy. The final sample consists of twenty-nine respondents of mixed ages from a wide range of educational backgrounds in which females slightly outnumber males.

4. Results

4.1 Sense of humour

Humour is very much in the eye of the beholder, as finding something funny or amusing depends on a wide number of variables which are connected not only with an individual's tastes, but above all with his or her personality.[24] The first thing we did in the questionnaire was therefore to ascertain respondents' attitudes to jokes in general, and secondly to jokes which are less than politically correct.

---

[24] Cf. Willibald Ruch, *The Sense of Humor: Explorations of a Personality Characteristic* (Berlin: Mouton de Gruyter, 1998), pp.5-12.

Over three quarters of the sample claimed that they liked listening to jokes, with the remainder being indifferent to them. As not a single respondent answered that they actually disliked listening to jokes, we can be reasonably certain that the sample was, to a greater or lesser extent, open to humorous discourse. However, what is more significant here is the respondents' attitudes to jokes which are politically incorrect. In fact, 13 respondents claimed that they were "uncomfortable" with such jokes. Interestingly, seven people had "no problem" with them while three atypical respondents actually claimed that politically incorrect jokes were their favourite kind of joke. The remaining respondents were indifferent.

As for jokes in which Italians are depicted negatively, only six respondents did not approve of them. In fact, most respondents answered that they "did not mind" such jokes, while five people actually enjoyed listening to them. Thus we can fairly say that, with regards to jokes, the sample was made up of a fairly open-minded set of people.

4.1.1 Reaction to ethnic stereotypes in jokes

Respondents were asked about their attitudes to the six themes frequently found in Italian ethnic jokes, namely: the "Italian Stud"; incest; superfluous hair; military cowardice; organized crime; excessive interest in food; close family ties and disorganization. They were asked to mark a point on a Differential Semantic Scale whose extremes were "Amusing" and "Offensive" according to how they felt about such subjects. The mid-point on the scale was "Indifferent".

4.1.1.1 Offence

The joke subject matter which caused most offence was clearly incest. 69% of respondents were affronted by the link between Italianness and jokes based upon incestuous behaviour. This is of course hardly surprising if we consider the highly emotive nature of the subject.

Second to incest, respondents were most offended by jokes in which Italians were linked with organized crime. Again, this is hardly unexpected if we consider the public indignation in the USA caused by a series such as *The Sopranos* (see 2.2) as well as strong reactions against many commercials and films containing this stereotype. After all, incest and organized crime are hardly laughing matters. Joking about the former could be considered "sick" and about the latter "black" or "dark"; furthermore to be a perpetrator of either is undoubtedly being profiled more negatively than as simply stupid, dirty or even cowardly. Thus strong joke content obtains strong reactions.

4.1.1.2 Amusement

The stereotypical Italian behaviour occurring in jokes which most amused respondents was food, with jokes about families in second position. Italians are extremely interested in food and pay great importance to family ties. It would appear that they find joking about these matters fairly entertaining. The attribute "fairly" is necessary because none of the stereotypes received especially high scores, with food and families scoring a consensus of 51.7% and 48.3% respectively. In other words, respondents' amusement was by no means excessive. In addition, 31% of the sample found jokes about "Italian Studs" amusing too, presumably because sexual prowess is seen as an extremely positive trait in an Italian male.

Interest in food, large, happy families and sexual dexterity are by no means negative personal or social attributes, thus it is permissible to laugh at these features, even if, or possibly *especially* if, possessed by one's own ethnic group. Laughing at positive attributes such as love of good food or a talent for seduction, is very different from laughing at negative undertakings such as incest or organized crime.

4.1.1.3 Indifference

Respondents displayed indifference to jokes about Italian disorganization, in all probability because it may well be the cliché containing most truth. Disorganization may even be seen as in some way endearing. More surprisingly, the sample was also generally more indifferent both to jokes about female hairiness and to those regarding military cowardliness.

4.2 Reaction to stereotypes in advertisements

Respondents were shown five short TV advertisements for Italian food products and were asked to express their reaction to each one by means of a series of Differential Semantic Scales which elicited reactions in terms of extremes. In other words each respondent had to judge each clip in terms of being either "Sad" or "Funny"; "Entertaining" or "Dull"; "Clever" or "Stupid"; "Appealing" or "Irritating" and "Flattering" or "Insulting" with "Indifferent" as a central point in each scale.

4.2.1 The advertisements

4.2.1.1 Walls Cornetto

A classic ad from the mid-seventies shows a young man on a Gondola singing "Just one Cornetto..." (an ice cream) to the tune of the Neapolitan classic *'O sole mio*. As he approaches another gondola coming in the opposite direction carrying a young woman dreamily eating a Cornetto, apparently love struck by the baritone's serenade. The Latin Lover snatches it from her and moves on singing "Give me Cornetto from Walls ice cream."

4.2.1.2 Goodfella's Pizza (A)

In this commercial for Goodfella's Pizza two elderly gentlemen are sitting at a café in an Italian square and one is complaining about his grandson who he is about to disown because of his failure to bake pizza in the UK which is as good as the frozen pizza made by the company being advertised. The advertisement is in Italian with English voice-overs, in other words the original can be heard beneath the translated version which is in almost simultaneous overlap. The final slogan reads "Looks like closing time for pizzerias."

4.2.1.3 Goodfella's Pizza (B)

Intertextually linked with Goodfella's Pizza advertisement (A), this commercial shows the grandson's pizzeria with no customers because of the existence of Goodfella's frozen pizza. The grandson explains his attempts at making the restaurant a success in almost incomprehensible English. Of course he had no chance against the goodness of the frozen product and it "Looks like closing time for pizzerias."

4.2.1.4 Bertolli Oil (A)

A parody of the opening credits of eighties soap *Dallas*, where Texan plains are substituted by Tuscan fields and herds of cattle are replaced by a single goat, Bertolli advertises the family industry in terms of the "Oil barons of Italy". A large extended family is seen enjoying a meal under the Tuscan sun.

4.2.1.5 Bertolli Oil (B)

Another Bertolli commercial which features a sprightly octogenarian Pietro who manages to run fast enough to save a baby in a pram rolling down a steep cobbled road in the style of the "Odessa Steps" sequence in Eisenstein's *Battleship Potemkin*, then returns home to serve lunch to his elderly wife who is waiting with an expression of jealousy on her face.

4.2.2 Reactions

After watching each commercial, respondents were asked to express their reactions on five Differential Semantic Scales. Each scale contained a positive and a negative pole measuring from +6 (positive) to -6 (negative) with a mid-point of zero indicating indifference. Respondents were asked to judge each clip in terms of being

  a) "Sad" or "Funny";
  b) "Entertaining" or "Dull";
  c) "Clever" or "Stupid";
  d) "Appealing" or "Irritating" and
  e) "Flattering" or "Insulting".

Thus positive attitudes could accomplish a maximum score of 6 while negative attitudes could score as little as minus 6.

4.2.2.1 Reactions to stereotypes

Summing the scores of each pair of polar adjectives across the five clips revealed that they correlated very strongly with each respondent generally expressing similar reactions for each commercial. The values of these correlations are reported in Table 1 where it can be observed that all the possible correlations of reaction to stereotypes are positive and highly correlated and thus indicating that respondents tend to rate the five Differential Semantic Scales in the same direction. Furthermore, while many respondents gave maximum and minimum scores on some of the scales, they did not give these scores consistently. This resulted in generally positive scores across the board, with funniness being the feature which gained the highest score and flattery the lowest.

Table 1: Correlations of reactions to stereotypes.

	Funny vs sad	Entertaining vs dull	Clever vs stupid	Appealing vs irritating	Flattering vs insulting
Funny vs sad	1.000				
Entertaining vs dull	.913**	1.000			
	(.000)	.			
Clever vs stupid	.825**	.844**	1.000		
	(.000)	(.000)	.		
Appealing vs irritating	.748	.881	.814**	1.000	
	(.000)	(.000)	(.000)	.	
Flattering vs insulting	.611**	.648**	.716**	.812**	1.000
	(.000)	(.000)	(.000)	(.000)	.

Number of cases: 29
** Correlation is significant at the 0.01 level (2-tailed), values in brackets.

4.2.2.2 Reactions according to generation

With regard to our hypothesis that first-generation migrants would feel more strongly about stereotypical ethnic humour, we found that, according to this sample, the reverse was actually true and that first-generation respondents tended to allot higher scores than subsequent generations, thus revealing more positive attitudes in original migrants than we had initially expected (Fig.1). In some cases, in fact, the scores are vastly different between the two groups. If we take the "appealing/ irritating" dichotomy for example, we find a gap of 9.64 between settlers and offspring. Again, where first-generationers gave a mean score of 13.15 on the "entertaining/dull" Semantic Scale, subsequent generations gave a lower 6.46 resulting in a gap of 6.69. Thus, in general, scores imply that second generations appear to be somewhat more averse to these stereotypes. Why this should be is difficult to imagine. Perhaps first-generation "settlers" have mixed emotions regarding the host culture, so that feelings such as gratefulness and reverence become tangled with those of resentment towards a form of humour which is less than positive about them. In other words, they may not have the emotional distance to be able to judge such humour objectively. But again, the same could have been true if they had answered in the opposite way, only in the latter case, the emotional distance would have been attributable to issues connected to identity and self-image rather than the relationship with members of the host culture. The first generation know that they are foreigners and it is this which possibly enables them to feel a certain amount of respect towards the host culture. If this is the case it is hardly surprising that the second generation find these jokes and stereotypes less acceptable than their parents.

With regards to the reaction of subsequent generations, these subjects are almost bound to have been exposed to such jokes and stereotypes since they were children. It is not unlikely that Italian ethnic jokes and gibes were even used against them as material for playground banter and teasing. If this is the case, then they are more likely to see such humour as a barrier to being fully accepted as citizens, something they desire more intensely than their parents who may still possess the myth of return.

Fig. 1: Comparison of reaction to stereotypes between first generation and other generation.

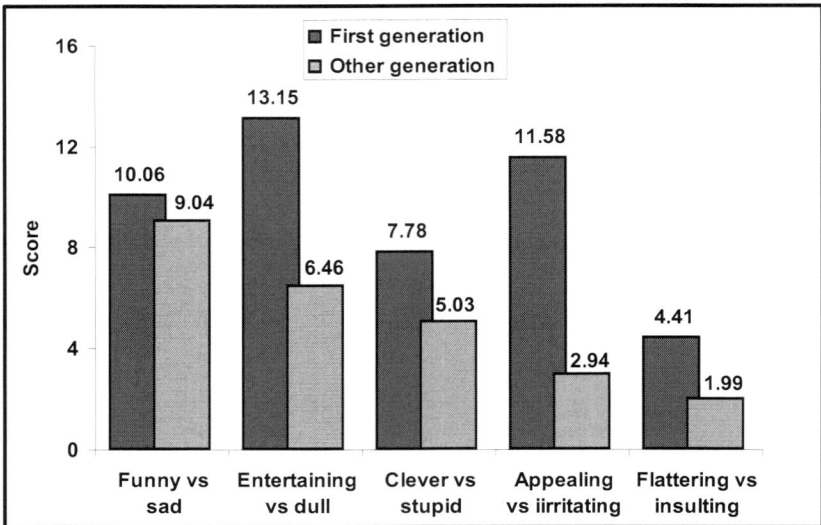

4.2.2.3 Reaction to context

Respondents were asked to rate how they reacted to ethnic jokes when they were heard at home with family and with friends, in social encounters with friends and at work, in terms of whether they reacted openly and positively with laughter or smiling, openly but negatively displaying irritation or offence or whether they were unconcerned. What we were trying to learn was whether respondents felt at ease about expressing discomfort at a politically incorrect joke or stereotype aimed at themselves in the company of others who did not always belong to their ethnic group.

As might be expected, when faced with an occurrence of Italian ethnic humour which they found irritating in a home context, respondents tended to display their annoyance openly. However, it would appear that the sample felt slightly less confident about expressing irritation in social situations such as in a bar or at a party with friends, or in more formal contexts such as work. The sample admitted to responding either with open irritation in the home situation, or with no reaction at all, but as the context moved towards a more formal setting, both the response of indifference and open laughter and smiling tended to rise, while an open display of irritation tended to fall, though not drastically. In fact, we found that if at home nobody laughed or smiled openly and 86.2% displayed irritation, in a work context only 58.6% openly objected to such humour while 24.1% admitted to displaying some kind of positive reaction.

The index derived from our data ranged from a minimum of -5.00 to a maximum 4.00 with a mean of -3.24 and a deviation standard of 2.44. As a result it seems that respondents are indeed annoyed by ethnic jokes regarding themselves and are unafraid to display their irritation. Interestingly, data also revealed that the more positively respondents reacted to stereotypes, the more likely they were to display irritation or offence openly in social situations. In fact, as can be observed in Table 2, all the correlations are negative and among them clever versus stupid is statistically significant at a level greater than 0.01.

One reason for this reaction could be that respondents feel that while it is possible for *them* to laugh at texts which poke fun at themselves, it is less acceptable for others to do so and especially in their company. What they are highlighting is a kind of request for respect for their ethnicity and *their* stereotypes -- even if comic in nature. Furthermore, why the "clever/stupid" pair was more significant than others may be explained by considering that a humorous text which is not especially clever but which simultaneously makes fun of the respondent's ethnic origins, could be seen as being particularly annoying. Thus, a text which is considered "stupid" may cause its recipient to express overt criticism of it in public.

Table 2:

	Funny vs sad	Entertaining vs dull	Clever vs stupid	Appealing vs irritating	Flattering vs insulting
Reaction	-.425*	-.392*	-.538**	-.265	-.227
	(.022)	(.036)	(.003)	(.165)	(.236)

* Correlation is significant at the 0.05 level (2-tailed).
** Correlation is significant at the 0.01 level (2-tailed).

5. Conclusions

It would appear from this survey that Italian migrants are generally well disposed towards Italian stereotypes in both jokes and humorous advertisements. Furthermore, contrary to our initial hypothesis, first-generation migrants are less disapproving of Italian ethnic humour than subsequent generations. Of course, we must bear in mind that the sample we are working with is a small one; a larger sample might well have produced very different results. However, this sample does clearly lead us to suppose that subsequent generations are more likely to need acknowledgment by the host culture than their parents.

When jokes were especially politically incorrect, such as those about incest and Mafia-style organizations, they generally caused offence to respondents while adverts based on more positive stereotypes like Latin Lovers, active senior citizens and so forth were by and large appreciated, thus underscoring the point that aspects which put forward a positive image of Italy and Italianness gained overall consensus. However, focusing on offence, we should bear in mind that part of the appeal of much humour lies in its very political incorrectness. One only has to consider the enormous popularity of entire genres of jokes such as blonde jokes and disaster jokes to understand that part of their appeal lies in their very impropriety. To think that someone who tells a joke about an Italian thug actually believes all Italians are criminals is no more true than believing all blondes are promiscuous or that 9/11 jokes reveal unhealthy mindsets. Thus to take personal offence, while perfectly understandable, may be seen as a sign of overreaction. Perhaps the answer is in the context of situation, in that while sensitive individuals may be more careful in their choice of humorous discourse and gauge it according to the company they keep, copywriters might do well to consider restricting their use of Italian stereotypes to more positive ones in order to avoid angry reactions of entire communities.

However, to sum up, it would be interesting to repeat this study, perhaps using Web-based technology and questionnaires, to investigate the attitudes of a more robust sample of Italian migrants and their offspring, especially in view of the fact that, at least as far as the discourse of advertising is concerned and despite the present climate of political correctness at all costs, negative Italian stereotypes appear to be the only ethnic stereotype which copywriters continue to exploit.

Bibliography

Alvin, Julius, *The New Treasury of Gross Jokes* (New York: Kensington Books, 2004)

Blame it on the Bellboy, dir. by Marc Herman, 1992.

Ballanzone, *Le 331 migliori barzellette* (Milan: Omega, 1982)

Chiaro, Delia and Giuseppe Nocella, 'Anglo-Italian Bilingualism in the UK: A Sociolinguistic Perspective', Paper given at the 2nd International Symposium on Bilingualism, University of Newcastle-upon Tyne, UK, April 1999.

———., 'Translational and Marketing Communication: A Comparison of Print and Web Advertising of Italian Agro-food Products', in *Key Debates in the Translation of Advertising Material*, ed. by Beverly Adab and Cristina Valdés, *The Translator* (Special Issue), 10 (2004), 313-328.

Davies, Christie, 'European Ethnic Scripts and the Translation and Switching of Jokes', *Humor, International Journal of Humor Research* 18. *Humor and Translation* (Special Issue), ed. by Delia Chiaro (Berlin: De Gruyter, 2005), 147-160.

———., 'The Right to Joke', *Research Report* 37, The Social Affairs Unit, 2004, http://socialaffairsunit.org.uk/digipub.

———., *Jokes and Their Relation to Society* (Berlin: De Gruyter, 1998)

———., *The Mirth of Nations* (New Brunswick, NJ: Transaction, 2002)

De Mooij, Marieke, 'Translating Advertisements: Painting the Tip of an Iceberg', in *Key Debates in the Translation of Advertising Material*, ed. by Beverly Adab and Cristina Valdés, *The Translator* (Special Issue), 10 (2004), 179-198.

Hofstede, Geert, *Cultures and Organizations: Software of the Mind* (London: McGraw Hill, 1991)

I Love You to Death, dir. by Lawrence Kasdan, 1990.

Italic Institute of America, The Image Research Project, New York, 1995.

Mintz, Larry, *Humor in America: A Research Guide to Genres and Topics* (Westport, CT: Greenwood Press, 1998)

Oring, Eliot, *Jokes and their Relations* (Lexington: University Press of Kentucky, 1992)

Ruch, Willibald, *The Sense of Humor: Explorations of a Personality Characteristic* (Berlin: Mouton de Gruyter, 1998)

The Italian Job, dir. by Peter Collinson, 1969.

Dutch Tulips in Unexpected Colours:
Humour in Dutch Migrant Writing: Kader Abdolah,
Sevtap Baycılı, Khalid Boudou, Edgar Cairo

Michiel van Kempen

Dutch society is renowned for its multiculturalism. Yet it has also come under critical scrutiny through recent political developments and violent events. Four examples of Dutch migrant writing, that of Kader Abdolah, Sevtap Baycılı, Khalid Boudou, and Edgar Cairo, show different forms of a humorous engagement with issues of migration and integration. While Baycılı employs the female Turkish outsider's look at things, Cairo's writings show a subversive encounter of Dutch normality with a Black Surinamese presence and patois. The exiled Iranian Abdolah prefers grotesque forms of fictional cultural encounters which relativise both the migrant's and the host culture's positions. The Moroccan Boudou opts for yet another form of intercultural engagement through a trickster-like figure manipulating his environment, but also his own story and history. These examples show that hybrid humour can come in significantly different forms -- despite its engagement with similar issues.

On Friday 17th January 2003, Sevtap Baycılı was one of a series of writers invited to *donderpreek* ("preach fire and brimstone")[1] at the international literature festival "Winternachten" in The Hague. Turkish-born Baycılı (1968) studied philosophy at the University of Istanbul. She settled in the Netherlands in 1992 and after some years started to write in Dutch. In her "fire and brimstone sermon" she took up the public debate which had raged in Holland since the attack on the Twin Towers in September 2001 and the murder of Dutch politician Pim Fortuyn in May 2002. It is not for me, thus Sevtap Baycılı opened her speech, to say here in angry, plaintive tones what is wrong "met de mensen van dit o zo schattige liberale democratische volk. [...] Weten jullie niet dat een niet te emanciperen, onderdanige Turkse vrouw de minst geschikte persoon is om boos te worden en dus geen donderpreek kan houden?"[2] ("... with the people of this oh-so-lovely liberal democratic people. [...] Don't you know that a non-emancipatable, subservient Turkish woman is the last person to get angry and so cannot preach fire and brimstone?") She went on to focus on the norms and values applied in the Netherlands and she touched upon the tolerance which goes so far that children have the right to kill themselves, without anyone really caring about them in their

---

[1] All translations are by the author, unless otherwise stated.

[2] Sevtap Baycılı, 'Donderpreek', *10 jaar Winternachten* (Den Haag: Winternachten, 2005), p.61-66 (p.61).

youthful despair. Baycılı's final remarks:[3] "Maar over zoiets essentieels durf ik eigenlijk niet tegen jullie te preken. Want, ik ben een Turkse vrouw. Ik moet eerst maar eens Nederlands leren." ("But on such an essential matter I do not dare to preach to you. Because I am a Turkish woman. First I should go and learn Dutch.")

The power of this speech arises of course from the fact that a philosophically trained migrant of Turkish descent presents herself as a traditional Turkish woman. Extra effect is added by her last remark -- made in Dutch -- that she has to learn Dutch. After all the author had already proven with her first book how perfectly she had mastered the Dutch language. *De Markov-keten* (The Markov-chain)[4] is the story of a lonely person considering the here and now, locked away from other people, pondering the nature of feelings of guilt that are rooted somewhere in the past. Anyone who had not read the jacket blurb would consider this story to be the history of a Turkish migrant in Holland, and the first-person narrator to be an *alter ego* of the writer. The blurb however steers the reader in another direction: a confused man is imprisoned, he reflects on a life devoid of sharp contours, and assessed by himself as absurd. Both perspectives lead to a useful reading of this serious, philosophical text. But what would be the fate of both the reader and the text if by accident the dust jacket of the book would disappear? That indeed would be a good joke.

Graeme Dunphy warns:[5]

> We risk the barrenness of a reductionist interpretation if we insist that all writings by migrant writers must be understood in terms of migrant problems. Rather, *De Markov-keten* is to be seen as an experimental and perceptive exploration of the human psyche which happens to have been written by a migrant author, though it need not have been.

However true these words may be in principle, I think in the case of *De Markov-keten* it is inconceivable that the text could have been written in any other context than that of Sevtap Baycılı's migrant experience.[6]

---

[3]   Baycılı, 'Donderpreek', p.66.

[4]   Sevtap Baycılı, *De Markov-keten* (Breda: De Geus, 1998).

[5]   Graeme Dunphy, 'Migrant, Emigrant, Immigrant: Recent Developments in Turkish-Dutch Literature", *Neophilologus*, 86 (2001), 1-23 (pp.15f).

[6]   Dunphy also touches upon the fact that the main character is not able to express himself, a problem that operates on two levels; the internal dimension: the inability to formulate his story for his own benefit; and the external dimension: to speak aloud and to enter into a discourse with his carers. "This block [...] is clearly a psychological and not a physiological one" (Dunphy, pp.14f). In this matter too the migrants' psyche seems to me to be clearly present.

In her second book, *De nachtmerrie van de allochtoon* (The nightmare of the resident alien),[7] Baycılı attempts a new criticism of Dutch society from a migrant perspective.[8] In this book she uses a radically different form: that of a (pseudo)-scientific report, purportedly commissioned to investigate how best to deal with the integration of foreigners. The magical formula for this integration, the report states, can be found in the nightmares, "de onaangename dromen van allochtonen en de vele effecten daarvan op hun leven, waardoor het integratieproces van deze bevolkingsgroep nog altijd stagneert."[9] ("... the unpleasant dreams of foreigners and the many effects they have on their lives, because of which the process of integration of this segment of the population is still stagnating.") What is an *allochtoon*?

> Een allochtoon is iemand die je bijna onontkoombaar laat denken: 'Vreemd.'" En: "Je bent een allochtoon, weet weinig, begrijpt weinig, denkt irrationeel, droomt stompzinnig, hebt een snor en bent lelijk. Je leeft met kreten, vaderlandse clichés, Nederlands namaakgeluk. Je leeft van je uitkering. Lekker schoon geld. Je credo is: 'Alles is shit of verandert tot shit als je het in je handen neemt.' Alles is een cliché voor je. Je bent zelf een cliché. Een allochtoon.[10]

> (An *allochtoon* is somebody who almost inevitably makes you think: 'Strange.'" And: "You are an *allochtoon*, know little, understand little, think irrationally, dream stupidly, have a moustache and you are ugly. You live with slogans, patriotic clichés, Dutch imitation happiness. You live from an allowance. Nice clean money. Your credo is: 'Everything is shit or changes into shit if you take it in your hands.' Everything is a cliché to you. You're a cliché yourself. An *allochtoon*.)

The first phase of the investigation exists in making an inventory of all the nightmares and commenting on them: language-use, norms of decency, unclear racism, the intellectual *allochtoon* (!), the western attitude, the fitted sheet, the naturist beach, the royal family, etc. A scene in an employment exchange goes like this:[11]

> Je consulente is een verlegen Chinees meisje. Of ze Nederlands tegen je spreekt blijft altijd een raadsel. Vragen of ze duidelijker Nederlands kan spreken durf je niet meer. Want dat maakt haar boos. De zachte Chinese blik in haar naar de zijkanten getrokken ogen verandert dan in een oer-Hollandse agressie. Ze kijkt dan scheel. Erg Nederlands. Maar in tegenstelling daarmee praat ze dan nog onduidelijker. Klinkt ze eerder

---

7   Sevtap Baycılı, *De nachtmerrie van de allochtoon* (Amsterdam: Van Gennep, 1999).

8   Dunphy, pp.16-19 analyses the book, as does Elma Nap-Kolhoff, *Turkse auteurs in Nederland: Verkenning van een onontgonnen gebied* (Tilburg: Wetenschapswinkel Universiteit van Tilburg, 2002), pp.71-82.

9   Baycılı, *De nachtmerrie*, p.15.

10   Ibid., pp.20, 129f.

11   Ibid., pp.109f. (The paragraphs in italics are the academic's commentary on the preceding nightmare.)

Chinees dan Nederlands. Als ze zo boos wordt, komt de directeur van het arbeidsbureau haar hele verhaal vertalen in het Nederlands. Ze zegt in het Chinees dat je Nederlands moet leren. "We hebben zoveel geld betaald voor die taalcursussen. Als je je best niet doet, dan kan niemand van ons je nog helpen." Wanneer haar ogen langzaam naar de oorspronkelijke Chinese plaatsen terug beginnen te vallen wordt ze kalmer. Ze wordt stil. Zegt niks meer.

Het is hopeloos.

Als de allochtoon in deze fase wakker wordt, dan staat hij op, pakt zijn "Delftse methode" en oefent zijn Nederlands. Ook als het midden in de nacht is. Tot in de ochtend.

Dit is een nachtmerrie die vooral door nieuwkomers gedroomd wordt. Niet door allochtonen die in ons land getogen zijn. Deze tweede groep heeft zijn eigen nachtmerries over de sociale dienst en het arbeidsbureau, waarin ze zelf de medewerkers bij deze instellingen zijn. De hierboven beschreven nachtmerrie vertelt ons dat we iets niet snappen over de verhouding tussen de allochtonen die hier opgegroeid zijn en degenen die op latere leeftijd naar ons land zijn gekomen. Er bestaat toch een probleem tussen deze twee groepen.

(Your consultant is an embarassed Chinese girl. Whether she is speaking Dutch to you or not remains a mystery. You can't ask if she can speak Dutch more clearly. For that makes her mad. The gentle Chinese look in her slanting eyes then changes to a primeval Dutch aggression. Then she has a squint. Ultra-Dutch! Yet, incongruously, she then speaks even more unclearly. She sounds more Chinese than Dutch. When she gets that mad, the director of the employment exchange comes and translates her whole story into Dutch. She says in Chinese that you should learn Dutch. "We've spent so much money on language courses. If you don't try your best, none of us can help you." When her eyes gradually begin to fall back into their original Chinese position, she becomes calmer. She falls silent. Says nothing more.

It's hopeless.

If the foreigner wakes during this phase, he gets up, grabs his copy of "The Delft method" and practices his Dutch. Even if it is the middle of the night. Until dawn.

This is a nightmare which is mainly dreamed by newcomers. Not by foreigners who were born in our country. This second group has its own nightmares about the social services and the employment exchange, in which they themselves are the staff of these institutions. The nightmare described above tells us that there is something we don't quite grasp about the relation between foreigners who grew up here and those who came to our country later in life. There is after all a problem between these two groups.)

The second phase consists in the construction of the ideal nightmare, offering the solution to start the process of integration. In the third phase the question arises how the ideal nightmare can be implanted in the subconscious of the resident alien. This, so the scientist monitoring the experiment states, seems not to be successful. Therefore the resident alien should be kept awake at night, to have him experience his life as a nightmare.

The form of a scientific report offers a plethora of possibilities of multi-interpretation. Baycılı's writing is infused with ironic comments with the result that objective reality disappears in a web of ambiguities. She gives a nice demonstration of this in the chapter "Carnival". The period of carnival is the best time of the year, since your headscarf no longer attracts any attention. The Dutch are so drunk that they even compliment you on your clothes. Roles are switched; resident aliens disguise themselves as extreme right-wing, racist Dutchmen, while right-wing liberal politician Bolkestein is disguised as a Pakistani. At one stage nobody knows anymore who's who. *En passant* the book also turns its black humour against the kind of sociological investigation from which it takes its form. A calculation has to be made of the average Turk. For this purpose 95 Turks are pressed into a bin, the mass sawn into 95 pieces, and the 95 monstrously disabled foreigners are subsequently invited to apply for state benefits: they might be eligible for the category of disabled persons as well as ethnic minority.

The landscape changes

The fact that after the publication of her two books Sevtap Baycılı was offered the position of literary critic in the prominent weekly *Vrij Nederland* reveals the changed position of migrant authors in the Netherlands. The year 2001 was the clearest marking point of this change in the literary landscape. The Book Week of that year was a cause of unprecedented commotion. The organizers of the event, the Foundation for the Collective Propaganda for the Dutch Book, were widely criticised for the fact that instead of a Dutch writer, Salman Rushdie was invited to write the Book Week's Gift. The theme for that year was the "writers in-between", writers with a non-Dutch cultural background, migrant-writers. This was not entirely well received by the people in whose honour the party was held. Grumbling was heard from migrant writers in Holland. Somalian Yasmine Allas voiced the unexpected opinion: "Schrijverschap kan sowieso aan geen enkele cultuur worden verbonden."[12] ("Writing cannot be connected to any culture.") Suddenly for Hafid Bouazza, author of the Book Week's Essay "Een beer in bontjas" (A bear in a fur coat)[13] his Moroccan origins didn't matter anymore. He claimed the free space of the imagination and wanted to be read as a "normal" writer. No more whining on about his Moroccan roots -- although "Een beer in bontjas" tells in detail about his youth in Morocco, Moroccan culture and the way they get the imagination going. His argument, basically, was that a writer writing in Dutch belongs to Dutch literature, a rather simplistic position defended already 27 years earlier by the grandfather of all migrant writers, the then 71-year-old Surinamese Albert

---

[12]   Cile Schulz, 'Interview met Yasmine Allas en Kader Abdolah: Boven de culturen', *De Geuzenkrant VI*, published in the Boekenweek 2001, and distributed with *Vrij Nederland*, 10 March 2001.

[13]   Hafid Bouazza, *Een beer in bontjas* (Amsterdam: CPNB, 2001).

Helman.[14] Many critics and writers spoke out on the subject. In essence all endorsed what Bouazza in his Book Week's Essay said: the writer doesn't have any limits and claims the whole space of free imagination.[15]

This resistance to the "annexation rage" is an essential writer's theme, or rather, an artist's theme. That writers would resolutely shake off every form of labelling in advance was to be expected. It was some time before it became clear that in the meantime the Book Week's theme generated huge publicity for the "new Dutchmen", which would have been unthinkable twenty or even ten years previously. When later that year the royalties statements were sent to the writers, there was no murmur of protest to be heard -- at least in this they had assimilated to good old Dutch customs. The "foreign" writers of only a generation ago could only have dreamt of being put into the spotlight, having the book pages of the newspapers take notice of them, being welcomed in all public forums and earning royalties, and seeing heaps of their books on sale in the grubby book shops of the train stations.

The generation of the seventies and eighties -- before that time migrant writers were lone wolves -- saw the first wave of writers offering the increasingly multicultural society a literature in Dutch, but of a completely different nature. Foreign writers of the time came for the most part from the Dutch Caribbean. The appreciation of "different literature" was growing at the beginning of the seventies, starting with the editors of publishing houses. In 1968 the Surinamese Leo H. Ferrier made a remarkable debut with his novel *Átman*, followed in 1969 by Bea Vianen's *Sarnami, hai*. In 1973 Antillean Frank Martinus Arion wrote his successful novel *Dubbelspel* (published in German translation in 1982 and only in 1999 in an English version: *Doubleplay*). In the same time the Surinamese Edgar Cairo and Astrid Roemer settled in the Netherlands, and gradually started developing their oeuvre. The Turkish Halil Gür had considerable success in the second half of the eighties with books written in Dutch and won several literary prizes. The Antillean Tip Marugg and Boeli van Leeuwen had made their first appearance much earlier, before 1973, but their "tsunami" would come in 1988 when Tip Marugg was listed among the five nominees for the prestigious AKO Literary prize with *De morgen loeit weer aan* (Against the Roar of Dawn). Boeli van Leeuwen would

---

14   Cf. Albert Helman, 'Over 'nationale' letterkunde', *Sticusa Journaal*, 4 (1974), 3-6.

15   This debate on migrants' literature in the Netherlands is portrayed by Marnel Breure and Liesbeth Brouwer, 'Schrijven tussen twee culturen wordt het thema van de Boekenweek; Een reconstructie van het debat rond migrantenliteratuur in Nederland', in *Kunsten in beweging 1980-2000*. Cultuur en migratie in Nederland 2, ed. by Rosemarie Buikema and Maaike Meijer (Den Haag: Sdu, 2004), 381-396. A survey of migrant literatures in Holland can be found in Bert Paasman, 'Een klein aardrijkje op zichzelf, de multiculturele samenleving en de etnische literatuur', *Literatuur*, 16 (1999), 324-334.

also have been part of the company with his novel *Het teken van Jona* (The Sign of Jonah), had the jury not judged two Antilleans among five nominees to be too much of a good thing, so J.J. Oversteegen, a member of the jury, later told me.

Nevertheless migrant literature still wasn't a mass phenomenon. *Dubbelspel* by Frank Martinus Arion, *De morgen loeit weer aan* by Marugg and *Over de gekte van een vrouw* (On the Madness of a Woman) by Roemer sold well, but it was the generation of the nineties who managed to fight their way through to the mainstream. Books by Abdelkader Benali, Hafid Bouazza and others were highly acclaimed for the self-confident way these youngsters requisitioned the Dutch language. Nearly all Dutch cities were transformed into multicultural cities and the art world was subsumed in these changes. Writers like Kader Abdolah, Cynthia McLeod, Clark Accord, Mozes Isegawa, Lulu Wang quite easily found their place in Dutch literary life, and this despite the fact that Isegawa and Wang didn't write in Dutch. And then there was the Book Week of 2001.

In this essay I should like to shed some light on this development, sketched so far only in broad lines, by looking at the humour in the work of writers of subsequent generations. As a representative of the generation of around 1980 I shall take the work of Surinamese Edgar Cairo. To show the divergent positions of the youngest generation, I will put next to Sevtap Baycılı two more immigrants: the Persian Kader Abdolah and the Moroccan Khalid Boudou. How did these four authors put their migrant experiences into language and how was this appreciated by the readers in the Netherlands around 1980 and twenty years later?

Edgar Cairo: Ies not toe iet!

In twenty years of publishing activities (1969-1989), Edgar Cairo, born in 1948 in Paramaribo and deceased in 2000 in Amsterdam, produced an extensive oeuvre: poems, short stories, columns, essays, theatre, novels -- the most important perhaps being *Dat vuur der grote drama's* (*That Fire of Great Dramas*).[16] In all these genres he shaped and reshaped a problem he never let go of: the "negerverdriet" ("negro-sorrow") or "bestaansverdriet" ("existence-sorrow"). This concept is best understood as a curse on the black man: a lack of self-esteem and self-confidence, and a fatalism of life that makes people fall back into a closedness towards everything and everybody, an armour preventing every normal type of communication. Man is tied to his history, and everyday

---

[16] A fragment of this novel has been translated into English by Scot Rollins; cf. *Callaloo*, 21 (1998), 689-692. The only novel translated in its entirety is *Temekoe/Kopzorg* (Haarlem: In de Knipscheer, 1979). Transl. by Peter Gobets as *Mindworry: A Surinamese Story of Father and Son* (Amsterdam: In de Knipscheer, 1993, only published as a Courtesy Edition).

life -- home or far away -- is always governed by the interaction between past and present. First and foremost Cairo depicted the life of the negroes, in whom he saw the entire sorrow of colonized humanity. He depicts the traumas in all their appearances, sketches with the blackest of his ink the enslavement of the mind resulting from the cultural imperialism of the colonizer. But always too he seeks the nuance; he is very self-critical and thus avoids the trap of racist black-and-white thinking.[17]

In the way he did this, Cairo became one of the great language creolizers and he may be bracketed together with Patrick Chamoiseau, Raphaël Confiant and Alice Walker. He belongs to the most important writers in Sranantongo -- the language of the Afro-Surinamese -- but also plunged the Dutch language into a Surinamese bath, the effects of which went far beyond the Surinamese-Dutch spoken in Suriname. Cairo spoke of his variant of Dutch as "gecreoliseerd Nederlands, inheems Nederlands"[18] ("creolized Dutch, indigenous Dutch"). In its vocabulary and syntax "Cairojan" is strongly determined by Dutch as spoken in Suriname. The author also tries to put as much of the timbre of Surinamese-Dutch in his texts by using a phonetic orthography ("dalek", "nèks" instead of standard Dutch: "dadelijk" "indeed", "niks" "nothing") and many exclamation marks, accents, elisions, italics, onomatopoeia, interjections ("aaj", "baja", "ehm", "san") and exclamations. Cairo's language furthermore knows some phenomena aimed at enriching Surinamese-Dutch by an intentional creolization. Often he takes words, proverbs, phrases or even syntactical constructions from Sranan.

A classic back-yard scene is this one from Cairo's novel *Temekoe/Kopzorg*:[19]

Een van die vrouwen van ons erf waar we woonden, had heftige ruzie met d'r man. Ze heette Sjako. Sjako en d'r man vochten (hoe kon dat ding anders) om een andere vrouw. Sjako bezat een kip. Die andere vrouw had ook een kip als d'r bezitting, die ze op na hield. Die twee kippen leken precies op makaar.

Enkele dagen voor Bedaki, Kerst! Dan die vrouw, ze gooide d'r kip in d'r pan. Mooi braaien! San? Met zwarte peper en nootmuskaat smoorde ze die *titi*. Onverwachts hoorde ze iemand d'r m'mapima geven! Dus iemand schold haar uit. Hmmmm? Wat zo, gedaan dan?

17   An overview of the author's life and work with a primary and secondary bibliography: Michiel van Kempen, 'Edgar Cairo', *Kritisch Lexicon van de Moderne Nederlandstalige Literatuur*, 36 (1990) and Michiel van Kempen, *Een geschiedenis van de Surinaamse literatuur*, 2 vols. (Breda: De Geus, 2003). The rise of Surinamese migrants' literature is extensively dealt with in vol. 2, pp.1085-1098.
18   Hijlco Span, 'Tussen vaderland en moederland; Surinaamse literatuur in Nederland', *Literama*, 22 (1987), 62-70 (p.63).
19   Cairo, *Temekoe/Kopzorg*, pp.103-104. Trans. by Peter Gobets.

Die scheldvrouw was... Sjako! Het was al zo, dat Sjako dat mens reeds op het hart had. En nu zo, met goeie gelegenheid, schrobde ze haar de dijen schoon! Allerlei "m'ma's", van die zwarte scheldtermen over moeders. En dat allemaal, omdat die vrouw die kip van Sjako fo d'r eigen kip had aangezien.

Die hele ochtend, razen, tieren. Halen en trekken, zoals mensen 't zo mooi zeggen. Die vrouw deed op 't laatst niets anders, dan dat zij die volle pan met kippevlees pakte en fo Sjako d'r deur zette. Hoor wat ze uitspoelde, met mond vol van tabak: "De!: neem! Is van jou door god gegeven! Laat die kippenek je keelgat steken! En die kip z'n vlees moet frotten in je schijtbuik!"

Ma' Sjako, met tienmaal zoveel schelden! Kos'kosi!, schelden! Je oor werd doof van 't! Dan was 't net, ofdat 't kind dat Sjako in d'r buik droeg, vuur stookte. Want ze nam die ijzeren bolle pan, en gooide alles zo, laat die honden jarig worden! Ija, want als je zag hoe honden rondgang hadden, met kippevlees! Die kinderen daar konden de honden doodbijten van haternij en jaloezie. Zoveel vlees had zo'n hond nog nooit gezien, laat staan gegeten met z'n bekwerk! Baja...

(One of the women on our backlot where we lived, had a terrific quarrel with her husband. Her name was Shacko. Shacko and her husband (what else would it be) was fightin' about another woman. Shacko owned a chicken. The other woman also had a chicken as her possession, that she kept. Them two chickens looked exactly alike.

A few days before Bedaki, Christmas! That woman, she threw her chicken in her pan. Nicely fried! What? With black pepper and nutmeg she stewed that *titi*. Unexpectedly she heard somebody givin' her shit! That is, somebody was swearin' at her. Hmmmm? What had she done, éh?

That cussin' woman was... Shacko! It so happened that Shacko already had somethin' against that person. And now, with a good opportunity, she scrubbed her thighs clean for her! All kinds of of mother's, them heavy-duty four letter words about mothers. And all of that because that woman had mistaken Shacko's chicken for her own.

That whole mornin', rantin' and ravin'. Pushin' and pullin', as people put it well. At last that woman did nothin' but grab that pan full of chicken meat and put it in front of Shacko's door. Listen to what she spit out, with her mouth full of tobacco.

'Here!: take it! It's yours given by the Lord! Let that chicken neck stick in your throat! And that chicken's flesh should rot in your shit gut!')

In his linguistic usage Cairo always aims at language conservation and language renewal. With his work in Surinamese-Dutch as well as in Sranan he wants to document the richness of both languages, conserve them and revive them. In the respect for Surinamese languages he sees the beginning of the respect for his own culture and identity -- ideas not far off from those of Frantz Fanon. Language makes the nation and therefore a kind of Dutch should be developed which maximises the Surinamese uniqueness and keeps the greatest possible distance from the language of the former colonizers.

In 1968 Edgar Cairo came to the Netherlands, at the age of twenty. Ten years later, in 1978, he started writing columns in the national newspaper *de Volkskrant*, later collected in *Ik ga dood om jullie hoofd* (I am dying for your head) and *Als je hoofd is geboord* (If your head is drilled).[20] Thus he became one of the first foreign authors ever to write prominently on a regular basis in a Dutch newspaper. Critically and wittily Edgar Cairo sketched how Holland was confronted with its former colony in the West Indies: the mistakes emerging from linguistic and cultural differences, everyday life and the big and small dreams of the migrant, prejudices and how people deal with them. In the column "Is not toe ieeeet!" for instance he sketched how he himself goes to buy cat litter in a supermarket, and a lady starts shouting at him: "No! No! Ies not toe ieeet!" Making him react: "Mevrouw! Ik ben academicus! En neerlandikus ook nog, alsjeblieft!" ("Lady! I am an academic! And a *neerlandicus* as well, if you please!") She finally answers him in an Amsterdam accent: "Nou? Vreet dan maar die zak op, zeikerd!" ("Indeed! Well stuff the bag yourself, asshole!")[21] Thus human concern is turned into vulgar Amsterdam coarseness.

Cairo initially composed his work in a baroque language, not always characterised by clearness of expression until his public began to show signs of irritation. The readers of his *Volkskrant* columns made it clear that they found his language incomprehensible. Sometimes it even provoked extreme reactions. In a letter to the editor four Surinamers wrote: "Die stukken hebben een kinderachtig beeld van de Surinamer gekweekt en daar lijden mensen onder. Die stukken hebben niet het effect wat u dacht. Men lacht om die stukken en de kinderlijkheid die Cairo naar voren brengt in zijn stukken. U weet net als ik dat Hollanders gedegenereerde lieden zijn zonder emoties." [22] ("These pieces create an infantile image of the Surinamer and people are suffering from them. These pieces have not had the effect you thought they would. People laugh about them and about the infantile impression Cairo gives in his pieces. You know as well as I do that Dutchmen are degenerate people without emotions.") Precisely this last "argument" makes clear how right Cairo was when in the prelude to his first collection of columns he stated that the negative reactions of Surinamers were not primarily a rejection of his language, but a colonial complex, rooted in jealousy, misunderstanding, doubt, racism, stupidity, lack of intelligence, fear, ignorance, unfamiliarity with certain phenomena and/or repression.[23] Anyway, the editors of *de Volkskrant* asked him to continue writing in a somewhat more accessible Dutch -- which he did from June 1980 onwards. Communication was

[20]   Edgar Cairo, *Ik ga dood om jullie hoofd* (Haarlem: In de Knipscheer, 1980); Edgar Cairo, *Als je hoofd is geboord: Krantecolumns 2* (Haarlem: In de Knipscheer, 1981).

[21]   Cairo, *Ik ga dood om jullie hoofd*, p.97.

[22]   Letter signed by D. Forster, A. Soekdeew, T. Resida and R. Ahmad Ali, cited in 'Cairo, kun je geen ABN schrijven?', *de Volkskrant*, 14. June 1980. Reactions were published in *de Volkskrant*, 21. June 1980.

[23]   Cf. Cairo, *Ik ga dood om jullie hoofd*, pp.9-47.

also essential to Cairo and an important conclusion was to be drawn from this: he was slowly moving away from the Surinamese situation.[24]

Edgar Cairo is descended from the race of Negroes from the Para, the district in Suriname where the population had conserved much of the old Afro-Surinamese culture, and thus he speaks a deep, authentic Sranantongo, not affected by standardised languages. At the same time he grew up in a former Dutch colony where the Dutch language continued to play a strong "umbrella" role because of the great diversity of the population. Since 1876 Dutch had been imposed through the educational system the hard way; Suriname had a genuine compulsory education long before the Netherlands! Of course this situation had a disastrous effect on the self-confidence of people using their own vernaculars.[25] On the other hand this also meant that in the long run vast groups of Surinamese emigrants had no language problems whatsoever when they arrived in Holland. Cairo sucked up Dutch at school and became aware -- as he states at many places in his books -- that only a variant as strongly Surinamese as possible could narrow the gap between the strange language and the Surinamers' own psyche. Starting from Standard Educated Dutch he hollowed out the language of the colonizer, to fill it up with Surinamese individuality. Furthermore he used that language to imagine the historical and contemporary world of the Surinamers, in their own land and overseas. It was this imagination that he offered on the Dutch literary market, and it was only when he noticed communication problems arising that he started watering the wine, and restructured his language instrument in the direction of a more easily understandable Dutch.

Kader Abdolah: Neighbour without underpants

Kader Abdolah was born in 1954 in the Iranian city of Arak as Hossein Sadjadi Ghaemmaghami (Farahani). He became active in the resistance against the Shah-regime and after 1979 against the regime of Khomeini, fled to Turkey in 1985 and more by accident than design he arrived in Holland in 1988, where he was granted political asylum. Thus he started to learn Dutch only at the age of 33.[26] Five years later, in 1993, his first collection of short stories was published

---

24   Cf. interview with Span, p.64. Cf. *de Volkskrant* 21. Nov. 1978, 14. June 1980, 21. June 1980.

25   Language policy and the effects it had on the population of Suriname are described in detail in Lila Gobardhan-Rambocus, *Onderwijs als sleutel tot maatschappelijke vooruitgang: Een taal- en onderwijsgeschiedenis van Suriname, 1651-1975* (Zutphen: Walburg Press, 2001) and van Kempen, *Een geschiedenis van de Surinaamse literatuur*.

26   A survey of life and work with a primary and secondary bibliography is provided in Ton Brouwers, 'Kader Abdolah', *Kritisch Lexicon van de Moderne Nederlandstalige literatuur*, 67 (1997).

in Dutch: *De adelaars* (The eagles), followed two years later by *De meisjes en de partizanen* (The girls and the partisans).[27] In 1996 -- twenty years after Edgar Cairo -- he started writing columns for *de Volkskrant*, collected in *Mirza* (1998) and *Een tuin in de zee* (A garden in the sea, 2001).[28] In 1997 his first novel was published, *De reis van de lege flessen* (The voyage of the empty bottles),[29] followed by four other prose books.

De reis van de lege flessen became one of the most successful novels ever written by a migrant author in Dutch. The plot in broad lines: Iranian refugee Bolfazl is undergoing his naturalization process in a Dutch village where he comes to live next door to René, who happens to be homosexual. In continuous flashbacks to his past in Persia, in drifting apart from his wife who follows western modernity, and in his mother's visit Bolfazl experiences how his life is turned upside down. René throws himself under a train. Bolfazl has a far less contact with his new neighbour, although he is very much interested in the man's radio transmitter.

To Kader Abdolah, Dutch and Dutch culture had to be conquered, and the same applies to the main character of *De reis van de lege flessen*, Bolfazl. This is reflected in the style of the novel. The persons communicate in phrases of only a few words. Linguistically the first contact with neighbour René takes place in a hesitant way. Language and reality form one identity, but they are both strange to Bolfazl. In the eye of European readers the confrontation of the refugee with western lifestyle and thinking has unmistakably tragicomical traits. The green of the surroundings, the mist and the showers, the nakedness of people: "Aan die blote benen, buiken, borsten, billen en aan de taal moest ik wennen. En René, mijn buurman, zou ik zonder onderbroek moeten accepteren."[30] ("I had to get used to those naked legs, bellies, breasts, buttocks and to the language. And René, my neighbour, had to be accepted without his underpants.") The first-person narrator is made painfully aware of the cultural discontinuity because of the fact that his wife masters the Dutch language quicker than he himself does.[31] If language and reality do form a unity, then the consequence is that Bolfazl has to learn a language that is not thinkable in Persian:

---

[27]   Kader Abdolah, *De adelaars: verhalen* (Breda: De Geus, 1993); *De meisjes en de partizanen: verhalen* (Breda: De Geus, 1995).

[28]   Kader Abdolah, *Een tuin in de zee: Mirza* (Breda: De Geus, 2001).

[29]   Kader Abdolah, *De reis van de lege flessen* (Breda: De Geus, 1997).

[30]   Ibid., p.11.

[31]   Cf. Ibid., pp.16, 85, 109.

Zijn die borsten in de spiegel van jouw dochter?
Zo'n zinnetje zou nooit in het Perzisch bij mij opkomen. In het Nederlands kon ik het
ook nooit uitspreken. Maar het op papier zetten lukte wel.[32]

(Are those breasts in the mirror your daughter's breasts? Such a phrase would have been
impossible for me in Persian. I couldn't say it in Dutch either. But I could put it down on
paper.)

In other words: in the act of writing the new reality takes refuge in the new
language and is thus rendered harmless. For the meaning of Kader Abdolah's
writing, this passage seems to me of crucial importance. Bolfazl's mother, who
comes to visit him for a short time, cannot see the necessity of getting to know a
new world let alone of redefining the language. She vigorously distances herself
from the neighbour, who in her eyes is decadent, when she has seen him in bed
with his boyfriend. Bolfazl quizzes his mother:

Lagen ze in bed, moeder?
Stonden ze op het bed?
Deden ze iets wat niet mocht?

(Were they lying in bed, mother?
Were they standing on the bed?
Did they do something indecent?)

But these questions are restricted to the written language of the novel, they don't
cross the border to the reality of the mother: "Bij ons was het ongepast om
zulke vragen te stellen. Zo'n gesprek kon tussen ons nooit plaatsvinden."[33]
("With us it was inappropriate to ask such questions. Such a conversation could
never happen between us.")

If Cairo's work is a feast of abundance, a feast of language virtuosity, *De
reis van de lege flessen* is the book of the silence following the questions. Those
questions structure the path of Bolfazl's language acquisition, but at the same
time take on a sadder meaning in the political story of the refugee: "Typische
eigenschap van ballingen: zwijgen. Een balling zwijgt omdat hij weet dat de
gebeurtenissen soms anders kunnen lopen. Vaak twijfelt hij en stelt liever
vragen."[34] ("Typical characteristic of exiles: silence. An exile remains silent
because he knows that things may go the other way. Often he is unsure of
himself and prefers to ask questions.") Asking questions is only possible where
there's confidence. That is what he experiences with René, but not with the later
neighbour, when suddenly the problem arises which questions can be asked and

---

[32] Abdolah, *De reis van de lege flessen*, p.18.
[33] Ibid., p.21.
[34] Ibid., p.57.

which cannot.[35] With this new neighbour, Jacobus, silence at once takes on another meaning. His radio transmitter catches unexpected voices from the sky and sometimes an Iranian voice (the reverse of what happens in the title story of *De meisjes en de partizanen*, where singing voices from the West represent the far-off free world to the listening boy). In a completely different way the radio silences of Jacobus' transmitter accentuate the position of the exile Bolfazl.

Kader Abdolah didn't start from a position where he had been confronted with the Dutch language since childhood. He had to conquer everything anew: the language, but also the reality and the public. His only anchor was a past with a form and a language not communicable in his new surroundings. He had nothing left but a complete exchange of his literary armamentarium. In his *Volkskrant* column of 11th June 1996 he wrote:[36]

> De Nederlandse taal is een vijand. Een bezetter. Duitsers in de Tweede Wereldoorlog. Ik ben beroofd door vreemde woorden. [...] In de bergen van mijn vaderland ligt het graf van mijn broer leeg. De bezetter heeft het lijk van mijn broer meegenomen en begraven in de grond van de Nederlandse taal.

> (The Dutch language is an enemy. An occupier. Germans in the Second World War. I've been robbed by strange words. [...] In the mountains of my fatherland the grave of my brother lies empty. The occupier took the body of my brother with him and buried it in the soil of the Dutch language.)

What had to be transferred from his old reality, Abdolah tried to crochet up into the new language; he wove old stories into the new story, knowing that part of the old reality could never be spoken, would ever remain inexpressible. "Voor wie weg is, heb je geen woorden meer"[37] ("You have no words anymore for those who have gone"), says Bolfazl of the disappeared René, but by extension these words do have at least as much power for the characters from the Persian past.

In the case of Kader Abdolah one might ask whether much of the wit of the story isn't rather in the eye of the beholder, and whether in fact the writer has intentionally put it into his text. The almost objective or naïve way of observing by an adult sheds an alienating light on things which are completely normal for

---

[35]   Cf. Abdolah, *De reis van de lege flessen*, p.128.

[36]   Isabel Hoving analyses this text and she calls the fragment as a sketch of the intercultural language situation "an unexpected harsh image". Isabel Hoving, 'Een leeg graf, een boze man, en een spraakmakende foto: De brokstukken van een Nederlandstalige reflectie over interculturaliteit', in *Tussenfiguren: Schrijvers tussen de culturen*, ed. by Elisabeth Leijnse and Michiel van Kempen (Amsterdam: Het Spinhuis, 1998), pp.50ff. Cf. also Kader Abdolah, 'Het Nederlands als mijn tweede vaderland', *Ons Erfdeel*, 39 (1996), 684-691.

[37]   Abdolah, *De reis van de lege flessen*, p.83.

any average European. Thus Kader Abdolah is holding up a mirror to the European, making him laugh at things one normally passes by.

Khalid Boudou: Sheep's head in a drawer

Khalid Boudou was born in 1974 in Tamsamane (Morocco). He came to Holland as a small boy, and had his entire school education there. In his first book, the novel *Het schnitzelparadijs* (The schnitzel paradise),[38] Boudou sketches the life of the "second-generation" Moroccans in Holland. Nordip has spent two years in apathy and decides to start working as a dishwasher in the restaurant "De Blauwe Gier" (The Blue Vulture) -- clearly modelled on a well-known chain of restaurants in the Netherlands, *Van der Valk* (The Falcon). The young kitchen staff confide in him their secrets, longings, frustrations and love-affairs. The rest of the personnel distrust him. What is this precocious dishwasher doing? Is he a spy for the management or the tax department? Things accelerate when the youngest member of the kitchen staff has three of his fingers chopped off in the meat machine, and the tax inspection office raids the restaurant. Throughout the story the reader is offered insights into the Nordip's home environment, and a couple of scenes in Morocco also highlight the expectations with which the migrants moved to Western Europe, and the contrasts in lifestyle which resulted.

Het schnitzelparadijs has been written with guts. It is a fast-moving story evoking the life of street youngsters, but at the same time a story of imagination, lifting events up to a literary level. Nordip, the main character, looks upon the world with healthy cynicism and youthful daring. The world wants to be cheated and will be cheated -- albeit within the margins of a scamp's mentality. In the character of Nordip, Khalid Boudou creates the modern version of the Moroccan Djeha (a variant of the shrewd fox Reynard, or also of the Hodya or Mullah Nasreddin in Turkey). This trickster-figure, this little outcast, manages to carry on thanks to his dodges and his big mouth: "Toen sloop ik maar helemaal weg, nadat ik bij die muggenlarf een bloederige schele schapenkop, traditioneel bij de keel afgesneden, in de la had gepropt..."[39] ("Then I sneaked away, after having put a bloody, squint-eyed sheep's head, cut off at the throat in the traditional way, into the drawer of that mosquito larva..."). Boudou manipulates new variants of old humorous techniques. In hilarious scenes which make you think of what you might see in the popular theatre, he sketches how Nordip, who hates dogs, takes care of the little doggy of an old woman, covers the poor beast with syrup and rubs it with scouring powder. That Morocco is not really the

---

[38] Khalid Boudou, *Het schnitzelparadijs* (2001; Amsterdam: Maarten Muntinga/Vassallucci, 2003).
[39] Ibid., p.80.

ideal place to be for the narrator is shown in a chapter telling the story of the way Nordip's nephew got married by a kind of gamble.

Boudou uses a virtuoso and baroque language. He creates new words ("ik salamiseer" -- "I salamize"), and by a flashing alternation of observations and interior monologue puts things into perspective. The migration of his father to Holland is described as follows:[40]

Teleurgesteld kwam hij weer terug, op de camion, met een verdienste van brood, vleesstomaat en een kilo sardine in de knapzak. Hij gaf zich over aan de armen van zijn snikkende moedertje. Grootvader sloeg een wandelstok op zijn harde hoofd kapot, en voordat hij zijn zoon warm, omhelsde, zei hij grienend: "Vóel je dat, mijn zoon? Vóel je dat? Dat zijn nog zachte klappen vergeleken met die jij me hebt gegeven. Kijk, elke dag dat jij er niet was heb ik met een bot mes in mijn hoofd gekerfd. Er is helemaal niets meer van over."

Maar vader legde zichzelf er niet bij neer. Wat had hij te verliezen?

Wat had ikzelf te verliezen gehad, toen ik besloot twee jaar lang te gaan slapen, een leven begon als "Weerwolfman"?

"Wat had ik te verliezen, Nordip, kleine shjodimieter? Twee balen stro, een hangoorezel die protesteerde tegen de te hoge werkdruk en de Hollandse koe Beatrijs, die zich maar niet wilde aanpassen aan de verzengende hitte en alle van de zon trillende dagen alleen maar stond te loeien -- nog geen druppel zure melk kreeg je uit haar…!"

Hij zou nu niet gaan voor een beter zuiden, voor sinaasappelen of stenen stapelen in Algiers, maar verder, veel verder, door middel van een contract dat Allah hem aanreikte uit handen van een oom, een zekere Boechaib.

Boechaib was een grote man met een dikke heerserssnor, een gezicht gegroefd door de jaren en de eenzaamheid. Boechaib genoot aanzien in het dorp. Hij was een van de eerste dorpelingen die zijn heil over zee had gezocht… Ze hadden Boechaib daar warm ontvangen, in dat grote Parijs, en meteen gehuld in een Citroën-overall. Hij werd bewapend met een Japanse dopsleutel om daarmee de volgende twintig jaar op zijn dorps om de realiteit heen te draaien: *Ik wil, ik heb, ik heb alles. Ik blijf willen hebben.* "Hebzucht is een bodemloze put, Nordip. Het einde is zoek. Hoe zoek je het beste naar het einde? Wordt vervolgd? Zulke verhaaltjes verkondigde Boechaib daar allemaal, totdat hij vorig jaar stierf aan de suikerziekte." In een tijd waarin de landverlaters werden uitgelachen, kwam deze Boechaib te weten dat mijn vader brandde van verlangen om te vertrekken, om een kijkje achter de zeedeur te gaan nemen.

(Disappointed, he returned on the lorry with his wages in the form of bread, beef tomatoes and a kilo of sardines in his knapsack. He abandoned himself into the arms of his sobbing mother. Grandfather broke a walking-stick over his hard head, and before he embraced his son, warmly, he said, blubbering, "Do you feel that, my son? Do you feel that? Those are soft blows compared with the one you gave me. Look, every day that you weren't here has been carved into my head with a blunt knife. There is nothing of it left."

---

[40]   Boudou, pp.154-6.

But father didn't lie back and take it. What did he have to lose?

What might I have had to lose myself, if I decided to go to sleep for two years, a life begun as "werewolf man"?

"What did I have to lose, Nordip, little bashtard? Two bales of straw, a floppy-eared donkey which protested about its heavy workload and the Dutch cow Beatrijs, which didn't want to adapt to the scorching heat and any day the sun blazed down just stood there mooing – not a drop of sour milk could you get from her…!"

He would not now go looking for a better south, to pile up stones or pineapples in Algiers, but further, far further, because of a contract that Allah had given him out of the hands of an uncle, a certain Boechaib. Boechaib was a large man with a thick ruler's moustache, a face furrowed by the years and the loneliness.

Boechaib was well esteemed in the village. He was one of the first villagers to seek his fortune overseas… They had received Boechaib warmly, in that great Paris, and at once dressed him in Citroën overalls. They armed him with a Japanese box spanner so he could spend the next twenty years turning his village towards reality: *I want, I have, I have everything. I'll keep wanting to have.* "Avarice is a bottomless pit, Nordip. The end is seeking. How do you seek the best after the end? Do you continue? Boechaib proclaimed such matters until he died of diabetes last year." At a time when the emigrants are mocked, this Boechaib learned of my father's burning desire to depart, to take a look behind the gates of the sea.)

Mockery and self-irony are Boudou's weapons. He continually refers to the bourgeois culture of Holland and the prejudiced way of looking at Moroccans, and takes advantage of them by intermingling asides, thus ironically parodying narrow-minded viewpoints, as well as Moroccan culture itself: "Mijn broer Kariem, toen nog vreselijk creatief omdat hij nog niet getrouwd was […]" ("My brother Kariem, at the time still terribly creative because he was not yet married […]"). And: "[Ik] keek mijn vader aan, die helemaal Delft blauw werd van de bordjes aan de muur."[41] ("[I] looked at my father, who went completely Delft-blue from the dishes on the wall.")

Prizes, no prizes

Four migrants in Holland, writing as though their lives depended on it, but what a world of difference in background, linguistic art and public appreciation too. Edgar Cairo, without doubt one of the most creative migrant writers ever to have lived in the Netherlands, never received any literary, royal or presidential prize or honour, neither in the Netherlands nor in his native country. In the eighties he made a name for himself by his steady stream of new books, his columns and his many performances, but he didn't acquire a vast reading public, and after his death silence surrounded his work. The public couldn't identify with his language and didn't recognize it as a reflection of the Surinamese-Dutch vernacular, both because of the dense concentration of Surinamese-Dutch

---

[41]   Boudou, pp.173, 175.

linguistic characteristics, and because of the neologisms of Cairo-workmanship. In Suriname Cairo became a widely-read author, especially with his first novel *Kollektieve schuld* (Collective guilt),[42] but appreciation was not unanimously positive. In his homeland Cairo was seen first and foremost as a migrant, writing for a situation eight thousand kilometres away. On the other side of the ocean the Dutch reading public seemed to realize that after so many Cairo books only Surinamers could see through the essence of his literature. And so Edgar Cairo fell between two stools.

Kader Abdolah has never lacked an appreciative audience. For his first book, the collection of short stories *De adelaars*, he was awarded the Gouden Ezelsoor (Golden Dog-ear), an award for the best sold Dutch debut book. Then he was granted the Charlotte Köhler scholarship for *De meisjes en de partizanen*, a collection that put him onto the short-list of the two awards with the highest prize money in Holland, the AKO and the Libris. For his columns in *Mirza* he was awarded the Media prize 1997. He later won the E. du Perron prize for *Spijkerschrift* (Cuneiform, 2000) and also a royal honour. This recognition came from the Dutch community. The Iranian supporters appreciated his work far less; obviously this was partly because Abdolah chose to write in Dutch rather than Persian, but also because he said things he would never have dared say in his native tongue.

In *De reis van de lege flessen* Kader Abdolah evokes the landscape of the IJssel-river in all its green space in a way no Dutch writer could have done better. This quality brought him a vast reading public, a public he drew from the IJssel-river up to the mountains of Persia. It was not until his sixth book, *Spijkerschrift*, that Abdolah situated a story almost completely in his country of origin.

No matter how intensely writers drag in their homeland in their plots and their way of storytelling, some writers simply want to belong to Dutch literature because they are writing in Dutch. Kader Abdolah, however, does not seem to jump to such a conclusion, according to his last book, *Portretten en een oude droom* (Portraits and an old dream).[43] The novel tells about a Persian journalist living in Holland, Dawoed, who on a journey in South Africa is besieged by phantoms of long ago, personified in five friends, three of whom have been executed. Out of the tissue of thoughts and stories of Dawoed and one of his friends, present-day South Africa is linked to Persian travellers' tales and reflections on the distance to Holland. In an interview Ed van Eeden held with Kader Abdolah on the occasion of the presentation of the book on 23rd February 2003 in Utrecht, the writer explained:

---

[42]   Edgar Cairo, *Kollektieve schuld of wel Famir'man-sani* (Baarn: Het Wereldvenster's/ Gravenhage: Novib / Brussel: NCOS, 1976).
[43]   Kader Abdolah, *Portretten en een oude droom* (Breda: De Geus, 2003).

Het voelde alsof ik Nederland had verraden. De zon in Zuid-Afrika voelde op mijn
huid als de zon in Iran. Deze zon was een andere dan die in Nederland. Hij bracht
herinneringen terug. Jarenlang dacht ik dat Nederland mijn tweede thuis was, maar nu
begreep ik dat het niet zo was.

(It felt like I had betrayed Holland. The sun in South Africa felt on my skin like the
sun in Iran. This sun was different from that in Holland. It brought back memories. For
years I had thought Holland was my second home, but now I understood it is not so.)

Cairo, from his post-colonial position, and Abdolah, from his position as forced
migrant, both struggled with comparable problems: the conquest of a new
language, the mental processing and literary rewriting of the past, the
exploration of a new reality. Both did so with a good feeling for humour -- in
Cairo roaring with laughter as soon as he dispensed of the shades of the Negro's
sorrow, in Abdolah smiling. The work of both testifies to a great feeling of love
for the little man in the street with all his annoying ways and great qualities. But
on decisive points their poetics choose completely divergent directions.

With Sevtap Baycılı and Khalid Boudou things are different again.
Baycılı's two books have not been a resounding success in the bookshops.
They simply contained too little narrative. They were books for an educated
public, a public prepared to put in the intellectual effort required to see
through the texts and to reconsider their own position in a critical way. Many
Turkish authors in the Netherlands write in Turkish. Baycılı has not been able
to break the pattern that the Turkish literature in Holland is developing "in
fits and starts."[44] Two more books by Baycılı have been announced, but so
far they have not appeared. Nevertheless she is an author who counts for
something in the literary world, if the invitation to speak at the
Winternachten festival is anything to go by.

For Kader Abdolah language brought a new reality, for Baycılı the
transformation has been less radical: "Het leren van een nieuwe taal opent
nieuwe deuren in de geest en ook in het leven. [...] Maar wat ik uiteindelijk
schrijf komt toch eerder voort uit mijn persoonlijkheid dan uit mijn
tweetaligheid."[45] ("Learning a new language opens new doors in the mind
and in life as well. [...] But what I ultimately write emerges from my own
personality, rather than from my bilingualism.") It is true that in *De*

---

[44] Dunphy, p.1. Besides Dunphy also Henriette Louwerse, 'The Way to the North or the
Emergence of Turkish and Moroccan Migrant Literature in the Dutch Literary Landscape',
Dutch Crossing, 21 (1997), 69-86, and especially Elma Nap-Kolhoff, *Turkse auteurs in
Nederland: Verkenning van een onontgonnen gebied* (Tilburg: Wetenschapswinkel Univer-
siteit van Tilburg, 2002) wrote on the tentative beginnings of Turkish literature in the Neth-
erlands.
[45] Jinke Hesterman, 'Sevtap Baycılı schrijft voor de zappende lezer', *Overijssels Dagblad*, 13.
March 2001.

nachtmerrie van de allochtoon Baycılı wrote of the migrant's existence, but her tone has nothing plaintive about it, and in her intellectual distance from the objects she describes, she steps effortlessly into a Cartesian tradition. Because she makes the problem of narration an object of her text and sheds an absurd light on reality, Dunphy has pointed to the connection with Samuel Beckett. He rightly states that although she is "a relatively recent intellectual migrant, her attitudes are in many ways close to those of a second-generation migrant." He calls her "an author who is capable of producing qualitatively the best migrant literature we have yet seen," and insofar as her mastery of the Dutch language is concerned, he compares her to German-Turkish writers Akif Pirinçci and Renan Demirkan.[46]

In 1998 Khalid Boudou was awarded the El Hizjra Literary prize (for Dutch writers of Moroccan origin) and he received in 2002 for *Het schnitzelparadijs* the Gouden Ezelsoor. The book has been turned into a film in 2005. With his novel he won a broad and also young public -- in Holland, certainly not in Morocco. In 1999, five years after the remarkable upsurge of Moroccan-Dutch authors like Mustafa Stitou, Hafid Bouazza and Abdelkader Benali, Ton Anbeek stated that they had become victims of their own fatal success; literary critics had a far more critical attitude towards the follow-up of the first series of best sellers.[47] That conclusion seems to have been rather premature; meanwhile quite some authors have fought their way through to the first ranks, and an author like Khalid Boudou was among those who made the stream of Moroccan-Dutch literature broader, and also more widely accepted than before.

The black splits

How in nearly twenty years time could such a turn in appreciation of migrant writing in the Netherlands take place? A complex combination of factors explains this.

In the first place there is the mere nature of the work of Edgar Cairo itself. His literary activities started from a sharp self-consciousness and an implicit (often also explicit) demand for self-inquiry on the part of his public. He sought confrontation, he held up a mirror to his audience reflecting a history

---

[46] Dunphy, pp.19f.
[47] Ton Anbeek, 'Fataal succes: Over Marokkaans-Nederlandse auteurs en hun critici', *Literatuur*, 16 (1999), 335-342 (p.341). Somewhat rewritten his essay also appeared as Ton Anbeek, 'Doodknuffelen: Over Marokkaans-Nederlandse auteurs en hun critici', in *Europa buitengaats: Koloniale en postkoloniale literaturen in Europese talen*, ed. by Theo D'haen, vol. I. (Amsterdam: Bert Bakker, 2002), pp.289-301. On the upcoming of Moroccan migrant literature, cf. also Hassan Bousetta, 'Kunst, cultuur en literatuur in de Marokkaanse gemeenschap in Nederland', *Migrantenstudies*, 11 (1996), 182-194, and Louwerse.

"that is black, that is black". The form he chose was original, but referred constantly to a number of elements from Afro-Surinamese culture. The imaginative world of Edgar Cairo is linked to a deep Afro-Surinamese experience. It is precisely the rapprochement of two cultural worlds -- in elementary terms *winti* (voodoo) versus Christianity, or tradition versus modernity -- that belongs to the essence of the Afro-Surinamese identity. But how to shape this imagination, when the Afro-Surinamese philosophy of life does not in any way appeal to the perception of the environment of the reading public in Holland? Standard Educated Dutch always remained a colonial language for the man from the colony, a language that had to be transformed to express the deepest feelings of the Surinamers. Unlike Kader Abdolah he didn't gratefully make use of the language of the host to enter "the world of freedom", no, in his perception it was precisely that colonial language constituting the lack of freedom.[48] He was Caliban, coming to occupy the language of the ruler and trying to give it another form. And the reading audience wasn't a fixed phenomenon either, neither in his own country where a reading culture was *in statu nascendi*, nor even in Holland, where a willing public was to be found, albeit a public unable to judge Cairo's virtuosity on its merits.

Cairo had no mission transmitting cultural information, he didn't want to preach a historical sermon to make Dutch readers realize the damage colonialism had done. First and foremost Cairo wanted to tell stories that hadn't been told before, retelling a history which was also part of the history of the Netherlands, from a different point of view. He did this on behalf of the people who always had been the losers, and he wanted to do so from the inside and with as few linguistic adaptations as possible for readers on the outside who were prepared to listen to this rewritten history.

Much of the humour of Edgar Cairo requires some insight in the social context of Suriname or in minority groups in the Netherlands, and quite some knowledge of the way he plays with Sranan, Surinamese-Dutch and his own "Cairojan". In the fragment cited above, for instance, Cairo says: "Onverwachts hoorde ze iemand d'r m'mapima geven!" ("Unexpectedly she heard somebody givin' her shit!"), and he explains the expression thus: "Dus iemand schold haar uit." ("That is, somebody was swearin' at her.") Now, what is not clear in his own Dutch explanation, nor in the English translation, is that he uses an expression not known in Surinamese-Dutch, but playing with abusive Sranan *yu m'ma pima*, meaning: "your mother's cunt". This expression is part of every-day-life of the people of the Surinamese backyards. Edgar Cairo is rendering the

---

[48]   A comparison between the language strategy of Cairo and Abdolah gives Michiel van Kempen, '23 december 1978; Edgar Cairo's eerste column voor de Volkskrant. 23 januari 1996; Kader Abdolah's eerste column voor de Volkskrant; De Nederlandse taal als onderdrukker en bevrijder', *Kunsten in beweging 1980-2000*, pp.19-35.

Sranan term of abuse into a new (Surinamese-)Dutch expression. Already the Sranan words, although thoroughly coarse, are rather comical, but spoken as they are among "bigi uma" -- big ladies -- they take on an even more comical effect, the more so in the combination with "chicken" where of course an old well-known metaphor for woman is present. In an essay in the weekly *De Groene Amsterdammer* Cairo claimed another motivation for his way of dealing with language, specifically applicable for the minority position of Surinamers in Holland. There he states that preserving authentic linguistic elements can create a "buffercultuur voor minderheden"[49] ("buffer culture for minorities"). The stigma of being less advanced than Dutch culture is thus put into perspective. The self-respect of the Surinamese Dutchmen and their pride in their own culture can be preserved and it is even possible for the author to make a contribution from Holland to the "mother culture", so reinforcing Dutch language as it is spoken in Suriname. In the introduction to his first collection of columns, *Ik ga dood om jullie hoofd*, he had already argued that in this way a Surinamese contribution to the language and culture of Holland should become possible.

Although many of the successful migrants writing after 1990 had to fight their way into Dutch culture, they do not generally expect from the reader a readiness to accept a new kind of Dutch. To writers like Kader Abdolah, Sevtap Baycılı, Yasmine Allas and Faroud Laroui, Dutch is their second language. They do not introduce their own language -- Persian, Turkish, Somalian, French -- into their Dutch, unless perhaps with a few small, easily understandable lexical elements. Writers like Hafid Bouazza, Abelkader Benali, Khalid Boudou and Moustafa Stitou came to Holland at an early age and developed their literature entirely in the Dutch language. An author like Hafid Bouazza takes up the Dutch literary tradition, by picking up all kinds of linguistic variants in older Dutch authors and breathing new life into them. Khalid Boudou does not go that far, but takes up modern Dutch and conjures with it, fully respecting -- unlike Cairo -- the grammatical rules of the Dutch language. Cairo asked for an active willingness by the reader to accept his language renewal. With Boudou the reader does not have to know anything of the Riffian language to follow his texts perfectly; the few Moroccan lexical elements are explained in a list at the back of the book.

Another explanation for the up-turn in appreciation for literature by "foreign" writers can be found in the noticably changed social constellation of the Netherlands. In the twentieth century Holland saw the arrival of three major groups of immigrants, all three finding their place in Dutch society without causing any great disruption; people from Indonesia before and following

---

[49]   The essay is reprinted in Cairo, *Als je hoofd is geboord*, pp.13-19.

Indonesian independence in 1950; Turks and Moroccans as *gastarbeiders* from the end of the fifties.[50] Edgar Cairo was a representative of the Surinamers who definitely did make their presence felt from about 1970 onwards, with some important gulfs at the time of Surinamese independence in 1975 and the military *coup d'etat* in 1980. However it was not until the eighties and nineties that Holland turned into a migration country not only for *gastarbeiders* or people from the overseas territories, but for refugees from all over the world. Gradually members of the "old" immigrant groups took up their positions in all segments of the society. Nowadays there is hardly any political party without an ethnic minority member of parliament.

This had a profound impact also on cultural life in the Netherlands. At the end of the twentieth century the public at large has become acquainted with Surinamese and Moroccan faces on television and in the theatres. Theatre companies like De Nieuw Amsterdam, Cosmic Theatre and Made in da Shade provide for a continuous stream of black repertoire. Cabaret performers of non-Dutch origin have acquired a broad, multicoloured audience.[51] Rapper and stand-up-comedian Ali B. (Ali Bouali) caused a commotion with texts like

> Je hoort Ali B., hardcore to the bone
> Ben hellemaal leip zelfs al doe ik gewoon
> Wil je een show? Geef me 'n microfoon
> Ik bust rhymes van hier tot Bergen op Zoom
> Iedereen weet ik ben altijd straight, als je likt aan m'n reet
> Ben ik altijd wreed
> Want ik schijt in je bek als een duif op je kop
> Jij bent een sukkel, maar je wijf, die is top.

> (You hear Ali B., hardcore to the bone
> Am totally weird, even if I do the normal stuff
> Do you want a show? Give me a mike
> I bust rhymes from here to Bergen op Zoom
> Everyone knows I'm straight, even if you lick my ass
> I'm always cruel
> Cause' I shit in your face like a pigeon on your head
> You are an asshole, but your wife she's top.)

---

[50] Migration numbers are given by Jan Lucassen & Rinus Penninx, *Nieuwkomers nakome-lingen nederlanders: Immigranten in Nederland 1550-1993*. Migratie- en Etnische Studies (Amsterdam: Het Spinhuis, 1994), John Schuster, *Poortwachters over immigranten: Het debat over immigratie in het naoorlogse Groot-Brittannië en Nederland*. Migratie- en Etnische Studies (Amsterdam: Het Spinhuis, 1999), and Leo Lucassen, 'Een kort overzicht van de immigratie naar Nederland in de twintigste eeuw', *Kunsten in beweging 1980-2000*, pp.429-443.

[51] To mention some names: Jörgen Raymann, Amar el-Ajjouri, Esma Abouzahra, Jetty Terborg, Bodil de la Parra, Najib Amhali, Anousha N'zumé, Monique Hoogmoed, Nilgün Yerli.

In the newspapers there are now literary critics of non-Dutch origin like Mustafa Stitou, Sevtap Baycılı, Abdelkader Benali, Ellen Ombre. Columnists like Anil Ramdas, Kader Abdolah, Khalid Boudou and Clark Accord have found their place in national newspapers. Particularly the E. du Perron Prize, for people who encourage a better understanding between different groups of the population, has brought foreign writers to the foreground. In 2003 Abdelkader Benali won the prestigious Libris Prize, while Hafid Bouazza got the Golden Uil a year later. In the past the only publishing houses interested in authors of non-Dutch descent were In de Knipscheer and De Geus. With the increasing success of these writers, ever more publishing houses made efforts to broaden their author lists.[52] Alongside all these phenomena, the work of migrant authors has caught the attention of literary critics; since 1995, scholarly studies have gradually proliferated, and the concept of the "writer in-between" has been analysed.[53] Since Holland became *Schwerpunkt* at the Frankfurt Book Fair and the Salon du Livre in Paris, there has been an overwhelming interest in literature for the Netherlands from abroad. In this "hausse", books by many migrant authors have been translated into other languages. Kader Abdolah and Khalid Boudou were both translated into English, German and French. During his lifetime Edgar Cairo saw only a handful of his prose texts and a couple of poems published in English translation.[54]

In a key essay, Albert Helman proposed a model for the development of national literatures, with special reference to Third World Countries. In the last-but-one phase -- just before the internationalization of the national literature -- he saw writers taking distance to themselves and their environment, and the introduction in literary texts of humour, self-mockery and a drive to put things into perspective. This is an interesting observation. One problem with Helman's development model is that it does not account for the influence migrant authors have on the literature of their homeland. It

---

[52] Cf. Lisa Kuitert, 'Niet zielig, maar leuk; Nederlandse uitgevers van multiculturele literatuur', *Literatuur*, 16 (1999), 355-364.

[53] In the essay-collection *Tussenfiguren*, the phenomenon was commented upon by some twenty literary scolars, analysing the works of among others Lafcadio Hearn, José Maria Arguedas, Albert Cohen, Nedim Gürsel, André Schwarz-Bart en Ishmael Reed. On the rise of the study of migrant literature cf. also Henriette Louwerse, 'Handle with Care: Politics and Power-relations in the Study of Migrant Literature', *Mutual Exchanges: Sheffield-Münster Collo-quium I*, ed. by R.J. Kavanagh (Frankfurt am Main: Lang, 1999), pp.257-269. The five-volume series *Cultuur en migratie in Nederland*, appearing since 2004, counts with a whole range of essays for different aspects of multicultural change in twentieth-century Holland.

[54] Alice C. van Romondt, 'Bibliography of Caribbean literature in English from Suriname, the Netherlands Antilles, Aruba, and the Netherlands', *Caribbean Literature from Suri-name, the Netherlands Antilles, Aruba, and the Netherlands: A Special Issue. Callaloo*, 21 (1998), 704-713.

is well known how important this influence is in countries of the British Commonwealth, in francophone regions and in the Caribbean. Migrant authors stand detached from national cultures, but in some cases they are also in with one leg. Some national cultures derive much prestige from the reputation writers have built up abroad: Saint Lucia from Derek Walcott, Trinidad & Tobago from V.S. Naipaul, Martinique from Patrick Chamoiseau and so forth. Although Helman's model does not account for the development within migrant cultures, it does offer a clue to understanding why things went differently in the case of Edgar Cairo as opposed to Kader Abdolah, Sevtap Baycılı and Khalid Boudou. An important writer like Cairo has been a main figure in the migrant literature of Holland, as well as in the literary history of Suriname. The continuous interaction of his work with the culture of Suriname meant that he was never entirely detached from his native country. He wanted to open a window on the culture and the history of his fatherland, but at the same time knowledge of that culture and history was necessary to appreciate fully what he was doing. Voilá, his cultural splits. For Abdolah, Baycılı and Boudou there has never been the need to make the same splits. Abdolah and Baycılı certainly do come from another world, and for their writing the contrast between "there" and "here" is of essential importance, but they do not write for "there". To Boudou, practically completely educated in two languages, the situation isn't ambiguous either: he reasons like a youngster in a remote corner of Holland who mocks the folkloristic happenings of his locality and at the same time cherishes it, reforging what he sees into a narrative material which he wants to bring to a larger audience. All the same, being a critical mind he wants to confront his readers with the mirror of their self-satisfaction. Loyalty and Cartesian esprit: a field of tension all migrant authors have to struggle with, and with which they make new literatures flourish. Dutch tulips but with unexpected colours springing up from the bulbous root.

Bibliography

Abdolah, Kader, *De adelaars: verhalen* (Breda: De Geus, 1993)
——, *De meisjes en de partizanen: verhalen* (Breda: De Geus, 1995)
——., 'Het Nederlands als mijn tweede vaderland', *Ons Erfdeel*, 39 (1996), 684-691.
——., *De reis van de lege flessen* (Breda: De Geus, 1997)
Abdolah, Kader, *Een tuin in de zee: Mirza* (Breda: De Geus, 2001)
——., *Portretten en een oude droom* (Breda: De Geus, 2003)

Anbeek, Ton, 'Fataal succes; Over Marokkaans-Nederlandse auteurs en hun critic', *Literatuur*, 16 (1999), 335-342.

――., 'Doodknuffelen: Over Marokkaans-Nederlandse auteurs en hun critici', in *Europa buitengaats: Koloniale en postkoloniale literaturen in Europese talen*, Ed. by Theo D'haen (Amsterdam: Bert Bakker, 2002), pp.289-301.

Baycili, Sevtap, *De Markov-keten*, (Breda: De Geus, 1998)

――., *De nachtmerrie van de allochtoon*, (Amsterdam: Van Gennep, 1999)

――., 'Donderpreek', *10 jaar Winternachten*, (Den Haag: Winternachten, 2005), 61-66.

Bouazza, Hafid, *Een beer in bontjas* (Amsterdam: CPNB, 2001)

Boudou, Khalid, *Het schnitzelparadijs*, 2001, (Amsterdam: Maarten Muntinga/Vassallucci, 2003)

Bousetta, Hassan, 'Kunst, cultuur en literatuur in de Marokkaanse gemeenschap in Nederland', *Migrantenstudies*, 11 (1996), 182-194.

Beure, Marnel, and Liesbeth Brouwer, '14 maart 2001; Schrijven tussen twee culturen wordt het thema van de Boekenweek: Een reconstructie van het debat rond migrantenliteratuur in Nederland', in *Kunsten in beweging 1980-2000. Cultuur en migratie in Nederland 2.* Ed. by Rosemarie Buikema and Maaike Meijer (Den Haag: Sdu, 2004), pp.381-396.

Brouwers, Ton, 'Kader Abdolah', *Kritisch Lexicon van de Moderne Nederlandstalige literatuur* 67 (1997)

Buikema, Rosemarie, and Maaike Meijer, *Kunsten in beweging 1980-2000, Cultuur en migratie in Nederland 2* (Den Haag: Sdu, 2004)

Cairo, Edgar, *Kollektieve schuld of wel Famir'man-sani* (Baarn: Het Wereldvenster's / Gravenhage: Novib / Brussel: NCOS, 1976)

――., *Temekoe/Kopzorg* (Haarlem: In de Knipscheer, 1979)

――., '*Ik ga dood om jullie hoofd*' (Haarlem: In de Knipscheer, 1980)

――., '*Als je hoofd is geboord*': *Krantecolumns 2* (Haarlem: In de Knipscheer, 1981)

――., *Mindworry: A Surinamese Story of Father and Son.* Trans. by Peter Gobets (Haarlem: In de Knipscheer, 1993)

――., *That Fire of Great Dramas*, excerpts trans. by Scot Rollins *Callaloo*, 21 (1998), 689-692.

Dunphy, Graeme, 'Migrant, Emigrant, Immigrant: Recent Developments in Turkish-Dutch Literature', *Neophilologus*, 86 (2001), 1-23.

Gobardhan-Rambocus, Lila, *Onderwijs als sleutel tot maat-schappelijke vooruitgang: Een taal- en onderwijsgeschiedenis van Suriname, 1651-1975* (Zutphen: Walburg Press, 2001)

Helman, Albert, 'Over 'nationale' letterkunde', *Sticusa Journaal*, 4 (1974), 3-6.

Hestermann, Jinke, 'Sevtap Baycılı schrijft voor de zappende lezer', *Overijssels Dagblad*, 13. March 2001.

Hoving, Isabel, 'Een leeg graf, een boze man, en een spraakmakende foto: De brokstukken van een Nederlandstalige reflectie over inter-culturaliteit', in *Tussenfiguren: Schrijvers tussen de culturen*. ed. by Elisabeth Leijnse and Michiel van Kempen (Amsterdam: Het Spinhuis, 1998), pp.47-61.

Kempen, Michiel van, 'Edgar Cairo', *Kritisch Lexicon van de Moderne Nederlandstalige Literatuur* 36 (1990).

———., *Een geschiedenis van de Surinaamse literatuur*. 2 vols (Breda: De Geus, 2003)

———., '23 december 1978; Edgar Cairo's eerste column voor de Volkskrant. 23 januari 1996; Kader Abdolah's eerste column voor de Volkskrant; De Nederlandse taal als onderdrukker en bevrijder', in *Kun- sten in beweging 1980-2000*. Cultuur en migratie in Nederland 2. ed. by Rosemarie Buikema and Maaike Meijer (Den Haag: Sdu, 2004), pp.19-35.

Kuitert, Lisa, 'Niet zielig, maar leuk: Nederlandse uitgevers van multi-culturele literatuur', *Literatuur*, 16 (1999), 355-364.

Leijnse, Elisabeth and Michiel van Kempen, eds, *Tussenfiguren: Schrijvers tussen de culturen* (Amsterdam: Het Spinhuis, 1998; repr. 2001)

Louwerse, Henriette, 'The Way to the North or the Emergence of Turkish and Moroccan Migrant Literature in the Dutch Literary Landscape', *Dutch Crossing*, 21 (1997), 69-86.

———., 'Handle with Care: Politics and Power-relations in the Study of Migrant Literature', in *Mutual Exchanges: Sheffield-Münster Colloquium I*, ed. by R.J. Kavanagh (Frankfurt am Main: Lang, 1999), pp.257-269.

Lucassen, Jan and Rinus Penninx, *Nieuwkomers nakomelingen neder-landers: Immigranten in Nederland 1550-1993*. Migratie- en Etnische Studies (Amsterdam: Het Spinhuis, 1994)

Lucassen, Leo, 'Een kort overzicht van de immigratie naar Nederland in de twintigste eeuw', in *Kunsten in beweging 1980-2000*. Cultuur en migratie in Nederland 2, ed. by Rosemarie Buikema and Maaike Meijer, (Den Haag: Sdu, 2004), pp.429-443.

Nap-Kolhoff, Elma, *Turkse auteurs in Nederland: Verkenning van een o-nontgonnen gebied*, (Tilburg: Wetenschapswinkel Universiteit van Tilburg, 2002)

Paasman, Bert, 'Een klein aardrijkje op zichzelf, de multiculturele samen-leving en de etnische literatuur', *Literatuur*, 16 (1999), 324-334.

Romondt, Alice C. van, 'Bibliography of Caribbean literature in English from Suriname, the Netherlands Antilles, Aruba, and the Netherlands', *Callaloo. Caribbean Literature from Suriname, the Netherlands Antilles, Aruba, and the Netherlands: A Special Issue*, 21 (1998), 704-713.

Schulz, Cile, 'Interview met Yasmine Allas en Kader Abdolah; Boven de culturen', *De Geuzenkrant VI*, 'Boekenweek', *Vrij Nederland*, 10. March 2001. pp.1-2.

Schuster, John, *Poortwachters over immigranten: Het debat over immigratie in het naoorlogse Groot-Brittannië en Nederland*. Migratie en Etnische Studies, (Amsterdam: Het Spinhuis, 1999)

Span, Hijlco, 'Tussen vaderland en moederland: Surinaamse literatuur in Nederland', *Literama*, 22 (1987), 62-70.

Beur Hybrid Humour

Hédi Abdel-Jaouad

Beur culture in France, the presence of second and third generation descendants of North African or Maghrebian migrants, has developed strikingly diverse humorous manifestations. This is partly the result of a complex negotiation of identity that neither wants to be French nor North African. Equally importantly, Beur humourists and comedians have taken French anti-Beur attitudes by the horns and reversed them in order to make fun of mainstream French misconceptions. The cartoonist Farid Boudjellal offers, through humour that incorporates his own experience as a disabled migrant, fictional glimpses of possible co-existence, mutual understanding and respect. The stage comedy of Rachida Khalil revolves around Arab women, specifically Moroccans. Jamel Debbouze, another comedian and actor, has become a pop icon in both France and the Maghreb because of his topicality, improvisational skills, and linguistic inventiveness. Beur film makers have also achieved national recognition and success -- often through films that employ humour. Beur bands such as Carte de Séjour (CDS) and Zebda employ humour as a mode of resistance. The prolific Azouz Begag provides humorous perspectives on Beur existence in his novels. There is even Beur cyber-humour on the Internet.

> ... To be labeled is already sad. But then you strive to conform to what is on the label. To make it tell the truth. You are as constrained as the one who must toe the party-line.[1]

> Ane, m'appelle pas beur, car ce mot m'écoeure[2]

In an increasingly ethnic, diverse "New Europe", migrant minorities have for a long time remained voiceless, disenfranchised, and docile; yet now they are clamouring ever more stridently for effective and meaningful visibility and representation in the public space from which they feel they have been marginalized, if not excluded, for both real and imagined reasons. Nowhere has this urge and surge of public outcry for ethnic participation been more sustained, pressing, and evident than in France, home of the oldest and largest migrant community in Europe. To outside observers, this new sociological development may indeed seem a historical twist of irony considering that France, a former imperial centre, has, over a relatively short period of time, become host (if not, in the eyes of many cynics and ultranationalists, hostage) to migrants from its former colonial periphery. Given this historical and cultural dis-placement, and the unease and tension that lie in the problems, as well as the solutions, of this new "political football," it is understandable that

---

[1]   Boris Vian, *Automne à Pékin* (Paris: Editions de Minuit, 1964), pp.233-234.
[2]   *Bye, Bye*. Director: Karim Dridi. 1995.

ethnic diversity and multiculturalism have become current issues of contention in France.

Unsurprisingly, France's migrant minorities, especially the increasingly
restive and vociferous youth, seem less prepared to accept a *status quo ante*
that perpetuates discrimination and joblessness, especially given their deep, if
not permanent, roots in their new homeland. This new combative attitude has
become the hallmark of a class of disenfranchised French citizens known
collectively as Beurs, the so-called second and third generation descendants
of North African or Maghrebian migrants. One can argue that a specific and
definable Beur consciousness and sensibility, shaped by the experience of
racism and marginalization, indeed exists in France.

What makes the Beurs' predicament even more precarious, however, is
that this Beur consciousness is both fluid and changing. The fact remains that
Beurs are still searching for some form of belonging, an identity that anchors
them in French society and culture; they feel neither accepted by their fellow
citizens nor by those relatives on the other side of the Mediterranean, in what
Azouz Begag calls "le pays non natal." Acceptance by others has emerged as
their most arduous problem and most ardent desire; they attempt to construct
a semblance of identity from this double negation. Since the mid-70's, Beurs'
proactive challenge to the status quo has taken many forms and shapes ranging from peaceful sit-ins and demonstrations to sporadic rioting acts of violence. Similarly, their advocacy for change has been carried out in both the
socio-political sphere and the cultural and literary arena. The latest mode of
resistance to emerge, which has already attracted some critical media interest
and attention, is the work of artists, specifically humorists. Humour, in its
diverse and multifarious manifestations (art, literature, stand-up comedy,
etc.), both as salve and critique of social and ethnic mores, has emerged as
the latest and perhaps most potent weapon in their arsenal. Through a combination of protest and education, humorists hope to shame, and thus reform,
the bigot while encouraging the youth to shed old prejudices. Like other
minorities Beurs seem to have moved from their initial counterproductive
rage against suppressed social angst to a more positive and self-affirming
posture. Increasingly, they have resorted to humour as the most effective and
universal form of communication conveying their own sense of the political,
social, and cultural alienation.

Whether in stand-up comedy, cartoons, films, plays or fiction, humour
has done more to advance Beurs' social and political agenda than any other
public expression. Today's Beur generation, in all its diversity and complexity, is "tickling" and "pricking" back; it has also slowly and seriously begun
challenging the established misconceptions of the mainstream French population as well as those of their own community with malicious, if not perverse,

pleasure. This generation has thus begun reversing a long and unchallenged trend that made North Africans "the butts" of France's jests and jokes.[3] Beur humorists have already, by their sheer presence in the media, broken down the biggest stereotype of all: they are now seen as individuals fighting back to alter the media (which ironically become the "miraculous weapons" that they turn against the system that employs and gives them a venue for their humour) in order to create a more balanced and fairer perception of themselves and their community. I propose to analyze this new type of humour through its manifestations in the various works of artists and writers, with the intention of delineating not only its contour and content but also, and more importantly, its specificity.

Humour and the namesake

By now it is a truism that Beur humour begins with the term "Beur"; a hybrid, nebulous, multicultural identity wherein Beur artists of all types derive their creative material, and furthermore find their niche. The Beur story began with a hybrid namesake whose origin no one seems to remember. Historians and etymologists of the term have provided countless and sometimes conflicting versions; nonetheless, they all agree that the term "Beur" is essentially a self-made namesake, monosyllabic, easily pronounced and remembered, and connoting light-heartedness and playfulness.[4]

The moniker "Beur" is itself rooted not only in racial but also in linguistic hybridization, more exactly *verlan*, that is French for "pig latin." *Verlan* is supposedly the reverse phoneticization of the word *l'envers*. Accordingly, the term "Beur" is the verlan of the *verlan* of the twice-removed word "Arabe" (an earlier iteration is "rebeu" which, when reversed again, gave "beur"). It has come to designate young Frenchmen of Arab extraction. In other words, a Beur is an Arab who is not only *à l'endroit* (at his place), but doubly so: he is an Arab of no place and who, of necessity, must find his own space. Slanguish and colloquial, this word was never meant to be written -- the Beur, unless s/he is *écrivain intégré* (assimilated writer) prefers the spoken to the written word; it belongs to the language and culture of the street, to an oral, vernacular but also marginal culture. And when spoken, it connotes, at least homophonically, "butter" in French (*beurre*). Only when written does it carry

---

3   Driss Chraïbi was the first to denounce racism against North African migrants in France with biting humour and sarcasm in his novel significantly titled *Les Boucs* (Paris: Gallimard, 1955). English translation: *The Butts* (London: Lynne Rienner Publishers Inc, 1983).

4   Michel Laronde gives the fullest and most convincing account of the history and the many semantic complexities of the term *Beur* in his book *Autour du roman beur: Immigration et identité* (Paris: L'Harmattan, 1993), pp.51-2.

the humorous charge of a homophone. When uttered, the term inevitably elicits a smile even by those who find the term demeaning, if not dishearten-ing.[5] It would not be excessive to postulate here that Beur humour is born in homonymy, precisely in the discrepancy between the spoken and the written word, between sense and sound, between France and its dis-placed Others. It is in humour that Beurs seem to have more successfully staked out a new "in-between" space wherein they have initiated a new discourse about themselves and others, beginning with their own neologism: BEUR. Like other minori-ties, namely gays and lesbians, Beurs use humour as a means to "come out" of their "closeted identity" and to come to terms with their "difference".

Interestingly, this self-designation, purposefully self-deprecating, is an invention of necessity if not adversity. It was meant to pre-empt and counter the negative "étiquetage" (Boris Vian) or labeling of others in a culture where brand-naming is paramount. Beurs' undeclared motto is clearly ideological: "If we don't represent and define ourselves, others will." From the beginning, one may postulate that humour and Beur seem indeed coextending. This is a rare, if not unique, case whereby humour creates an over-arching conscious-ness for all the disenfranchised in contemporary France, so much so that the term has come to encompass children of immigrants as a whole, regardless of their ethnic or cultural background. Such a term strikes one as a tongue-in-cheek act of supreme self-derision; a word born in humour will, more easily if not inevitably, lend itself to copy-catting. The hybridization or "beuriza-tion" of proper names has become a fashionable trend especially among those in the entertainment business. The "rock'n Raï" singer Karim adopted the *nom d'artiste* R'mic, which, we are told, is double *verlan* of "Karim"; "Karim", which pronounced a certain way sounds like *crème* (another word for *beurre* in French) that, when reversed, gives "R'mic". Likewise, the Rap singer Ridan is the *verlan* of his real name Nadir. The Toulouse-based rock group Zebda has, tongue-in-cheek, changed the metaphoric "beur" back to a simple "metonymy" [*beurre*], but translated back into Arabic.

Not surprisingly, the term has given rise to proliferating word-plays, puns and all kinds of playful and humorous reinventions: *Beurette*, supposedly feminine form of Beur, *Jambon beur* (refers to children born of interethnic couples known as *coupés* or *croisés* (crossbreed), but also recalls the famous Parisian ham and butter sandwich or *Paris Beurre*, a symbol for the crossing and interplay of the sacred and profane, *hallal* and *haram*, Christians and Muslims). In the Lille region a *Jambon beur* refers to *Français maghrébins sur-intégrés* (over-integrated Franco-Meghrebians). There is also the expres-

---

[5]   Mouloud, the Beur protagonist in Karim Dridi's film *Bye Bye*, speaks for many who find the term "Beur" loathsome: "Stupid, don't call me Beur, this word makes me want to puke."

sion *Beur noir* (as in "beurre noir"), *Beurgeois* or *Beurgoisie*, and *Beur pourri* (for pot-pourri, the *p* is pronounced *b* by immigrants; it also means a "Beur gone bad, in trouble"). In her novel *Parle mon fils, parle à ta mère*[6], Leïla Sebbar, herself a Beurette, pokes fun at the new mythology that surrounds the contradictory but ever-proliferating etymology of the word:[7]

> Je sais pas pourquoi ils disent Radio Beur, pourquoi ça beur, c'est le beurre des Français qu'on mange sur leur pain? Je comprends pas. Pour la couleur? Ils sont pas comme ça, c'est pas la couleur des Arabes. Les jeunes savent, moi je ne sais pas, j'ose pas demander.... Peut-être c'est *le pays.... El Ber*, chez nous en arabe ça veut dire le pays tu le sais mon fils, c'est ça ou non.

> (I have no idea why they say Radio Beur, why beur, is it the *beurre* [butter] of the French that we use on their bread? I don't get it. Because of the color? They aren't like that, it's not the color of Arabs...the young ones seem to know, I don't, I don't dare ask... Perhaps it's the country....El Ber, for us Arabs it means the homeland, do you know that my son, is this it or not.)

For Beurs, this designation functions, at least subconsciously, as an epistemological break of sorts; a definite cultural marker from the culture of their parents. More importantly, it represents their way of distancing themselves from the term "immigrant" that both defines their parents and robs them of equal justice and opportunity in France. Young Beurs in particular, albeit citizens of France, continue to be seen and treated by the mainstream as perpetual immigrants or *immigrés à perpétuité*. Appropriating the pejoratively connoted *Arabe*, and turning it literally around and recharging it with a new identity (their own identity) signifies their want and desire to divest it of the colonial legacy that kept their parents marginalized. Equally, the term "Beur" functions as a foil to the French monogenealogy and ethnic purity, the very symbol of French national identity. From the ruins of an inoperative identity, a double negation of the stereotypical *Arabe* and *beurre*, they have attempted to construct a contemporary, youthful and relevant identity without abandoning the positive aspects of their double heritage. The term incorporates both the old and the new. "Beurness" has become at once a cultural marker and de-marker, a form of decolonization and new enfranchisement.[8]

It is also instructive to note that humour, in the Beur context, is inherently

---

[6]   Leïla Sebbar, *Parle mon fils, parle à ta mère* (Paris: Stock, 1984).

[7]   Ibid., pp.27.

[8]   Obviously, this has not come about *ex nihilo*, there was a precedent in a literary and artistic movement during colonial times: Negritude. Paraphrasing Senghor's definition of Negriture, one may say that "Beurness" is the sum total of the values of being Beur. However, unlike Negritude poets, Beur artists extol a new identity different from that of their parents, rooted in their own social and cultural environment.

a hybrid genre. In this regard, hybrid is most often seen only in opposition to the Metropolitan canon and never as an addition to, or an enrichment of this canon. Because it questions established rules and values, hybrid Beur humour is naturally iconoclastic and "transgressive"; it often heralds the hetero-geneous at the expense of the homogenous, and always with the intention of challenging and ultimately "altering" the status quo. Clearly, this "altering," is understood in the etymological sense of "other-ing," of ethnicizing this humour both culturally and racially. Beurs wittingly and unwittingly yearn to "tan" (*bronzer*) and *épicer* (spice) their new humour, giving it the colour of their faces and the savour of their food. A brand of humour, however, that eschews "aesthetitization," for "functionalism," and one that also draws on and resonates with the humour of other minorities. As the "Cultural Other", *par excellence*, Beurs have come to embody, in the eyes of many, the most direct threat to French national identity. Survey and evidence shows that the French are more racist toward North Africans than toward Sub-Saharan Afri-cans. This pervasive stereotyping and stigmatization of Beurs occurs daily and furthermore is relentlessly reinforced by an often complacent, if not complicit, media.[9] How does one rectify this overwhelming if not hopelessly negative situation? This is obviously a challenge for any ethnic humorist to tackle, especially in a country such as France that has no tradition for admit-ting, let alone valorizing, ethnicity and diversity. To illustrate Beurs' multi-faceted humour, we will examine a number of manifestations from many varied fields and genres such as cartooning, comedy, film, music, fiction and, most recently, cyber humour.

Farid Boudjellal: Rather be the cartoonist than the cartooned

A cartoon is said to be worth a thousand books or treatises because both its text and image are tinged with a dose of humour. This self-evident, invalu-able truth resonated with a number of artists who took up cartooning pre-cisely to explode, rectify and correct the many implicit and explicit racist stereotypes embedded in the French cartoons such as *Tintin* and *Astérix et Obélix*. Their message is clear: expose and combat prejudice through hu-mour, the most effective antidote to ethnic stereotyping. Ironically, Beur cartoonists will re-use the same stereotypes but will cheeckily return them to the French.

Farid Boudjellal represents the best and most prolific of Beur cartoonists. Born in Brest, France, in 1953 to Algerian immigrant parents, Boudjellal has

---

[9]   One such example is the recent hysteria in the RER incident caused by the false anti-semitic aggression by a group of Beurs, totally invented by Marie Leblanc in July 2004.

been attracted since his youth to drawing. In spite of his physical handicap (he contracted polio when he was eight years old, which later became the subject of one his cartoons), he completed his university education with a degree in Art. Boudjellal has created comic books with a decidedly Beur viewpoint, but always with a biting sense of humour. He seems to have discovered early on in his career that only through humour can an audience be receptive to his message. Although focusing on Beurs, Boudjellal's humour derives from his own personal life (as reflected in his comic book): "Arabe, Handicappé, Chômeur."[10] Through exaggerations, distortions and reversals, Boudjellal attempts to make all these perceived deficiencies the inspiration and material of his humour. It is through his personal experience that his humour touches a raw "nerve" in everyone, regardless of their ethnic background. He has dared to take his audience outside their comfort zone, and beyond their perception of their physical and mental home, to let them directly experience the predicament of the "distant other". Not surprisingly then, Boudjellal's cartoons are didactic and even pedagogical. From them we derive pleasure, amusement and also profit, for we gain psychological insights and sociological perspectives on immigrants and their children, and also on French society as a whole. By providing broad contextualization for his material, clearly Boudjellal intends to reach a diverse audience, specifically those among the French who feign to find his culture opaque, if not impenetrable.

The titles of his comic books, in and of themselves, speak volumes of the general Beur predicament and inter-ethnic relations in today's France.[11] Whether in *Jambon Beur*, *Le Beurgeois*, *Ethnik ta mère*, a word play on "Nique ta mère" ("F...* your mother"), *Black Blanc Beur*, or *Gags à l'harissa*, humour always begins with the title. Moreover, the titles suggest that his biting humour is not only politically incorrect, but that it also spares no one. His "shooting gallery" includes such targets as Jews, Blacks, French, Arabs, and the handicapped. In his cartoons, he has ripped into such current and controversial issues as immigration, xenophobia, racial profiling, religion and cultural differences, and joblessness, all conveyed with lucidity and transparency. He articulates those weighty issues without being pedantic or dogmatic and shows that the so-called "clash of civilizations" is caused more

---

[10]   His comic book *Petit Polio* (Toulon: Soleil Productions, 2000) for example is based on his own handicap, polio.

[11]   *Les soirées d'Abdulah* (Paris: Futuropolis, 1985), *Petit Polio*, *L'Oud* (Toulon: Soleil Productions, 2000), *Juifs-Arabes* (Toulon: Soleil Productions, 1998), *Jambon Beur* (Toulon: Soleil Productions, 1998), *Gags à l'harissa* (Paris: Humanoïdes Associés, 1989), *Ethnik ta mère* (Toulon: Soleil Productions, 1996), *Black Blanc Beur* (Cachan: Tartamudo, 2004), *Les Beurs* (Paris: Albin Michel, 1985), *Les Beurgeois* (Toulon: Soleil Productions, 1998).

by ignorance than hatred.

To give just one of many examples of Boudjellal's hybrid humour, I would like to consider a cartoon entitled *Jambon Beur*, whose subject is clearly stated in the subtitle, *Les couples mixtes*, a children's piece that also appeals to adults.[12] This comic book has a clear message that is optimistic about ethnic relations in the "New France", one which is quite a rarity of its kind.[13] Boudjellal explodes graphically and dramatically the root cause of negative stereotyping: xenophobia, that is fear of the other and the foreigner (the main sources of interethnic tensions and misunderstandings) often results from ignorance of and disrespect for the culture of the Other. Moreover, through *Jambon Beur*, he shows that there is no better way to exorcize the demons of fear and prejudice than through a healthy dose of derision aimed at both the self and the other. Although set against the haunting ghosts of the Algerian war, *Jambon Beur* purports to be a love story; one that defies race and prejudice and overcomes the enmity of the past. As such *Jambon Beur* stands as a metaphor for uneasy yet possible Franco-Algerian coexistence, a model of interethnic harmony. By focusing on a "mixed marriage," Boudjellal offers an autopsy of racism and has no qualms wringing both his French and Algerian characters inside and out to reveal their most unvoiced racist thoughts, and their innermost fears and prejudices. In many respects, *Jambon Beur* could be conceived as a Beur retake of *Guess Who's Coming to Dinner*, the landmark film about racial prejudice.

Patricia's mother, Eliane, is extremely excited about meeting her daughter's fiancé: "Eliane sait que sa fille a choisi le gendre idéal..." ("Eliane knows that her daughter has chosen the ideal son-in-law"), an excitement tainted, however, with apprehension. She prepares herself psychologically for the worst. She would accept her daughter's choice, provided that: "Il n'est ni ARABE, ni HANDICAPPE, ni CHOMEUR". As expected, her worst nightmare turns out to be true. Patricia's new love could not be more stereotypically "Arab": Mahmoud Slimani, an Algerian, who happens to be handicapped (like Boudjellal himself), and unemployed (if not, as suggested in a musing *aparté*, ethnically "unemployable"). Faced with her daughter's choice, and past initial shock, Eliane rationalizes her "exaggerated" fear through a series of well-meaning yet equally racist observations: "ARABE? Ce n'est pas de sa faute...S'il s'appelait MAURICE, personne ne devinerait ses origines...". Similarly, the Slimani family is also unhappy about their son's exogamous choice. Having already lost two daughters, one committing suicide for having been prevented from marrying the Frenchman she loved,

---

12 Farid Boudjellal, *Jambon Beur* (Toulon: Soleil Productions, 1998).
13 It is interesting to note that this particular comic book was highly recommended by M.R.A.P (Mouvement contre le Racisme et pour l'Amitié entre les Peuples).

and another marrying a Senegalese Christian, they reluctantly acquiesce to Mahmoud's engagement to Patricia, hoping all the while "that the other children will marry Arabs".

Jambon Beur is not only about "couples mixtes" but also about how one's dilemmas culturally manifest themselves through children, such as "name-picking." For Boudjellal, names represent the main marker of one's identity. He argues that Beurs' "problem" is not necessarily the color of their skin or their "faciès" but their names; consequently, naming is both a cultural and political component of this intercultural contention. For Mahmoud and Patricia, the birth of their new child triggers a second interethnic crisis that threatens their marriage. Even before the concerned parents began choosing a name, the interfering grandmothers, as upholders of tradition, each decided on a name, Charlotte for Eliane, and Badia for Mrs Slimani; two names for two cultures in conflict. The mainstream sees onomastic homogeneity as the most visible sign, if not a *sine qua non* to assimilation, whereas Beurs still seem reluctant to surrender the last marker of their parents' identity. Increasingly, however, Beurs are opting for trans-ethnic names (such as Sami, Ramsey or Adam) to blur their ethnic identity, some resorting to *verlan* (such as Rmic for Karim and Ridan for Nadir).

In *Jambon Beur* the intense rivalry between the grandmothers is staged out as a vaudeville comedy, a series of amusing vignettes that underscore the question of naming in a multicultural society. Mrs Slimane seeks to upstage her rival by claiming the identity of her grand-daughter: "Comme elle est belle ma petite Badia". Incidentally, "Badia" also means "beautiful" in Arabic. But Grandmother Eliane will not be outdone by her rival's maneuver, retorting that it was only natural that the child should be named after her own deceased mother: "Mais ma chérie ...Tu ne devrais pas l'appeler CHARLOTTE?" But grand-mother Slimani finds her proposition absurd. For her, naming is patrilineal: "Pourquoi CHARLOTTE, c'est pas la fille de CHARLOT". Here the unintended joke ("Charlot" is a clear reference to the comedian Charlie Chaplin known in French as "Charlot") somewhat vindicates Mrs Slimani's impeccable logic. The joke comes, however, at her expense, for the reader laughs at her ignorance.

As a couple, Mahmoud and Patricia manage to stay remarkably above their interethnic fray; they succumb, however, to the onomastic pressure of their respective cultures. By way of a compromise, they finally settle on both names: Badia will be the "secret", private, ethnic name, but Charlotte will be the public, acceptable name. This onomastic duality, perceived by adults as an enrichment of identity, proves to be a confusing source of schizophrenic proportions for Badia/Charlotte. Partaking in both cultures is a problem for the child. Although Badia/Charlotte participates in both cultures with disarming innocence, she belongs in neither and is thus doomed to an untenable *entre-deux*. Both cultures in conflict are revealed through the innocent and naive eyes of this child. Through derisive vignettes, both cultures are also shown as caricatures which render their clashing claims with superficiality and utter meaninglessness.

In *Jambon Beur*, the cultural confrontation is clearly meant to help establish a kind of *terrain d'entente* and foster a modicum of understanding. Only through transcendence of religion and nationality can there be, it seems, hope for peaceful and productive interethnic coexistence. If French society will take long to reform and adjust to the new "hybrid" reality, Boudjellal advocates beginning the long process of ethnic enfranchisement with the individual. Mahmoud speaks to and for many Beurs when he declares that he refuses to be scapegoated for the seemingly open-ended Franco-Algerian bone of contention, nor will he take the blame for it: "FRANÇAIS, ARABE! J'en ai rien à foutre PATRICIA!". Through love and a sharp sense of humour, he will triumph over prejudice. His declaration of love for Patricia reads, ironically, like the Beurs' Bill of Basic Rights: *Pays, Visa, Carte de séjour*, the holy trinity that constitutes every immigrant's wish-list and dream. For Boudjellal, salvation seems only possible at the individual, personal level and always with a robust sense of humour: "Mon pays c'est toi", "Mon visa c'est tes yeux...", "tes lèvres ma CARTE DE SEJOUR..." and "J'émigre vers toi".

Jambon Beur is also a clear demonstration of the humanizing power of humour: Mahmoud Slimani is a Beur with a name, and a face, with a physical handicap. Even his joblessness is not perceived as negative. Moreover, in Boudjellal's exaggerated, idyllic vision, Mahmoud assumes the role of a homemaker, which further upturns yet another stereotype -- North Africans' machismo. Through the clever and apt metaphor *of Jambon Beur*, Boudjellal has successfully transcended (at least at the individual level) racial and cultural barriers.[14] Ironically, the Beur predicament is viewed by the mainstream through the distorting lens of fear and insecurity. Boudjellal offers, through humour and his own experience, the possibility of co-existence, mutual understanding and respect. His other cartoons convey, like *Jambon Beur*, the promise of the not so distant conciliation between France and its "ethnic"

---

[14] Undoubtedly, ethnic humour is in itself a subtle form of racism, it is always at the expense of another group. Hence the thin line that the humorist needs to maintain between vigilance and paranoia. Moreover, one may indeed find Boudjellal's cartoons racist. In poking fun at racist attitudes he may have committed the same sins as the ones he attempts to debunk. The portrayal of the Senegalese brother-in-law may be viewed as offensive if not racist. Clearly Boudjellal's intentions are not racist or injurious. His racism is functional. It is, in the Sartrian sense, an "anti-racist racism."

citizens. Reading and musing over Boudjellal's cartoons leaves us with a simple message: there is no room for bigotry in a multicultural society. More importantly, Boudjellal's humour represents an explicit exhortation to his fellow Beurs to take initiative in shaping their own image. Indeed, it took a great deal of courage for an "Arabe, Handicappé, Chômeur" to give his imagination free rein, and to be the cartoonist instead of the cartooned.

The Beur humorist as a young engage

> If Christopher Columbus had sailed up the Seine and crossed over the pont de Puteaux or the pont de Suresne, he would have discovered... my Harlem[15]

The last decade has not only seen the rise but also the rapid and unexpected consecration of many ethnic (or hybrid) standup comedians in France. The fact that such hybrid names as Smaïn, Fellag, Ramzy, Dieudonné, Elie Simoun, Michel Boujenah, Gad Elmaleh and Jamel Debbouze have become household names attests to the ascending popularity and acceptability of hybrid humour in France. The most recent and promising addition to this already popular collection of ethnic humorists is Rachida Khalil, the only female comedian of Maghrebian descent to have garnered national recognition. Unsurprisingly, Khalil's humour essentially revolves around Arab women, specifically Moroccans. Her most recent one-woman show *La vie rêvée de Fatna*, co-written with none other than Guy Bedos (France's premier humorist) features the tumultuous life of three women depicted through different but complementary experiences. The first is perhaps Khalil's self-portrait as the token French-born Arab female artist, who parades her "Arabness" in Paris only to ironically find herself cast and closeted in the only role possible for her type, that of a Beurette. Her nemesis is a Moroccan woman named Fatna, hence the title of the show, who dreams of going to France to escape the poverty, brutality, and capriciousness of her husband and his three terrorizing sons, provocatively named Saddam, Oussama, and Khadafi. This Arab two-some is joined by their French foil, Sophie, who represents mainstream French opinion vis-à-vis its ethnic population. Sophie indulges in unabashed patronizing and outrageous racial slurs, although expressed in a naive and somewhat lighthearted way. Unlike most of her fellow male comedians, Khalil loathes the idea of watering-down or glossing over reality. Playing safe with an audience, she argues, always runs the risk of stripping humour of its edge and specificity. One poignant but hilarious example of her uncompromising humour is the mock fashion show of parading tchador-clad

---

[15]   Richard L. Derderian, *North Africans in Contemporary France: Becoming Visible* (New York: Palgrave Macmillan, 2004), p.150.

models. This particular act provides mirth but also depth, for it allows us to partake in France's hotly debated issue of the "Muslim scarf". Khalil's reputation as a straight-shooter who refuses to play "the PC game", even when her own identity is at stake, seems well established. Rather than be labeled Beur she prefers to be called, unapologetically and unabashedly, Arab: "Beurette? Maghrébine? Mais c'est détestable. C'est trouillard. C'est l'hypocrisie de la peur. Je suis arabe." ("Beurette? Maghrebian? But that's awful. It's cowardly. It's the hypocrisy of fear. I am an Arab woman.")

A Star is Beur[16]: Jamel: 100% Debbouze

Among her male counterparts, the most talented and popular Beur comedian to have emerged lately is Jamel Debbouze. He has built a successful professional career on contemporary cultural politics and satirical use of negative, media-generated immigrant stereotypes. Raucous impersonations of his own people, and particularly of himself, are a staple of his humour.[17] While still targeting the other's foibles and mores, this other is, however, never a total outsider, for Debbouze seems as keen to direct and train his humour on himself and his community. Self-deprecating humour, as self-affirmation, has become Debbouze's most defining trait and most potent weapon as an *engagé* comedian. In this regard, his self-deprecating humour is far more critical than that used by mainstream French humorists often accused, unjustly as is the case of Guy Bedos, of being bigoted, if not downright racists.

Debbouze, whose parents, like those of Rachida Khalil, immigrated from Morocco, uses nervous, gritty, and edgy humour to face, and further explore, the fears and anxieties of being ethnically and culturally alienated in today's France. The eldest of seven children, Debbouze was born in Paris in 1975 but grew up in Trappes, an economically depressed immigrant *banlieue*. Like Boudjellal, Debbouze is physically handicapped. When he was 13 he lost his hand in a train accident that crushed his best friend; a traumatic experience that he sought to overcome through humour. Like Farid Boudjellal, Debbouze's unabashed ability to tell uncomfortable "home truths" makes him a humorist with a mission. Through humour, he attempts to bridge two com-

---

[16]   This is the title of the one-man show by Beur comedian Smaïn (1986).

[17]   Debbouze's talent lies in his versatility; his ability to inhabit many personae is indeed amazing. The television program "Nulle part ailleurs" made him a celebrity. His first major film break was in *Zonzon* (directed by Laurent Bouhnik). He plays the idiosyncratic Egyptian architect, Numerobis, in *Asterix & Obelisk: Mission Cleopatra*. He also starred in *Le fabuleux destin d'Amélie Poulain*, as the grocer's assistant Lucien: "Et puis j'ai joué dans Amélie Poulain! Au début ils voulaient que je fasse le poulain! Lo!" (*Jamel: 100% Debbouze*). Debbouze is currently engaged in a film project entitled *Les indigènes* about Moroccan *tirailleurs*.

munities that have become separated by different experiences and misconceptions of racism: "If my work helps French people everywhere understand and embrace the humour and language of the banlieues, that's a small step toward closing the huge gap," he says. "My success is also a sign that humor and talent are universal, and capable of crossing social divisions." In the eyes of many on the media Jamel Debbouze has become, along with footballer Zinedine Zidane (known as "Zizou"), a symbol of positive integration into mainstream French society.

Debbouze's most recent one-man show *Jamel 100% Debbouze* has turned him into a pop icon in both France and the Maghreb. In 90 minutes of non-stop sarcasm and humour, yet with a touch of disarming sincerity, Jamel takes his audience on a raucous roller-coaster ride, creating shock waves of laughter but also pointed pain, as he rips happily and maliciously into such eclectic topics as his turbulent upbringing, his traditional immigrant family, his chaotic schooling, and his own professional "rags to riches" experience. No one seems immune or safe from his biting criticism and politically pointed jokes.

Although inspired by real events, Jamel's material represents an entire generation of Beurs who came from the French "hoods" in the eighties and nineties. Because Jamel is most attuned to the concerns of the young whose language he speaks intimately, his humour derives essentially from a playful, if not mischievous, mispronunciation of often simple and recognizable words or names (such as "Joney Star" for Joey Starr, "Neménemzz" for M&M's). His inimitable distortion of Zidane's name "Zimadime Zimdame" has become his comedic signature. This self-deprecating humour is directed specifically at the mainstream audience that often deliberately mispronounces Arabic names: "Si un jour j'ai un fils, je l'appelleria Zizou! Si j'ai une fille je l'appellerai aussi Zizou, elle se démerdera! Lo!"[18]

Furthermore, Debbouze's fame rests on his peerless verbal pyrotechnics as he often creates his own and unique language, known as *tchatche*. Not surprisingly, Debbouze has been crowned king of *tchatche* by his many Banlieue fans. The etymology of the term seems as volatile and vague as that of Beur. [19] In the idiom of the *banlieues*, a *tchatcheur* is a street-wise guy with the gift of gab, a smooth talker and a verbal ventriloquist who never tires of reinventing words that often sound like tongue-twisters. In many respects, the *tchatcheur* represents the modern *troubadour* of the *banlieues*

---

[18]   Jamel Debbouze, *Jamel: 100% Debbouze* (Sony, 2004).
[19]   The term *tchatche* is said to come from Provençal *cha-cha* (the song of the cicadas). Some claim it derives from the Spanish *chacharear*, "to chat".

and the Zone, also known as the Beur's Harlem (Mounsi).[20] Debbouze has become a master of the new *sabir*[21] of the French hoods or Zone, an idiom that meshes French slang with American words and expressions as well as cyber language ("Je te like Janet Jackson"), ("S'il y a des anglais: How do you doing?"). Moreover, Debbouze's popularity lies in the fact that his humour is always on the cutting edge of new modes of expression and communication.[22] In a surrealistic rewriting of Shakespeare's *Romeo and Juliet*, recast in the Banlieue, Romeo is a "mec" (a dude) of Danish origin who seems "as welded to Juliet as a Turk to his *Carte de séjour* [Green Card]."

Jamel's resourcefulness lies, above all, in his improvisational skills and language inventiveness, a combustible admixture of street slang and fast-paced dialogue. His sketches are punctuated by signature phrases of his own vintage such as "Dites moi pas que c'est pas vrai!" "Ah ça fait plaisir", often ending his phrases with the inimitable "Lo!". He "tchatches céfran" ("speaks French") like no one else. "Pornographie" is pronounced pedantically "pornographure", "effets spécifiques" for "effets spéciaux". Debbouze alters the French language in ways the French youth have come to appreciate and identify. He creates a unique language that his fans endearingly call *La Debouzzerie* -- a mixture of onomatopoeia, new and fresh elocution, funny neologisms, and disarticulated grammar.

A good example of Jamel's *tchatche* is the following episode from *Nulle part ailleurs*, a television show he hosted for years and which coincidently launched his comedic career. His guest for this particular episode was novelist Françoise Sagan, an iconic figure for rebellious teenagers in the 50s, who was eager to learn about the Banlieue *tchatche*. Playing the attentive and diligent pupil, Sagan relished in Jamel's crash course on the recent evolution of the French language: "A l'époque des *Visiteurs* avec Jean Reno, on disait 'Boutonnons-nous prestement car il risque d'y avoir moult diableries.' Dans les années 80, ça donnait : 'Cassons-nous, ça risque d'être chaud,' et dans les années 90, c'est devenu: 'Viens, on s' taille, ça risque d'être chaud.'" As Jamel explained to Sagan, *tchatche*'s aim is to speak a language not understood by parents or cops.

---

[20] "Inadequately translated as suburbs in English but closer to inner city in American parlance, *banlieues* in French typically conjures up frightening images of failed urban communities torn apart by violence, drugs, delinquency, unemployment, and above all North African youth. Exclusionary spaces or neighborhoods of exile, the banlieues are perceived as repositories for all of France's ills and unwanted populations" (Derderian, p.145).

[21] For Fellag, code-mixing and switching is the trademark of North-African speech: "Je dis 'bonjour' en kabyle et on me répond en arabe et la conversation s'engage en français."

[22] The English term "chat" is also called *clavardage*, *babillage* or *tchatche*.

Through humour Debbouze captures that which often escapes the keenest expert on Beur culture. Without pedantism or didacticism, Jamel Debbouze embodies, in his own way, the Beur as an *engagé* comedian committed to changing the general perception of the immigrant other. Although his strategy aims at shaking and waking his public, he does so without resentment or bitterness. Debbouze makes us laugh, cry, and most importantly think. He has successfully expanded, through a changing and ever more diverse repertoire, the narrow focus of racism against Beurs that includes all aspects of France's disenfranchised society.

Hello cousin!

In the context of Beur humour, one would be remiss to not include the work of filmmakers. Beur filmmakers have increasingly resorted to humour as a vehicle for portraying urgent issues of concern that affect their community. The films of Mehdi Charef, Abdellatif Kéchiche, Karim Dridi, and Yamina Benguigui (to name a few who have recently garnered major prizes for their films) all reveal novel approaches to the issues confronting Beurs. Paradoxically for these filmmakers, the decried marginality of Beurs is not without advantage; their "peripheral" perspective sheds a unique and insightful light on the "center". Humour affords the filmmakers a distant, and therefore "objective", view of what goes on in the Hexagon; but more importantly an equally distant and "objective" perspective on the "Polygon" (Algeria). They show the Banlieue as a complex and vibrant microcosm that can also be a site of love and creativity, and not the stigmatized social milieu as which it has been portrayed. In general, Beur filmmakers seem doomed to being iconoclasts who break and transgress all kinds of taboos and prescribed boundaries.

Although not technically-speaking Beur, Franco-Algerian filmmaker Merzak Allouache has in his recent films dealt with issues related to Beurs and their interaction -- or lack thereof -- with the culture of their parents in a serious but extremely humorous way. To further prove this point, I would like to consider two of his films, both starring the Moroccan-born comedian Gad Elmaleh.[23] Both represent immigrant stories laced with biting humour that delves into the unresolved identity of his Beur characters.

---

[23]   Gad Elmaleh performs a modern brand of burlesque, very much in the style of American stand-up comedians, a choreography of words and gestures, using as source for his material the many cultural displacements he encountered since he arrived from his native Morocco. His humour advocates a new cosmopolitanism beyond parochialism and jingoism. Gad Elmaleh's sketches, especially "Décalages" (1995) and "La vie normale" (2000) are inspired by his Jewish-Moroccan childhood in Casablanca. But he fuses this traditional lore

Salut cousin (1996) is a clever and funny Beur reading of Jean de la Fontaine's 17th-century fable, "The Town Rat and the Country Rat." It describes the story of Alilo, an Algerian *trabando*, or smuggler, on a "business" trip to Paris. While there, he is hosted by his French-born cousin Mok (whose real name is Amokrane), an aspiring rap singer. Through Mok he discovers the "other" Paris, that of the "Blacks, Blancs, Beurs". Mok's fascination with the lyrics of the famous 17th-century moralist, Jean de la Fontaine, is clearly more than an attempt to bridge the cultural gap that splinters his identity. Rapping on such a canonical text as la Fontaine's is meant as a provocation; his "beurization" of the classic fable is assimilation in reverse. Ironically, his brand of Rap fusion is met with disdain, if not with hostility, by those who, like him, clamor for more diversity. To his fans Mok is a "kissman" in the jargon of the Banlieue who panders to the establishment. We see in this film yet another ironic reversal of fortunes: the Algerian cousin settles in the city where the second generation Beur, who never went to Algeria and only speaks French, is deported back to the country of his parents' origin, Algeria, *le pays non natal*, without any real connection or understanding of the customs, traditions or culture of the people. This film highlights, among other themes, the absurdity of French immigration policies and politics, and the inanity and hypocrisy of the assimilationist Republican discourse of the French Left that has only succeeded in further marginalizing Beurs.

In his second Beur film *Chouchou* (2002), Allouache tackles yet another taboo head-on: the predicament of Beur gays, particularly transvestites. Chouchou, a Maghrebian transvestite, passes for a Chilean political refugee on the run because of his illegal immigration situation. Chouchou, short for Choukri, represents a French term of endearment. With the help of a priest, Chouchou lands a job as a receptionist for a psychoanalyst named Nicole Milovavich. Chouchou's search for his equally illegal immigrant nephew leads him to the cosmopolitan nightclub named "L'Apocalypse." Here, he encounters an array of people from Algeria, including his nephew who "waitresses" under the name Vanessa. "L'Apocalypse" becomes Chouchou's favorite hangout, the ideal place for all kinds of uninhibited *éclatements*. Notwithstanding its name, "L'Apocalypse" proves to be the only hospitable place for Chouchou: a haven, a miracle of an oasis where interethnic love and friendship can flourish. Chouchou's burgeoning love affair with Stanislas seems to transcend all barriers, and thus stands for a possible harmonious "marriage" between France and its immigrant community. This idyll, however, is threatened by Inspector Grégoire, a former and dangerous patient of

---

with Marceau-type mimicry and Chaplin's. His humour is about culture clash and ethnic fusion.

Doctor Milovavich. In both films, the message is clear: for Beurs, the French police are never too far behind.

In portraying a transvestite, a minority within the Maghrebian minority in France, Allouache shows the diversity and complexity within the Beur community. Moreover, through Chouchou (portrayed as a kind of Beur avatar of Voltaire's Candide) the audience discovers not only the mores of French society, but moreover its positive and humane face, as demonstrated by the priest and Stanislas. In both films, Allouache uses humour and the art of nuance to put to the lie, if not to rest, the ubiquitous clichés and stereotypes heaped upon Beurs who relish in showing the Manichean aspect of extremism, delinquency and "unassimilability."

And the Casbah rocks back!

It is instructive in this regard to consider, where the related question of Beur artistic contributions is concerned, the musical phenomenon called "Raï'n Roll," especially the contributions of such Beur bands as Carte de Séjour (CDS) and Zebda, particularly the solo performances of the bands's lead singers, Rachid Taha (CDS) and Magyd Cherfi (Zebda). Both bands use militant lyrics to denounce the living and working conditions of immigrants and their children, yet always with a touch of humour. It is unquestionably the sharp sense of humour that sets them apart from other French musicians. They employ humour as a mode of resistance to stake out a new creative space within a culture dominated by institutional and national strategies. CDS and Zebda are both telling names for Beur rock bands. From its inception, Carte de Séjour (CDS) has fused and "métissaged" sounds, infusing "French Rock'n Roll" with Oriental and African tunes and lyrics. This hybrid fusion has come to represent the new music scene known as "Raï'n Roll". An examination of CDS's early songs reveals the depth of their commitment in addressing concerns and sensibilities rarely engaged by mainstream musicians. They couch their biting social commentaries and serious issues in playful, ironic, and sarcastic language, as best demonstrated in their album *Rhorhomanie*. This title is meant as a provocation: "Rhorho" is another word for Beur, a pejorative term for "Arabs". It alludes to the Arabic phoneme *rho* that sounds barbaric to a French ear and is thus deemed "unpronounceable".

It is precisely at the intersection of clashing sounds, phonetics and lyrics that humour arises. Again, the hybrid titles of the songs are quite revealing: "Moda" and "Zoubida" (which is Arabic for Beurette).[24] But it was the pro-

---

[24]   Richard Derderian cogently observes: "Unlike most North African groups, *CDS*'s music was primarily in Sabir -- a mixture of French, Arabic, and an assortment of other languages spoken by North African immigrants. While the sound of electric guitars and drums of their

vocative reappropriation of a classic song by suave crooner Charles Trenet, "Douce France," that made him popular. Like the rap fusion based on la Fontaine's lyrics, CDS will de-territorialize the song by orientalizing it. Trenet's effusively romantic chanson about the "douceur" of France in the throes of the barbaric Nazi occupation is "Beurized" by CDS to express their frustration with a nation that refuses this same "douceur" to its "other" citizens. After CDS's demise, the group's creative soul, its raspy-voiced lead singer Rachid Taha, went solo with the same social and political commitment that made CDS popular among North African youths. With an ever vengeful and biting humour Taha states, "I take Western music, and read right to left." From his first solo album "Olé, Olé", Taha seems to court controversy and scandal. The cover of the album shows him as a "Boy George-like" transvestite with spiky blond hair and blue lensed-glasses. This provocation directly aims at the French's xenophobia, but also at his own community's homophobia. Again, Taha's album represented a work of "reappropriation" that catapulted him to the front of the French music scene. During Operation Desert Storm, American armed forces adopted as their rallying war song the Clash's "Rock the Casbah." It was macabre humour at its best. Thirteen years later, on the eve of the second Gulf war, Rachid Taha re-appropriated the song, with the title "Rock El Casbah," which not only corrected its misuse by the American military, but also recharged it with authentic Casbah sounds and flavors.[25] As in his early song "Zoubida," Taha's ire is directed against all kinds of fundamentalisms, particularly the Islamic one.

One of Taha's biggest influences was the Clash's lead singer Joe Strummer, to whom Taha pays homage by doing an Arabic version of "Rock the Casbah". "I loved Joe Strummer," he says, "and this is my tribute to him." This is not to say that Taha endorses the negative reading that could be, and indeed was, made of the lyrics of the song: "That song is very ironic, maybe even racist; it seems a parody of the West's view of the Arabic world as only an oil pump completely devoid of culture."[26] Although still searching for a sense of adjustment to this double identity, as suggested by the title of his sixth and latest solo album *Tékitoi* (*T'es qui toi*; Who the hell are you) while

---

first album was reminiscent of the Clash, the band gradually developed its own style. By combining traditional North African instruments with all the paraphernalia of a Western rock band, *CDS* created an entirely new blend of music" (Derderian, p.64).

[25] His frequent use of the mandolute, an instrument combining the sounds of oud and guitars, is significant. It symbolizes the fusion that he seeks between East and West: "It reminds me of where I come from and where I'm going."

[26] Clearly, some of its lyrics are irreverently provocative: "By order of the prophet/We ban that boogie sound/Degenerate the faithful/With that crazy casbah sound/But the bedouin they brought out/The electric camel drum/The local guitar picker/Got his guitar picking thumb/As soon as the shareef/Had cleared the square/They began to wail."

increasingly troubled by the post 9/11 anti-Arab and Islamic media frenzy, Taha's music always seems to reveal a glimmer of hope, even in the direst of situations.

With the rock group Zebda, humour also begins with the name and the group's mascot. *Le coq français* (the French Rooster), symbol of France's national identity, is drawn in the shape of an arabesque that reads the "cal-ligraph-ed" word *Zebda* in Arabic. The mascot represents a composite vin-tage of their Arabic and French heritage, which, in turn, they incorporate in their lyrics: "We who live by rock and rai and accordion/On the periphery of commercial hits". The Arabic name of Zebda is a homophonic translation of the word "Beur" (*beurre* [butter] in French).

Humour has emerged as a survival strategy to make their marginal, if not inferior, status somehow more endurable; it also represents a form of aware-ness used as a weapon against their adversaries. By forging and meshing diverse impulses into a celebratory and affirmative ethnic fusion, Zebda clearly staked out its own share of the national and public space: "When you hear people speak about immigration and integration, it's usually in a nega-tive context -- the problems, things that aren't working, and threats to na-tional identity," comments Magyd Cherfi, the band's lyricist and one of its three singers: "People hear our music and recognize the different influences as things they've grown up with and are used to. That indicates that these influences, which may have once been considered foreign, are now a part of the French cultural fabric. I think more people are becoming aware of that, and simultaneously realizing it's something to celebrate, rather than fear."

After the disbanding of Zebda, Magy Cherfi continued his solo career with equal success. His recent songs continue to reveal, through humour, the jarring discrepancy between the rhetoric and the reality of the so-called egali-tarian, colorblind discourse of the French Republic.

Begag's Beur Black Humour[27]

The most distinctive trait of Beur fiction writing is humour, but no one has used humour more frequently and effectively than Azouz Begag. Begag, hailed by critics as the most productive and prolific Beur writer, is the author of over twenty books. Like other writers and artists, Begag uses his autobiog-raphy to illuminate the Beurs' experience. Many of his own demons, whether autobiographical, cultural, or literary, resurface, albeit in a fictionalized form, through his main characters. Keenly attuned to the cultural and political dy-

---

[27]   For a more detailed study of Azouz Begag's humour, cf. my essay, 'Humour au Beur noir dans *Quand on est mort, c'est pour toute la vie*', *Expressions maghrébines*, 1 (2002), 109-127.

namics of France, Begag has explored pressing issues of social justice and identity politics in novels such as *Le Gone de Chaâba* (1986), *Quand on est mort, c'est pour toute la vie* (1995), *Les Chiens aussi* (1995), *Dis oualla!* (1997), and *Le Passeport* (2000). Although Begag takes stock in his narratives of the many confusions of Beurs through the lens of his sociologist identity, his relentless descriptions ooze with a humour that is both sociological and political. What the Franco-Algerian comedian Fellag says about his own brand of humour aptly applies to Begag's fiction: "L'humour permet, à travers des petites histoires, de raconter la grande Histoire et de toucher des points que l'on peut pas atteindre par d'autres voies." ("Through little stories, humor makes it possible to tell the big Story [Histoire] and to touch upon points that cannot be grasped in any other way.") Likewise, Begag holds up a humorous mirror to the life and tribulations of Beurs, a mirror that also reflects the dramatic changes and tenuous tensions of contemporary French society. From the title of his first novel, *Le Gone du Chaâba*, Begag seems to have set a light-hearted but grave tone that has become his unmistakable style; it encapsulates in a humorously serious way the *entre-deux* predicament of an entire ethnic group. *Gone,* meaning "child" or "boy", represents a specific reference to the Lyon patois, whereas *Châaba,* an Arabic word, refers to the place from where the parents originate. Begag's effectiveness as a humorist resides in his uncanny ability to tap into the common background and experiences of the restless and idle Beurs, those most attuned to "reading" the subtle codes of their alien and alienating society.

Yet Begag's humour, manifested in guises, is often dark; no celebration or "aesthetization" of this identity exists, only a mere attempt to come to terms, in a direct and raw fashion, with a particular predicament. This humour most clearly reveals itself through the oxymoronic title of one of his best and most representative novels, *Quand on est mort, c'est pour toute la vie* (When you're dead, it's for the rest of your life). This title further suggests the blackness and macabre of Begag's humour, which often conveys a sense of despair and bitterness. As with his other novels, the protagonist Amar, represents a Beur writer impelled by an urgent need to write about his current uneviable predicament.

Brought to its barest essentials, *Quand on est mort, c'est pour toute la vie* depicts a non-prosecuted crime narrated by Amar, a well-assimilated Beur writer whose younger brother Mourad is killed on the way to the airport by a cab driver seeking revenge for his unpaid fare. Mourad dreamed of emigrating to California to escape the dismal predicament that many young Beurs face in France. Adding insult to injury, the "justice of France" claims lack of evidence and refuses to prosecute Mourad's death. Amar's anguished despair at the loss of his brother, and his frustration with the judicial system, lead him to suspect that the murder was racially motivated. He thus engages in a series of provocative acts aimed at the police. At his parents' behest he journeys to Algeria, the ancestral but non-native land, *le pays non natal*, in search of some inner peace with what he calls his "Arabe Généalogique". Unfortunately, he is disappointed again; Algeria is in the throes of a vicious civil war. He cuts his visit to his family village short to journey back to "Douar Lyon,"[28] and instead embarks on an adventurous and hair-raising trip home through the desert. Again, Amar feels powerless; a foreigner in a country he does not comprehend.

All of Begag's novels are marked not by nostalgia but by absence, and illustrate the illusory return to one's perceived roots, which is essentially entertained by the parents. In his fiction, the Beur is by nature and culture, unlike his parents, a pro-active and pre-emptive strategist. The myth of ambivalence seems to be perpetuated by critics and outsiders. Interestingly, on this particular score a reversal of situations occurs, an ultimate ironic twist of fate in which Beurs try to assimilate their aging parents into mainstream French culture and society. His humour poignantly reveals the contradiction of *écrivain intégré*, or assimilated writer, both courted and rejected by French society. Perceived, if not often self-anointed, as the *interlocuteur valable* for his community, Begag's *écivain intégré* is considered a "traitor" by both communities. Rather than translating them, from the vantage of his borderline position, he relishes in betraying both.

Begag's fiction crackles with wiseguy dialogues and vignettes.[29] He abundantly uses pranks, puns, and wordplay to lighten up an otherwise unbearable situation, and always with the intent of working a pointed, if often veiled, social commentary. Another sample of his humour is the ridiculed immigrant speech heard through French ears, used in an exaggerated fashion,

---

[28] "Douar Lyon": Begag mixes Algerian and French toponomy, as in *Le Gone du Chaâba,* to express, humorously, the Beur's sense of perpetual displacement.

[29] The following exchange, in *Le Gone du Chaâba* (p.211), between the Beur pupil and his French teacher illustrates this type of humour:

  -- Il était journaliste dans la ferme de Barral.

  He [the father] was a journalist on Barral's farm.

  -- Journaliste? Dans une ferme? interroge le prof ébahi.

  Journalist? On a farm? asks the astonished teacher.

  Il éclate de rire avant de dire:

  He bursts into laughter before he says:

  -- Ah! Vous voulez dire qu'il était journalier?

  Oh! You mean he was a «journey man» [a day laborer].

  -- Je ne sais pas m'sieur. Mon père dit toujours qu'il était jounaliste. Alors moi je répète ce qu'il me dit.

  I don't know sir. My father always says he was a journalist. And I repeat what he tells me.

which becomes a form of self-deprecation and derision: "Tan a rizou, Louisa. Fou lidigage di la, zi zalouprix. Li bitaines zi ba bou bour li zafas".[30]

In Begag's work, self-deprecating humour aims also at debunking the official discourse and underscore the contradictions that undermine the claims that France is a democratic society (*Des mots crasses*). However, if humour provides unique insights about a society, it also reinforces certain prejudices, for humour without stereotypes does not exist. One may perhaps reproach Begag for his unbalanced and un-nuanced characterization of the French. Indeed, his French characters are often portrayed as stock men and women entrenched in their "Frenchness" prone to fanning religious and racial prejudice, pandering to widely held perceptions. Unsurprisingly, only a few positive French characters exist in his novels.

Beur Cyber Humour

If real public space constrains and limits, then cyberspace allows for un-precedented liberty for immigrants, and specifically Beurs, to express their ethnic differences. The World Wide Web has made it possible to display and broadcast one's ethnic specificity within and beyond the Hexagon's bounda-ries. Although they reflect a cultural and a nostalgic attachment to the Maghreb, these French websites militate with abundant humour in favour of cultural heterogeneity while striving for a new humanism of the "Other". In this sense, the web represents a form of communication in which transna-tional and transethnic expression supersedes any form of closure. More im-portantly, cyber space has become a boon to minorities within the immigrant minority: gays, lesbians, and Judeo-Maghrebians. Such sites as Kelma, Harissa, Zlabia, Dafina, Judeo-Maghrebian represent part of the cobweb-like tapestry that migrant consciousness has come to define. *Harissa*, *Zlabia* and *Dafina* all refer to food, emphasizing a cultural link to the Maghreb, whereas *Kelma*, meaning "The Word", attempts to turn a taboo-word ("homosexual-ity") into a form of gay pride.

Harissa is to the Tunisians what *beurre* is to the French: an integral part of both their national diet and identity. Ironically, *Harissa*, which has come to symbolize a pejorative stereotype refering to Tunisians in the Maghreb, now represents an object of ethnic pride, a badge of honor. In this regard, Harrissa's motto is a humorous and revealing rewriting of the French prov-erb: "les goûts et les couleurs se discutent". Not to be outdone by their neighbors, Algerian Jews have opted for Zlabia,[31] the famous traditional

---

[30] Azouz Begag, *Le Gone du Chaâba* (Paris: Seuil, 1986), p.50.
[31] Ironically the majority of Zlabia makers are Tunisian from Ghomrassen.

North African pastry. Dafina, named after a traditional Shabbat Moroccan dish, has become a forum for all those who want to "reclaim their emotional heritage." To Morocco, the fact that Judeo-Maghrebians identify themselves with non-French foods, is a subtle but clear repudiation of a form of French racism that expresses itself through a purported culinary superiority. Jacques Chirac's and Brigitte Bardot's infamous pronouncements about ethnic smells are perhaps the best known examples.

But it is the website Kelma, which has highlighted the plight of a long-forgotten minority within the Maghrebian immigrant community. This site purports to break a taboo by combining homosexuality with humour. Gay Beur humour represents perhaps the best example of the "de-ghettoizing" of the Beur.

The Beur gay community wraps itself in the Tricolor flags, but dyed unabashedly in more inclusive and representative hues: Black, Blanc, Beur. The humoristic hybridization of the national colors, to the chagrin and dismay of many French purists, is ethnic as well as linguistic. It is ironic that the term "Black", clearly an American import, seems more acceptable and respectable in France than *noirs*. For many Beurs, the model is no longer exclusively Parisian, Maghrebian or home-grown but global.

Conclusion

In an age where "political correctness" has become the yardstick by which tolerance is measured, the one jarring exception remains the ever-negative media coverage of Arabs in particular and Muslims in general. This burden has, above all, impacted heavily on the Beurs' perception and, even more troublingly, their self-perception, thus complicating and delaying further their integration into mainstream French society. Ironically, Beurs now suffer not from invisibility, but from an excess of negative media-generated visibility. What remains unreported and ignored is their many cultural, literary, and artistic contributions. It is precisely in the domain of creativity that Beurs have begun with a measure of success to shatter the silence that shrouds their many positive contributions to French culture and society. Because the older migrant generation was illiterate, therefore silent and voiceless, and perceived as humourless, Beurs have come to assume and occupy a significant space in the "communication" gap between France and its minorities.

This essay shows that creativity, among Beurs, always seems to evince a healthy dose of humour. The fact that Beurs have developed their own brand of humour shatters a prevalent myth in France concerning the inherent inadaptability and "unassimilability" of Beurs into French culture. Furthermore, Beur humour strives for proximity and neighbourliness, and in this capacity has served as a bridge across cultures. Wittingly or unwittingly, the Beur humorist has emerged as a cultural translator who navigates between antagonistic perceptions at the core of interethnic misunderstandings. Their contributed to narrowing the communal gap can no longer be ignored.

But, above all, humour provides a window on the thoughts and feelings of Beurs, who have long been left outside the mainstream of French politics and culture. Clearly, Beur humorists and artists have shown that integration is a two-way street. As Ridan notes cogently in a recent interview in *Le Monde*: "If they [Beurs] find it so hard to say they are French, it is because people don't believe them."

Increasingly, we see an attempt on the part of Beur humorists to "universalize" their condition; the Beur has become a kind of new modern picaro, a *redresseur de torts* whose mission is to unmask and debunk social and political hypocrisy, strictures, and double standards: the quintessential transient whose shifting sensibilities, fluid identity, and very non-fixed identity has become everyman's condition in the postmodern world. Where the media points to a "clash of civilizations", humour affords, on the contrary, rare moments of cultural syncretism and mutual understanding.

This brief examination of Beur humour also reveals that the Beur has made significant inroads in reaching out to a French mainstream audience that ignored him or her; no longer characterized as a type, but as a complex and even positive character. "Beurness," albeit not yet a badge of honour, has shaped a new national identity in France, not as a deficit, but as a surfeit of identity. The Beur humorist has placed himself/herself in the vanguard of his community, inexorably turned to the future, turning rage and despair into hope, with tears of pain and laughter.

Bibliography

Abdel-Jaouad, Hédi, 'Humour au Beur noir dans *Quand on est mort, c'est pour toute la vie*', *Expressions maghrébines*, 1 (2002), 109-127.
Allouache, Merzak, *Salut Cousin* (1996)
Allouache, Merzak, *Chouchou* (2003)
Begag, Azouz, *Les Chiens Aussi* (Paris: Seuil, 1995)
———., *Dis oualla!* (Paris: Mille et une nuits, 1997)
———., *Le Gone du Chaâba* (Paris: Seuil, 1986)
———., *Le Passeport* (Paris: Seuil, 2000)
———., *Quand on est mort, c'est pour toute la vie* (Paris: Gallimard, 1994)
Boudjellal, Farid, *Les Beurgeois* (Toulon: Soleil Productions, 1998)

Boudjellal, Farid, *Les Beurs* (Paris: Albin Michel, 1985)

———., *Black Blanc Beur* (Cachan: Tartamudo, 2004)

———., *Ethnik ta mère.* (Toulon: Soleil Productions, 1996)

———., *Gags à l'harissa.* (Paris: Humanoïdes Associés, 1989)

———., *Jambon Beur* (Toulon: Soleil Productions, 1998)

———., *Juifs-Arabes* (Toulon: Soleil Productions, 1998)

———., *L'Oud* (Toulon: Soleil Productions, 2000)

———., *Les soirées d'Abdulah* (Paris: Futuropolis, 1985)

———., *Petit Polio* (Toulon: Soleil Productions, 2000)

Chrabi, Driss, *Les Boucs* (Paris: Gallimard, 1955)

———., *The Butts*, trans. by Hugh A. Harter (London: Lynne Rienner Publishers Inc, 1983)

Debbouze, Jamel, *Jamel: 100% Debbouze* (Sony, 2004)

Derderian, Richard L., *North Africans in Contemporary France: Becoming Visible* (New York: Palgrave Macmillan, 2004)

Dridi, Karim, *Bye, Bye*, 1995.

Laronde, Michel, *Autour du roman beur: Immigration et identité* (Paris: L'Harmattan, 1993)

Sebbar, Leïla, *Parle mon fils, parle à ta mere* (Paris: Stock, 1984)

Vian, Boris, *Automne à Pekin* (Paris: Editions de Minuit, 1964)

Cold Turkey:
Domesticating and Demythologising the Exotic in the German Satires of Şinasi Dikmen, Muhsin Omurca and Django Asül

Graeme Dunphy

Recent critical discussions of German migrant and post-migrant literature has repeatedly focussed on the phenomenon of the exotic; where some writers seem consciously to exoticise their writing, exaggerating myths about Oriental culture and thus highlighting differences between East and West, perhaps with the aim of making foreigners exciting, likeable or deserving of sympathy, others react against this, rejecting clichés and highlighting continuities, apparently with the aim of making cultural boundaries traversable. Both are understandable strategies for dealing with displacement.

In this context I should like to adopt a term from quite a different discipline, Bultmann's concept of demythologising. In theology, demythologising means dissecting the "myth" – the sacred but implausible narrative – to distil from it a kerygmatic truth. If we regard the exotic as being, in this technical sense, the "myth", then it is not entirely devoid of a relationship to reality, but it cannot simply be read as "real". Thus demythologising is the opposite process to exoticising.

Drawing on satirical texts by four Turkish-German writers and cabaretists, this paper looks at ways in which this ethnic minority can use ironic self-depiction to capture and defuse the stereotypes with which it is confronted. Under the rubric "cold turkey", that is, Turkishness without the psychedelics, it shows how the satirists transpose clichés into everyday situations, where they become absurd.

The paper's conclusion is likely to be that hybrid communities are inevitably torn between a desire to highlight demarcation lines (exoticism) and a need to accentuate the potential for assimilation (demythologising). Humour, which in any case has a tendency either to underline or to debunk stereotypes, serves as a highly effective tool for working out this dichotomy, and as all four satirists have successfully reached main-stream German audiences, it would also appear to be a key mechanism in achieving inter-cultural understanding.

"There is nothing especially controversial or reprehensible", remarked Edward Said, about "domestications of the exotic".[1] All cultures hang their pictures of all other cultures on the convenient hooks of ready images which are memorable because they verge on the fantastic. Said's critique of western perceptions of the orient has often been misconstrued as a complaint that these perceptions are a construct, not properly representative of the "reality" of the East; however, if it is impossible to have a complete knowledge of any culture, if all views of the foreign are necessarily constructs, this is not in itself the problem. Rather, Said's complaint was that the orientalist construct was used -- and was so designed as to be easily used -- for the anchoring of

---

[1] Edward W. Said, *Orientalism* (1978; New York: Vintage, 2003), p.60.

imperial and post-imperial power structures. In itself, the addiction to the exotic would seem to be a harmless enough near-universal in cross-cultural projections.[2]

The word "exotic" means "foreign", "strange", perhaps "outlandish", but in modern usage normally has a positive slant: the exotic is exciting, fascinating, appealing, because of the mystery of its otherness: when we think of exotic birds, the bird of paradise may spring to mind. A sense of the exotic is often the pull which causes people to become fans of foreign languages and cultures, and in itself it can be a very constructive force.[3] What Said called the "domestication" of the exotic is its encapsulation in relatively unsophisticated images and accoutrements akin to those of travellers' tales, the second-hand experience of the foreign which conditions most people's perception of cultures they have not encountered directly. This is the exotic canned for the home market. Such a simplified exotic fascination with the cultures of the Middle East, for example, might begin with an enthusiasm for the tastes and styles and colours of the orient, which mingle in the mind's eye with an affectionate caricature of life in Cathay, all imbued with a whiff of the scent of Scheherazade. The attraction of the foreign is that it is conceived as in every respect utterly foreign, and is stylised as idyllic, magical or psychedelic. This may play on some of the same clichés which underlie prejudice, but in contrast to prejudice, a delight in the exotic is well-meaning, though it may be patronising. In essence, it is a love-affair with a half-understood, half imaginary otherworld.

For the ethnic minority in a European context, the element of the exotic is a double-edged sword. It is not necessarily a bad thing to be thought of as exotic: this may convey a desirable status. As an exotic entity, one has one's niche and is valued in it. It can therefore be rewarding as a foreigner to play a rôle in which one's foreignness endows an easy popularity; at any rate this may seem preferable to being in racial confrontation with the indigenous majority. It can also provide an opening through which more meaningful communication becomes possible. But this same dynamic also holds the exoticised object at a distance, artificially widening the gap which intercultural communication seeks to bridge. And it can backfire, since it feeds stereotypes which in turn may nurture xenophobia. It is therefore not surpris-

---

[2]   For recent work on the exotic, cf. for example *"New" Exoticisms: Changing Patterns in the Construction of Otherness*, ed. by Isabel Santaolalla (Amsterdam: Rodopi, 2000). In her prologue, Santaolalla argues for a more flexible approach to the concept of the "exotic" as "that simultaneous fear and fascination for what comes from beyond [our] limits" (p.9).

[3]   In German, this is complicated by the fact that the noun *Exot* can be used slightly disparagingly to refer to an "eccentric", but otherwise the semantic ranges of German *exotisch* and its cognates are generally parallel to those of the English forms.

ing that members of migrant communities may feel ambivalent about their own exotic plumage.

Recent critical discussions of German migrant and post-migrant literature have on several occasions focussed on the phenomenon of the exotic. In an essay on the novelist and poet Zafer Şenocak entitled 'Wider den Exotismus',[4] for example, Ulrich J. Beil described the exotic as "eine Verführung nicht nur für das westliche Publikum"[5] ("seductive, and not only for the western public"). Drawing on parallel work which has been done on presentations of Japanese culture, he expounds Irmela Hijiya-Kirschnereit's concept of *Selbstexotisierung* and applies it to the Turkish-German situation.[6] The basic observation here is that migrant writers, being aware of the predilections of their European readers, often choose to couch their cultural self-portraits in language and imagery which seeks to cash in on the good-will which western appreciation of the exotic appears to promise. The point at issue is whether this is legitimate: Şenocak thinks not.

This debate has also been observed in the context of German-Arab literature by Uta Aifan.[7] She proffers the helpful term "staging" exoticism to describe the approach of Rafik Schami, who works very consciously with exotic material, often employing the most explicit motifs from the Arabic folk-tale tradition as a platform from which intercultural prejudices can be disarmed. Schami's writing has found a very broad acceptance, but other writers such as Emine Sevgi Özdanar and Saliha Scheinhardt have on occasion been roundly criticised for pandering to the exotic. The opposite, anti-exotic tendency is characterised by Aifan as "demystifying" the exotic, which connotes the clearing up of a confusion. One might wonder if Bultmann's concept of demythologising might come closer to Aifan's intention,[8] for she means more than just the countering of misinformation; she means the dismantling of the exotic myth itself. In theology, demythologising means dissecting the "myth" – the sacred but implausible narrative – to distil from it a kerygmatic truth. If we regard the exotic as being, in this technical sense, the "myth", then it is not entirely devoid of a relationship to reality, but it cannot

4   Ulrich Johannes Beil, 'Wider den Exotismus: Zafer Şenocaks west-östliche Moderne', in *Zafer Şenocak. Contemporary German Writers*, ed. by Tom Cheesman and Karin Yeşilada (Cardiff: University of Wales Press, 2003), pp.31-42. Cf. my review of *Zafer Şenocak* in: *Modern Language Review*, 99 (2004), 1112-1113.

5   Ibid., p.31.

6   Irmela Hijiya-Kirschnereit, *Das Ende der Exotik: Zur japanischen Kultur und Gesellschaft der Gegenwart* (Frankfurt a.M.: Suhrkamp, 1988).

7   Uta Aifan, 'Staging Exoticism and Demystifying the Exotic: German-Arab *Grenzgänger-literatur*', trans. by Susan Tebbutt, in *German-Language Literature Today: International and Popular?*, ed. by Arthur Williams et. al. (Oxford: Lang, 2000), pp.237-253.

8   Though Said also speaks of "demystification", albeit in a slightly different context. Cf. Said, p.181.

simply be read as "real". Whereas staging domestications of the exotic involves exaggerating myths about Oriental culture and thus highlighting differences between East and West, perhaps with the aim of making foreigners exciting, likeable or deserving of sympathy, demythologising is a reaction against this, rejecting clichés and highlighting continuities, apparently with the aim of making cultural boundaries traversable. Both are understandable strategies for dealing with displacement.

Migrant humorists face this choice on a daily basis: do they manipulate exotic clichés about their home countries or eschew them? Three Turkish-German satirists of different generations, Şinasi Dikmen, Muhsin Omurca and Django Asül, provide an opportunity to observe some of the ways this question can be handled. All three first achieved public acclaim through their cabaret, all three have also published in book form. For the present purposes these three must stand as representatives of a strong tradition: other names which could as easily have been highlighted include Osman Engin, Kaya Yanar, Serdar Somuncu, Sedat Pamuk or Kerim Pamuk. The following discussion will focus on Dikmen's prose satires, Omurca's cartoon strips, and the CD recordings of Asül's stand-up comedy.

* * *

Şinasi Dikmen was born in Turkey in 1945, and came to Germany as part of the guest-worker programme in 1972;[9] he is one of the few German migrant writers who still use the term *Gastarbeiter*, which others find dated or politically loaded. Only after a decade in Germany, now in his late 30s, did he become the full-time humorist whom comedian Dieter Hildebrandt has described as a "satirischer Beobachter des deutsch-türkischen Mißverständnisses"[10] ("a satirical observer of the German-Turkish misunderstanding"). Alongside his television appearances with Hildebrandt in the comedy series *Scheibenwischer*, Dikmen is best known for his cabaret tours with Muhsin Omurca under the banner *Knobi-Bonbon* (garlic sweet), which ran for twelve years with five programmes (1985-97), and since 1997 for his solo-tours. In these solo performances, he appears on stage alternately as, for example, a

---

[9] Literature on Dikmen, and on German ethnic-minority cabaret generally: Karin Yeşilada, 'Schreiben mit spitzer Feder: Die Satiren der türkisch-deutschen Migrationsliteratur', in *Spagat mit Kopftuch*, ed. by Jürgen Reulecke (Hamburg: Körber-Stiftung, 1997), pp.529-564; Mark Terkessidis, 'Kabarett und Satire deutsch-türkischer Autoren', in *Interkulturelle Literatur in Deutschland: Ein Handbuch*, ed. by Carmine Chiellio (Stuttgart/Weimar: Metzler, 2000), pp.294-301; Will Hasty and Christa Merkes-Frei, *Werkheft Literatur: Şinasi Dikmen -- Zehra Çirak* (Munich/Atlanta: Goethe Institut, 1996).

[10] Dieter Hildebrandt, foreword, in Şinasi Dikmen, *Hurra ich lebe in Deutschland* (Munich: Piper, 1995), 7-9 (p.7).

German land-lord and a Turkish tenant, costumed and propped accordingly, soliloquising on cultural clashes in the dialect of Ulm and in the broken Turkish-German of the recent immigrant respectively. He has also established himself as the author of several volumes of satirical prose. His collection of stories *Hurra, ich lebe in Deutschland* (1995) will serve here a sample of his work.[11]

To demonstrate the tone of Dikmen's writing, we might take, to choose one at random, the story "Kein Geburtstag, keine Integration". Birthdays are important in German social life, especially for young adults, who are inclined to throw large parties in their own honour. The narrator, Şinasi, regularly has to think up excuses for not inviting his German friends to an annual birthday function, and has begun to feel that his inability to do so is the last great barrier to his integration. The reason for this rather unusual handicap -- unusual when viewed through the lens of western cultural expectations -- is quite simple: he has no idea when his birthday is. Of course there is the requisite entry in his passport, since the German authorities require a date of birth and the Turkish officials processing his immigration papers obligingly invented one. This phenomenon is picked up by other Turkish-German humorists, too: in his book *Sprich langsam, Türke*, Kerim Pamuk describes the astonishment of German civil servants who, while processing residence permits, discover that the majority of the Turkish population were born on the 1st January.[12] For Şinasi, the problem is acute because he cannot bring himself to enter into the spirit of party revelries on the wrong day. So, on his next trip to the village where he was brought up, he sets out to discover his actual date of birth.

Here in Turkey, however, he is confronted by different cultural expectations. His family and friends are bemused by his pedantic interest in such an odd point of trivia, and wonder if too much contact with Germanic precision has addled his brain. But they do their best to help. His mother is able to tell him he was born on the day the family's prize bull escaped, and is irritated that he cannot be satisfied with this. His older sister knows this was the same day when she had her first illicit tryst with her husband-to-be; but the brother-in-law has very different memories of this assignation and ridicules his wife's romantic notions: "die Weiber, die Weiber, die erzählen nie die

---

[11]   By the same author: Şinasi Dikmen, *Wir werden das Knoblauchkind schon schaukeln* (Berlin: EXpress Edition, 1983); Şinasi Dikmen, *Der andere Türke* (Berlin: EXpress Edition, 1986). However these earlier collections have been allowed to go out of print, partly because the most successful stories from them were recycled in *Hurra ich lebe in Deutschland*. Two of these stories also appear with lesson plans for the DAF classroom in Hasty and Merkes-Frei. The *Knoblauchkind* volume includes a transcript of one of Dikmen and Omurca's joint stage performances.

[12]   Kerim Pamuk, *Sprich langsam, Türke* (Hamburg: Nautilus, 2002), p.67.

wahre Wahrheit, sondern immer nur ihre eigene, weibliche, Wahrheit."[13]
("Women, women! They never tell the true truth, but only their own female
truth.") The irony here, of course, is that the superior husband's own information proves every bit as unreliable as that of his supposedly brainless wife,
which not only parodies gender prejudices -- a set-piece in Turkish diaspora
writing -- but also suggests that the whole community's concept of "truth" in
such a question is far removed from that of western thinking.

On one level, this is not unrealistic; work on the psychology of orality has
shown that non-literate or semi-literate societies do value different kinds of
information from that which seems important in the modern typographical
world, and that they order and retrieve this information in quite different
ways.[14] To this extent, the same story could have been told about a German
peasant community only a few generations earlier. However, the implicit
raising of simple-mindedness to a Turkish national characteristic coincides
too closely for comfort with Said's observations on the way the West has
sought to render Islam harmless by caricaturing Muslim populations as inca-
pable of advanced reasoning. At any rate, a recurring theme in Turkish-
German writing is the impression on the part of many Germans that Germany's Turks are simple. What some may find surprising here is that the
same prejudice can be encountered in Turkey. A large proportion of the
Turkish guest workers who came to Germany in the 1960s, including Dikmen
himself, came from peasant communities, and one of the recurring tensions
between the Turkish diaspora and its fatherland is that sophisticated urbanites
in Turkey often regard what they see as the country-bumpkin mentality of the
ex-pats in Germany with some distain. This adds great complexity to the
whole panorama of perception and reality.

The rural Turkey of this story, then, is the Turkey of German fantasy. It
has its roots in reality -- Dikmen himself does not know when his birthday is
-- but it is idealised, caricatured, made at once more appealing and more
remote, and the village is not inhabited by the flesh-and-blood villagers
among whom the author grew up.[15] As always in Dikmen's writings, the
humour points in two directions, the Germans and the Turks being parodied
equally, but it is nonetheless a humour of the stereotypes which exaggerates
the differences between the two cultures, and this romanticised rustic idyll
recurs in the story "Freundschaft", in which a German family seek the au-

---

[13]   Dikmen, *Hurra*, p.27.
[14]   Discussed, for example, in Walter J. Ong, *Orality and Literacy: The Technologizing of the Word* (London & New York: Methuen, 1984).
[15]   Cf. for example the July 1995 interview with Dikmen in Hasty and Merkes-Frei, pp.65-73; here p.66 (on his birthday) and p.72 (on the idealisation of the village).

thentic Turkish experience by holidaying in an Anatolian peasant village, but pack up and head home early when the exotic turns out to be overwhelming.

Interestingly, this sense of the exotic, like the humour itself, works in two directions in Dikmen's writings, for the cultural estrangement of a Turk looking at German culture is portrayed in very similar ways. One of the reasons why the German family in "Freundschaft" are overtaxed by their experience is that they find themselves the exotic westerners who are constantly the centre of the villagers' fascination. The title story "Hurra, ich lebe in Deutschland" has the form of a guest worker's letter home, in which the wonders of the occident are expounded for the amazement of the wide-eyed Anatolian villagers. Germany is the strange and fascinating land of the west where everything is different. The epistler describes toilets on which one can sit, buses in which a mysterious voice announces each stop, and a day of the week dedicated only to car-washing. These almost anecdotal details of German life may be accurate enough in themselves, but picked out of their contexts and reported in isolation they convey a sense of the totally alien. This itself is a "domestication of the exotic", but is compounded by a great deal of accompanying misinformation. The strange rolls of paper beside the sit-down toilets must, the letter-writer deduces, be for scribbling down notes to oneself, no doubt with the intention of harnessing all the great ideas which occur to employees during their "sittings" for the benefit of German industry; perhaps this is how the German economy recovers so quickly after the wars which they periodically lose. Or again, Germans always look sad on the bus home, because they can only be happy when at work:[16]

> Abends ist es im Bus sehr still, als ob jemand gestorben wäre. Niemand hat Lust, über irgendein Thema zu sprechen. Ich würde dir raten, falls du in Deutschland überhaupt arbeiten könntest, rede nach der Arbeit keinen Deutschen an, sonst bekommst du eine unpassende Antwort, vielleicht sogar eine grobe, unfreundliche. Am schlimmsten ist Freitagabend. Am Freitagabend sind sie wie wilde Tiere, die jederzeit zum Angriff bereit sind.

> (In the evenings it is very quiet on the bus, as though someone had died. No-one feels like talking about anything. I would advise you, if you ever do get the chance to work in Germany, never to speak to a German after the end of work, or you may get a short answer, perhaps even a rude, unfriendly one. Friday evening is worst of all. On Friday evening they are like wild animals, ready to attack at any moment.)

The reader is left to guess the real source of the irritability which the guest worker has observed. Obviously, all this is wildly exaggerated for the sake of its humour, but it is not meant entirely ironically: in an interview Dikmen

---

[16]   Dikmen, *Hurra*, p.17.

insists that this piece is based on letters which he really did receive from Germany before he emigrated -- "Die Gastarbeiter, die vor mir nach Deutschland gekommen sind, haben über Deutschland ungefähr so erzählt"[17] ("The guest workers who came to Germany before me spoke of it in more or less this way.") -- and other migrants tell how the sense of wonder evoked by such stories was part of what motivated them to leave their homelands. The key question here is the tone in which these convoluted travellers' tales are delivered: amazement, affectionate admiration, and a slight shiver of apprehension about contact with the utterly alien. Strange as it may seem to the German reader, Germany too can be exotic.

This story is a sequel to a piece in an earlier volume with a similar "letter-home" format entitled "Deutschland, ein türkisches Märchen" (Germany, a Turkish fairytale'),[18] and this title is telling. Its history would appear to be as follows. In 1978 Aras Ören had published collection of poems with this same title, *Deutschland, ein türkisches Märchen,* obviously in deliberate echo of Heine's *Deutschland ein Wintermärchen.* (Other book titles by Ören are also Turkish versions of western classics: *Berlin Savignyplatz* in allusion to Döblin, for example, or *Paradies kaputt* to Milton.) In 1979, Ören's title was used as the catch-phrase for an intercultural event in Ulm at which Dikmen was asked to speak, and the first version of Dikmen's story was read on that occasion.[19] The title itself, then, is not Dikmen's but its relationship to the material it inspired is nonetheless poignant. In an oriental context, the exotic element of a "märchenhaft", fairy-tale world conjures up visions of the *Arabian Nights* for most western readers. One might go as far as to say that the exotic orient is a "Märchen" of western invention. The idea that the Germany portrayed in Dikmen's story might be a "Märchen" originating in Turkish fantasy is neat reversal of this.

This reversible nature of the exotic is particularly obvious in its relationship to the erotic, which Dikmen himself expresses succinctly: "je exotischer desto erotischer"[20] ("the more exotic, the more erotic"). Said complained that an insidious feature of western orientalism was its belief in the sensuality and licentiousness of the oriental. Dikmen enthusiastically reproduces this cliché, the potency of the eastern man and the exhibitionism of the belly-dance, but matches it with what might be termed an occidental stereotype of the sexual willingness of the German woman.[21] These opposing exoticisms meet and collapse upon each other without any real resolution when it emerges that the

---

[17]   Hasty and Merkes-Frei, p.69.
[18]   Dikmen, *Koblauchkind*, pp.5ff.
[19]   Hasty and Merkes-Frei, p.66.
[20]   Dikmen, *Hurra*, p.158.
[21]   Dikmen, *Hurra*, pp.27, 95, 157ff.

"Egyptian" belly-dancer in the Turkish restaurant is in fact a German student earning some pocket money.

The primary focus of Dikmen's satire, then, is the clash of contrasting cultural assumptions. These contrasts allow criticisms to be made of both German and Turkish life. A nice example of humour at the expense of the Turkish side is the story "Eine Reise durch Griechenland", in which the narrator must spend a night in Greece on his way home to the Bosporus. He carries with him a racial profile of the Greeks as hateful and murderous and is able to confirm this prejudice through experience because he stubbornly misinterprets every friendly gesture. The message of this story obviously goes beyond the specific Greek-Turkish dynamic to speak of racial prejudice generally, but its focus is by no means accidental: the Greek question is a perennial irritant which calls liberal Turks to serious self-reflection. More frequently, however, social criticism is directed against Germany. Dikmen has spoken in interviews of his disillusionment with Germany: he describes himself as "ein enttäuschter Liebhaber", a disappointed lover, disappointed by the slowness of the German majority to warm to his attempts at integration.[22] While his stories do not blame the German side alone for the failure of communication, their reticence is obviously the problem which most frequently confronts him, and as Germans are his primary readership, it is this that he wishes to write to them about.

Dikmen's aim, then, is to deal with tensions across this divide. Almost all of his stories are told through the voice of a rather green and gullible immigrant who has a stylised view of the Germans, and himself corresponds entirely to a German stereotype of the Turk. Invariably the Turkish figure is warm and open-minded about the Germans, though sustaining this good-will in the face of a thousand setbacks requires considerable endurance, enough that one protagonist on the hunt for a new flat coins the proverb "As patient as a Turk in Germany."[23] Some of the Germans in the stories reciprocate this attitude by looking on the Turks with an equal benevolence, and an equal lack of real understanding. This mutual failure of understanding is the source of much of Dikmen's humour, as when German neighbours, out of pity for the poor migrants, bring unwelcome sacks of second-hand clothes, and the narrator's reluctant children are forced to wear these in order not to offend their benefactors. Frequently, though, we are made to sense that the friendliness of Germans is limited to a few exceptional individuals or to superficial contacts. Sometimes, indeed, the reader sees more than the narrator can, and recognises that what the naïve newcomer sees as heartiness may be ambiva-

---

[22]   Hasty and Merkes-Frei, p.67.
[23]   Dikmen, *Hurra*, p.71.

lence at best: in "Ein Türkenbub scheibt einen Brief an Onkel Goethe", the child-narrator repeatedly mistakes insults for complements and is thrilled by the warm reception he receives. And the piece "Wir werden das Knoblauch-kind schon schaukeln", the title story of an earlier volume which is reprinted in *Hurra*, parodies liberal German activists who wish to see themselves help-ing race relations but only reveal their own inherent prejudices.

Outright hostility is only occasionally the theme of Dikmen's writing, but in the story "Wer ist ein Türke?" which has been discussed thoroughly by Karin Yeşilada,[24] it is sheer racism which makes an elderly German couple refuse a Turk a place in a railway carriage, although there is space. The narra-tor -- if it makes sense to distinguish narrator from author in what turns out to be a recollection of an actual incident -- is the third passenger in the com-partment, and happens to be one of those Turks who look and sound German, as does Dikmen himself. When the woman explains that she has no wish to share a compartment with a Turk, the narrator can wrong-foot her by pointing out that she is already doing precisely this. Rather than re-examine her preju-dice, however, the woman refuses to believe that the narrator is Turkish; after all, he is reading *Die Zeit*. Dikmen's response to this mindless hostility is an irony which renders the woman absurd. The narrator ponders that if reading *Die Zeit* makes him German, perhaps those Germans who do not read *Die Zeit* become Turks?

It is perhaps significant that Dikmen's humour focuses almost exclusively on the Turkish-German dynamic. Even when he turns his attention to more general matters, the Turkish aspect is always present. For example, his short text in letter form, "Bölls Tod in Deutschland", inveighs against the outrage that the death on 16th July 1985 of the novelist Heinrich Böll, whom Dikmen so much admires, received less media coverage in Germany than Ronald Reagan's surgery for cancer of the colon, four days earlier. The fictional letter-writer, a German literary scholar, and an admirer of Böll's controver-sial critic Matthias Walden to boot, finds this normal, "weil der Arsch in Deutschland wichtiger als der Kopf ist"[25] ("because in Germany the arse is more important than the head"). It is of course the stock-in-trade of satirists to link such apparently unrelated items in order to comment on the upside-down priorities of society, but Dikmen -- almost gratuitously in this piece -- has a Turkish post-grad expose the discrediting state of affairs like Grimm's boy the emperor's nakedness, while the self-satisfied German expert mocks the Turk's naïvety. Dikmen's point-of-view, then, is unwaveringly that of the alien in Germany, whether the material requires this or not. And indeed this

---

[24]   Yeşilada, pp.534ff.
[25]   Dikmen, *Hurra*, p.156.

obviously coincides with reader-expectations, for despite the Turkish perspective in this story, Dikmen was criticised for writing about Böll, a *German* author.[26] This clear delineation may be considered a prerequisite for exoticism: for it could be argued that an author who moves easily between cultural spheres is less likely to accentuate the differences between them.

We see, then, that the world of Dikmen's *Hurra* is characterised by a fairly stark demarcation line across which Germanness and Turkishness are opposing poles. Although he himself is well able to merge into German society,[27] none of his Turkish protagonists are, with the exception of that one autobiographical narrator in the railway carriage. The differences between the cultures are constantly highlighted for humorous effect, whereas similarities and cultural continuities go unremarked. To facilitate this widening of the cultural gap, Dikmen's portrait of the Turks, is heavily endowed with exotic elements. There is the pastoral idyll of the Turkish village, the obedience of the Turkish wife, the emotionalism, illogicality and backwardness of the oriental, and generally the sights and sounds of the east, all of which are presented as unquestioned and at least ostensibly unquestionable.

One might wonder whether the innate irony of Dikmen's prose counteracts these features. In some cases it clearly does: when he calls the Turks "rückständig" ("backward"),[28] for example, the reader registers powerfully that the author is in fact rejecting, not asserting this prejudice. There is at least a whiff of the ironic in every paragraph of the book, and Dikmen himself has called irony "Haltung", an attitude rather than a technique, a constant in his manner of looking at the world.[29] A possible interpretation, then, would be that in presenting the exotic ironically, Dikmen is signalling that it is fake. The difficulty here is that he makes no attempt to put anything in its place. When he refers to Karl May, the 19th-century author of adventure stories for boys, as the greatest authority on the Turks,[30] for example, the tone is obviously ironic, yet far from undermining the exotic *per se*, the allusion calls to mind a whole new layer of exotic clichés which surface in the reader's perception and are never discredited. On the contrary, despite the fact that he is clearly not taking the exotic material too seriously, one is left with the impression that he is enjoying it rather than rebelling against it. It would seem, then, that there is no inherent contradiction between irony and the delight in

---

[26]   Hasty and Merkes-Frei, p.71.

[27]   In the foreword, Hildebrandt writes: "Şinasi sieht aus und wirkt so wie ein Deutscher, der türkisch gelernt hat. Erst seine Betrachtensweise des deutschen Alltags entlarvt ihn als Türke" (p.7).

[28]   Dikmen, *Hurra*, p.80.

[29]   Hasty and Merkes-Frei, p.69.

[30]   Dikmen, *Hurra*, p.110.

the exotic. With his irony, Dikmen warns the reader to question everything, especially when it seems simple, but the exotic remains a field with which both author and reader can be comfortable.

In a similar way, Dikmen's strategy of extrapolating *ad absurdum* for humorous effect may sometimes have the effect of rendering the exotic unreal; the behaviour of the guests in the story "Wir tun so als ob wir Deutsche wären", for example, who end up drawing knives and stabbing each other, cannot be described as "typically Turkish" without a reverse effect setting in in the minds of the readers. The exaggerated exotic should ring alarm bells. However, this is undermined by the fact that the exaggeration itself is portrayed as an Turkish trait: "denn jeder, Freund oder Feind, weiß, daß wir, die Südländer, eine grenzenlose Phantasie haben und übertreiben."[31] ("For everyone, friend or foe, knows that we Mediterranean peoples have an unbounded imagination, and exaggerate.") Thus any power that exaggeration might have to protest against the stereotype is negated when the exaggeration and the stereotype are so effortlessly reconciled. Like irony, exaggeration is a relativiser which makes it just a little bit harder for us to take the exotic material at face value, but without presenting an alternative, non-exotic picture.

Occasionally however, the exotic element is sharply reversed by a dose of cold realism, which really does tend for a moment to demythologise. In "Freundschaft", we are left wondering whether perhaps the German family in the Turkish village fled because they discovered that their view of the orient was inadequate -- do they in fact learn anything? Likewise, in "Bauchtanz", the revelation that the oriental dancer is really a German woman must suggest to the reader that the exotic cliché is flawed, or at least potentially deceptive. However such counter-thrusts are by no means found in every story. Only in "Wer ist ein Türke?", politically a key story of the collection, is the exotic entirely abandoned as a tool. In this case, the outright racism of the woman on the train is too blunt to be answered subtly. But in every narrative and technical sense, this story is untypical.

Perhaps the greatest challenge to an exoticised orient construction in Dikmen's writing is the fact that, as we have seen, the exotic element is reversible, the strange and fascinating eastern hemisphere being matched by a strange and fascinating west. The exotic is not a way of viewing one nation, but a way of viewing the world. It should of course come as no surprise that the excitement of looking across cultural boundaries can be reciprocal, but for most western readers, this is not part of their awareness. The reversibility of the exotic therefore has a strategic function: Dikmen's predominantly

---

[31]   Dikmen, *Hurra*, p.57.

German readership is invited to make the unexpected comparison and thus discover the subjectivity of their personal exotic fantasies.

All these caveats warn against letting exotic stereotypes get out of hand. Nevertheless, in Dikmen's writing the exotic is manipulated, not debunked. The story "Der Kebabstammtisch" is indicative of this. The Kebab, the Turkish speciality most beloved of Germans, is itself an exotic cliché. In this text, the narrator declares his intention to found a Kebab club at which Germans will learn to love the taste of the Turkish:[32]

> Der Kebab ist nicht nur ein Kulturgut, eine Folklore, eine Gaumenfreude, sondern auch eine Verständigungsmöglichkeit, eine Brücke sozusagen. Ich kenne keinen Deutschen, der nach einer Portion Kebab seine Feindlichkeit den Türken gegenüber aufrechterhalten hat. Hätte Sultan Selim der Zornige Luther eine Portion Kebab geschickt, in den Jahren, als Martin Luther seine 95 Thesen an der Kirchentür aufhing, wäre aus Martin Luther ein lammfrommer Türkenfreund geworden. Ich habe bei meinen eigenen Versuchen festgestellt, daß man nach einer Portion Kebab offener, entspannter, toleranter wird. Der Mensch, auch der Deutsche, macht sich dann auf, er ist dann bereit, seine Mitmenschen in seine Arme zu nehmen.

> (The kebab is not only a piece of culture, folklore, a delight for the palate, but also a means of communication, a bridge so to speak. I know no German who has succeeded in maintaining his hostility towards the Turks after a portion of kebab. If Sultan Selim the Furious had sent Luther a portion of kebab in the years when he was hanging his 95 thesis on the church door, Martin Luther would have become a committed turkophile. Through my own experiments I have discovered that after a portion of kebab people become opener, more relaxed, more tolerant. Even a German opens up and is willing to embrace his neighbours.)

The kebab strategy, which includes offering kebab of a variety of meats (bear, wolf, snake, spider and kangaroo) so that the Germans will realise that the veal kebab tastes best, is obviously typical of Dikmen's absurdly exaggerating comedy, but what the narrator seeks with his "Stammtisch" is precisely what the author seeks with his texts, to seduce German readers into an affection for the guest worker by giving them a taste for the exotic. On the whole, one has the impression that Dikmen enjoys the exotic status. He does make several attempts to relativise it and put it into perspective, but as long as its recycling for the German domestic market has the desired narcotic effect of numbing the irritants which lead to hostilities, he is happy to let it thrive.

*   *   *

---

[32]   Dikmen, *Hurra*, p.151.

Muhsin Omurca[33] was born in Turkey in 1959, and came to Germany at the age of 20. His career in stand-up comedy began with his twelve-year co-operation with Dikmen; after the break-up of the *Knobi-Bonbon* team in 1997, Omurca established a series of solo programmes entitled *Tagebuch eines Skinheads in Istanbul* (Diary of a skinhead in Istanbul, 1996), *Kanak-män* (1999) and *TRäume-alptrEUme* (Dreams-nightmares, 2004). Omurca is also known as a cartoonist, he drew the cover illustrations for Dikmen's books for example, and in his solo programmes he has pioneered what he calls "cartoon cabaret", a new concept in Germany, in which his drawings are projected onto the wall as he performs. The cartoons from the *Kanakmän* programme subsequently took on a life of their own, appearing first in the newspaper *Etap*, which was circulated free of charge to Turkish households throughout Germany, and then in the mainstream newspaper *taz*, where the comic strip received such reader acclaim that excerpts, fashioned into a continuous narrative, were published in 2002 as a 60-page comic booklet.[34]

The proactive use of the word *Kanake*, which properly designates a South Sea Islander (from Hawaiian *kanaka*, "man") but in today's German slang has become a racist epithet for "the" Turk, reminds us of Feridun Zaimoglu's volume of fictional interviews *Kanak Sprak* (1995) or Lars Becker's gangster film *Kanak Attak* (2001, based on Zaimoglu's 1997 novel *Abschaum*), both of which contain hard-hitting depictions of urban deprivation and young Turkish drop-outs in the sleazy North German drug scene, or of satirist Os-man Engin's novel *Kanaken-Gandhi* (1998) and his volume of stories *Ober-kanakengeil* (2001). In a similar way Omurca co-opts the word as an affirmative self-designation. The title-figure, "Kanakmän" (the *Umlaut* is intended to evoke an English as opposed to a German pronunciation of "man") is nothing less than a large-nosed, moustached and thus obviously Turkish Superman who flies in with his cape and vest -- adorned with the letter *K* where Superman has his famous *S* -- to aid the beleaguered guest-worker in his daily struggles. Unfortunately, Kanakmän is only a dream, or rather, an invincible self-projection, of the bumbling central figure, Hüsnü.

As the subtitle *tags deutscher nachts türke* suggests, it is the phenomenon of mixed identity which is the central theme of the cartoon narrative. The key-word of the booklet is *Doppelpass*. For many years, the issue of dual nationality has been on the German political agenda, but despite frequent representations from minority groups, the policy of successive governments of both complexions has been firm: foreign nationals who are long-term

---

[33] Pronounced *'mu:çsin o'mu:rd3a*. I am grateful to Muhsin Omurca for taking the time to discuss his cabaret with me, and for giving permission to publish photographic reproductions of his cartoons.

[34] Muhsin Omurca, *Kanakmän: tags deutscher nachts türke* (Ulm: omu Verlag, 2002).

residents may apply for German citizenship, but as part of the administrative process must normally give up their previous nationality. Like many Turks, Hüsnü cherishes what is for him the impossible dream of the double passport, acquiring the German documents which confer rights and privileges while retaining the Turkish escape-route, an official recognition of dual identity. He dreams of keeping these two passports in his two back pockets like revolvers in a cowboy's holster, ready to draw at a moment's notice. "Ich spüren die Macht und die Härte der beiden Staaten auf meinem Arsch! Meine Arschbacken sind in sicheren Händen!"[35] ([In broken German] "I feel the power and the strength of both states on my arse. My two cheeks are in safe hands.")

Hüsnü has his own unique angle on the nationality question. He desires dual citizenship because it will facilitate his innate wanderlust. In "Wir Türken sind Nomaden", he explains:[36]

> Das ist unsere Bestimmung. Wir müssen immer weiterziehen. Wie Wanderlachse! Also Türken nix stammen von Affen ab wie Deutsche. Wir vielmehr verwandt mit den Lachsen!

> ([In broken German] That is our destiny. We must keep moving on. Like migrating salmon! So Turks are not descended from apes like the Germans. Rather, we are related to salmon.)

Salmon, then, are the "Türken der Fischheit", leaving their homes in the river to head out to work in the oceans, and returning to spawn. The difference is that salmon do not need visas; Turks are more like salmon in an aquarium, hemmed in by glass right and left. And the problem is the Turkish passport, which does not open borders, not even to the "German provinces" of Austria, Switzerland and Holland.

So Hüsnü's hopes are fixed on the thought of a German passport, "ein Pass wie 'Viagra'!",[37] like Aladin's lamp.[38] The passport that will get you a Russian wife if no other women will have you. "Bist du ein Schlafwandler? Er ist dein Kompass! Kämpfst du gegen die Römer? Er ist dein Zaubertrank!"[39] ([In broken German] "Do you walk in your sleep? It is your compass! Are you fighting the Romans? It is your magic potion!") Hüsnü knows that the unbeatable Kanakmän is only a dream, but this dream convinces him

---

[35] Omurca, *Kanakmän*, p.5.
[36] Ibid., p.8.
[37] Ibid., p.10.
[38] Ibid., p.33.
[39] Ibid., p.38.

that he himself will be immune even to the racist violence of the skinheads if he can achieve citizenship.

So he applies for his German passport and is granted it, but his Turkish one is taken away, leaving him feeling as if he has been castrated. This association of Turkishness with masculinity is of course an implicit affirmation of the pervasive clichés of the over-sexed oriental, but there is no doubt that giving up Turkish citizenship, and with it a symbolic connection to one's roots, really is a difficult psychological step for many immigrants. This sense of loss makes it doubly important that the new passport should deliver what it promised, and the latter part of the booklet explores Hüsnü's disillusionment as he discovers that in fact it does not. "Deutscher Pass ist wie ein fliegender Teppich! Bei mir aber heben er nicht mal ab!"[40] ([In broken German] "A German passport is like a flying carpet. But mine won't even take off!"). The biggest problem is that even with the documentation, no-one believes he is German. No matter what the paperwork says, a Turk's Turkishness does not easily become invisible.

Illustration 1. *Kanakmän* 12.[41]

40 Omurca, *Kanakmän*, p.21.
41 [In broken German]: "Psst, Döndü! I dreamt about the double passport again. I felt super-strong. I wanted to try out my double passport and I went to Erfurt, the capital of the skin-heads. I didn't have to look for long. First I lured them with my Turkish passport. I let them come within two club-lengths of me. Then suddenly I waved my German passport under their noses, like garlic against vampires!" "And then?" "Then I woke up." "Thank Allah!"

From an intercultural perspective, the German verb *türken*, "swindle", is extremely interesting. It is said to originate from an 18th-century confidence trick involving a Turkish doll which was supposed to be able to play chess mechanically but in fact was controlled by a man hidden in a box. There are also other explanations of the origins of the phrase, involving ruses in the Turkish wars of the 16th century, but interestingly, what all the explanations have in common is that the original Turk-swindle was not perpetrated by Turks but rather by Germans manipulating an illusion of Turkishness. At any rate, to "Turk" someone is to cheat them, to "Turk" documents or statistics is to falsify them, and the adjective *getürkt*, often in the set-phrase "alles getürkt", means "fake". For the Turkish-German satirists, this linguistic quirk is too good to miss. Several unrelated books and films bear the title *Alles Getürkt*,[42] and Omurca plays on the same idea when he has Hüsnü's neighbour declare a Turk with a German passport (or should we say, a German with a Turkish name) to be "Ein getürkter Deutsche, eine Fälschung", in contrast to the real thing, the "Bio-Deutscher", the pure, organic crop, so to speak.[43]

This theme recurs throughout the *Kanakmän* strip in a series of variations. The Turkish assimilant may satisfy bureaucratic requirements, but can never really be more than a "Scheindeutscher",[44] a humorous neologism which may echo the term *Scheinasylant*, "fraudulent asylum seeker", so frequently banded about in the immigration debate. The concept of a pure-blooded German is of course particularly pernicious in view of its National Socialist overtones, but Omurca does not pursue this direction far; he is more interested in the corollary, the feeling of spuriousness engendered by not being native. Changing one's citizenship inevitably brings complex questions of identity to the surface, and an immigrant with a heavy accent is obviously naïve to imagine that an act of officialdom will allow him to become invisible in German society. A sense of being fake may well be pre-programmed no matter how the indigenous community reacts. What troubles Hüsnü, however, is that the Germans around him so pointedly reinforce the fault-line in his identity. His origins are a stigma from which he cannot escape; as

---

42 For example Osman Engin's collection of satrirical stories, *Alles getürkt* (Hamburg: Rowohlt, 1992) or the television police comedy *Alles Getürkt*, directed by Yasemin Samdereli (2002). An academic study with the same title is Margret Spohn, *Alles getürkt: 500 Jahre (Vor)Urteile der Deutschen über die Türken* (Oldenburg: Bibliotheks- und Informationssystem der Univ., 1993). In March 2004, ZDF broadcast a documentary report on copyright crimes perpetrated by Turks entitled *Alles Getürkt: Die Buchpiraten vom Bosporus*.
43 Omurca, *Kanakmän*, p.37.
44 Ibid., p.58.

Omurca puts it, being an "Ex-Turk" is tantamount to having a previous conviction.[45]

However Hüsnü has the answer to the disappointment of his semi-successful attempt at integration. In his super-hero fantasy, Kanakmän will change things. The Germans will have to adapt to *his* norms. "Gastarbeiterdeutsch" will be declared to be the standard language, and the annoying articles *der*, *die* and *das*, the source of so many headaches for foreign learners, will be prohibited: "Wer sie dennoch verwendet, werden wegen Hochverrat und Separatismus verklagt."[46] ("Those who persist in using them will be charged with treason and separatism.") Thus the failure of multi-culturalism is ultimately compensated for, if only in an oriental fantasy.

Illustration 2. *Kanakmän* 20.[47]

Although a vast array of cultural phenomena are touched upon, *Kanakmän* is focussed squarely on a single issue: dual citizenship. The reader, like the audience in the original cartoon cabaret, is led through the ins and outs of the quandary of the Turk who is forced to choose between two passports and

45   Omurca, *Kanakmän*, p.46.
46   Omurca, *Kanakmän*, p.36.
47   [Hüsnü's speeches in broken German] "No-one believes that I'm a German. Once for example at a traffic control." Policeman: "Stop! Oh oh oh, in quite a hurry! Papers! WHAT IS THAT?" Hüsnü: "My passport; my German passport." Policeman: "Italian or Russian?" Hüsnü: "What?" Policeman: "From the Italian or the Russian Mafia?" Hüsnü: "Not Mafia! Real German, honest!" Policeman: "Boss! There's a Turked (fake) German here! One of these doubled-up types! What should I do?" Voice from car: "Charge him twice!"

finds neither choice fully satisfactory. Dual nationality would resolve Hüsnü's problems, and it quite specifically is the object of Omurca's entreaty. In an interview he explains the importance of this question.[48]

> Ich verstehe die Angst derjenigen nicht, die sich gegen den Doppelpass einsetzen. Wie soll die doppelte Staatsbürgerschaft diesem Deutschland schaden? Darauf haben die Gegner des Doppelpasses noch keine Antwort gegeben. Doch sie schaffen es, tausende von Unterschriften im Nu zu sammeln, ohne ein solches Argument vorzubringen. Das ist ein interessantes Phänomen.
>
> Ich will nicht viel von den Deutschen, ich verlange nur Gerechtigkeit. Wir erfahren immer wieder, wie die versprochene Mietwohnung plötzlich vergeben ist, sobald der Bewerber einen türkischen Namen angibt, und das auch bei den Türken, die perfekt Deutsch sprechen.
>
> Das Wort "Integration" ist eine Hülse, es ist leer. Wenn die Türken sich beschweren, wird ihnen vorgeworfen, sie haben sich nicht integriert. Das ist leicht gesagt, und keiner muss so genau erklären, was es bedeutet. Mir geht es nicht um Integration, aber schon um Entgegenkommen. Aber das muss zweiseitig sein. Ich schulde den Deutschen nichts: wenn ich also einen Schritt mache, so sollen sie auch einen machen. Ich zum Beispiel führe mein Kabarett in deutscher Sprache auf. Damit komme ich den Deutschen entgegen. Dafür sollen auch sie was geben. Die doppelte Staatsbürgerschaft wäre eine gute Möglichkeit, den Türken entgegenzukommen.

> (I can't understand the fear of those who are opposed to the double passport. What harm would dual nationality do to this Germany? The opponents of the double passport have never given an answer to this question. Yet they can manage to gather thousands of signatures in no time without ever producing such an argument. That is an interesting phenomenon. I don't ask much of the Germans, I only demand justice. We experience time and again how the promised flat suddenly has already been let, as soon as the applicant gives a Turkish name, even from Turks who speak perfect German. The word "integration" is a husk, it is empty. When the Turks complain, they are reproached with a failure to integrate. That is easily said, and no-one needs to explain exactly what is meant. I am not concerned with integration, but rather with give-and-take. But that must go in two directions. I don't owe the Germans anything: so if I make a step, they should also make one. For example, I conduct my cabaret in the German language. That is a step which I take towards the Germans. In return, they too should give something. Dual citizenship would be a good way of making a gesture towards the Turks.)

Thus *Kanakmän* is a satire with a very clear agenda. The same is true of Omurca's other cabaret programmes: *TRäume-alptrEUme*, for example, focuses (as the capitalisation suggests) on Turkey's aspirations to join the European Union. All satire challenges its public to re-examine positions, but it is less common for a whole programme to be engaged a targeted polemic; the result is that Omurca's satire is tightly structured and very effective. Omurca estimates that his live audience is equally divided between Turks and

---

[48]   Muhsin Omurca, in conversation with Graeme Dunphy, 9 April 2005.

Germans, and the same may be true of the readership of the comics. For the former, *Kanakmän* is an affirmation of their right to persist in their citizenship claims, for the latter it is a persuasive argument not to resist this.

The use of the exotic in Omurca's booklet is far less complex than in Dikmen's volume: it is one-sided and consistently applied. The Turkish clichés are far more intense than Dikmen's, the gambling cliché, the kebab cliché, the nomadic cliché, the obedient wife cliché and many others. Throughout the story, Hüsnü reinforces the impression of the Turk as a creature from another world. The inclusion of elements of Arab culture reflects the lack of differentiation that has long been inherent the western sense of the eastern exotic; going a significant step further than Dikmen, Omurca plays with such Ali Baba images as the flying carpet, and Aladdin's genie. This mixing into the mythical Turkish identity of images from the Arab fairy-tale could be criticised as a simultaneous pandering to two different mechanisms of western orientalism, namely the smelting of the diversity of oriental cultures into a single orient and the stylisation of this orient as magical and unreal. All this Omurca takes on board. Nor is this play on the exotic mitigated, as it is in Dikmen's work, either by reversal in the sense of a Turkish perception of an exotic occident or by any counter-thrust surreptitiously undermining the exotic image and hinting that may in fact be misplaced. On the contrary, the traditional German domestication of Turkish exoticness is co-opted entirely to the service of the minority voice. "Ich bediene mich der Motive", he explains; "Aber ich verpacke darin meine Meinung, meine Kritik, und liefere sie mit den bekannten Motiven ab." ("I use the motifs. But I pack it with my own opinion, my critique, and deliver these together with the familiar motifs.")[49] Though the reader suspects that Omurca means much of this ironically, this is less explicit than with Dikmen, and it would be difficult to argue that the aim here is to disarm exoticism by laughing at it. Rather, Omurca's strategy is to win the German reader's sympathy for the Turkish *Mitbürger*, and specifically sympathy for his position on such causes as the dual-citizenship debacle, and in this he is no doubt successful given the popularity of his work, but in the process he takes on board the possibility that the reader is left believing that this -- perhaps in a slightly less exaggerated form, but still, on the whole -- is what Turks really are like.

* * *

Django Asül -- the stage-name of Ugur Bagislayici -- is the youngest of the three comedians under discussion here, and the only one born in Germany

---

[49]   Muhsin Omurca, in a conversation with Graeme Dunphy, 9 April 2005.

(Lower Bavaria, 1972). He too specialises in cabaret, and his oral-performance satire can be more comfortably studied than Dikmen's and Omurca's, as his three main touring programmes have been released on CD: *Hämokratie* (the neologism is a fusion of "haemorrhoids" and "democracy") in 1997, *Autark* in 2001, and technically his most polished performance, *Hardliner* in 2004.[50]

In all of these, he appears alone on stage, without costume or props, and speaks in alternating personas and voices; Asül has a principal persona in which he acts as a linkman and commentator for his whole act, and the relationship of this persona to the artist might be likened to that of the narrator to the author in written forms. In this persona he speaks in his natural voice, a strongly Lower Bavarian accent, but in grammar and lexis more standard German than dialect. From here he moves into a very convincing dialect to give voice to the typical Bavarian, rather less-convincing stylized accents to represent Germans from outwith Bavaria, and a broken and heavily accented Turkish-German to represent a stereotyped guest-worker, generally styled as the artist's father. These staged voices are all parodies, and it should be noted that Asül's speech-patterns only betray his Turkishness when he deliberately pokes fun at it.

In its inter-cultural dynamic, Asül's satire operates quite differently from that of Dikmen and Omurca. This is at least partly to be explained by his biography -- he is more clearly rooted in Germany than they are. The choice of a stage name is already a mock-exotic cultural mix,[51] and this hybridity is encapsulated in the fact that, even in his narrator voice, "we" can mean either Bavarians or Turks. Thus a large part of his programme deals with German or international issues from a Bavarian perspective, with both Schröder's Social Democratic national government and Stoiber's Conservative state government being lampooned for perceived economic incompetence, while US president Bush's military adventures provide a leitmotif in absurd comparisons of all kinds. In short, "Ein Terrorkommando regiert die Welt -- ein Errorkommando regiert Deutschland!"[52] This is the standard fare of political cabaret, and the overwhelmingly Bavarian audience finds the comedian

[50] All appear on the Zampano label. He has also published a book containing transcripts from *Hämokratie* and other short texts: Django Asül, *Oh Abendland!* (Viechtach: Lichtung Verlag, 1997).
[51] "Django" is a male nick-name familiar in several Western European countries, which nevertheless has exotic or glamorous overtones; one thinks of the Belgian-born jazz guitarist Django Reinhardt (1910-1953) or the spaghetti western *Ein Fressen für Django* (Eduardo Mulargia, 1996); "Asül" looks and sounds Turkish, though in fact it is not a normal Turkish surname and presumably contains a deliberate echo of the German word *Asyl*, "political asylum".
[52] Asül, *Hardliner*, track 1.

speaking for them, giving voice to their own frustrations. There are no Turk-ish aspects in much of this, and even when Asül assumes the broken German of the "father", he is not necessarily pursuing minority interests. The fact that for much of his act, the rôle which he plays, and in which he is accepted by the audience, is in no sense the "other", greatly increases the complexity of the reception process. It means that when he does turn to Turkish themes, as he does in a little under half of all the tracks on the CDs, the German audi-ence are listening from a position of prior identification and are thus forced either to stay with the artist and experience an intimacy with Turkish perspec-tives or to draw back and experience a sharp discontinuity. Either way, the potential fluidity of ethnic identities comes home to the German listener in what may often be a surprising way.

This fluidity receives a clear expression in *Autark*, where the shades of *de facto* cultural integration are humorously contrasted with the relative mean-inglessness of paper distinctions:[53]

> Meine Mutter hat seit letztem Jahr übrigens einen deutschen Pass und schaut den gan-zen Tag türkisches Fernsehen. Das heißt, erstmals in ihrem Leben beschäftigt sie sich mit fremden Kulturen. Überhaupt bin ich derjenige in der Familie, der am schlechtes-ten Türkisch spricht, aber ich habe als letzter noch einen türkischen Pass. Ich bin bei mir daheim praktisch eine Randgruppe, und als einziger Ausländer in einem deutschen Haushalt, ... man hat es nicht leicht.

> (My mother got a German passport last year, by the way, and she sits all day long watching Turkish TV. That means that for the first time in her life she is taking an in-terest in foreign cultures. In fact, of all our family I am the one who speaks the least Turkish, but I am the last one who still has a Turkish passport. At home, I am practi-cally an ethnic minority, and when you're the only foreigner in a German household, life's tough.)

The humour here obviously rests on the inversion of expectations, and raises the inevitable question, what *is* a German, what *is* a foreigner? Asül's im-pressive ability to move easily between these categories is typical of many well-adjusted second-generation Germans of Turkish extraction. And here too, the listeners are drawn in, because much of the play on identities re-volves around the traditional inner-German rivalries: Bavaria versus North Germany, with side-sweeps at Hessen and Baden-Württemberg; Upper Bava-ria versus Lower Bavaria, with side-sweeps at the Bavarian Franks and the Upper Palatinate; and obviously the glance across the border to the great rivals of the south:[54]

---

[53] Asül, *Autark*, track 14.
[54] Ibid., track 3.

Ich komme aus Niederbayern und ich stelle mich [*sic*] schon so lange die außenpoliti-
sche Frage, wie soll es mit dem Österreicher weitergehen? Und vor allem warum?

(I come from Lower Bavaria, and for a long time now I've been struggling with the
foreign policy question, what future is there for the Austrians? And why should they
have one at all?)

Subsumed in this maze of ethnic fun-poking, which is an innocuous and
almost ritual part of German life, comes a similarly structured exploration of
the far more sensitive Turkish-German relationships, and the audience, who
have been won over by the familiar game, are inclined to accept the Turkish
dynamic on a similar basis. All the familiar clichés about both nations are
rehearsed, and generally the effect is to house-train the differences and render
them harmless. Thus the Turk becomes amiable.

On occasion this allows Asül to make a very poignant exposé of the overt
racism of the German right. There is a sequence in *Hämokratie* in which a
Turkish voice comments on the series of arson attacks on hostels for asylum-
seekers in the early 1990s. His take on this is to distinguish between asylum-
seekers and guest-worker, maintaining that only the former are the targets of
the violence -- and rightly so!

Wie man sagt auf Deutsch? Brenzlige Situation! Naja aber ich glaube, diese Männer
vorher auch schon schwarz. Naja, vielleicht besser ohne Asylheim. Weißt du, sonst
immer hat gegeben Missverständnis. Leute nichts haben gewusst, was ist Asylant, was
ist Gastarbeiter.[55]

([In broken German:] How do you say in German? Tricky [lit. burning] situation! But,
well, I think these men were black already. Perhaps we're better off without the hostel.
You know, before there were always misunderstandings. People didn't know who was
an asylum-seeker and who was a guest worker.)

He then proceeds to recount such a misunderstanding from his own experience. Three young men try to burn down his house. From his window he
shouts "He, Nichts Asylant", but they don't believe him. So they all go together to the local authority office, the *Einwohnermeldeamt*. Here, the
speaker's status as a guest-worker is confirmed. Now the three men realise
their mistake and to make amends they give him a voucher for a beer festival.
In Turkish culture, if you receive a gift you must give one, so the narrator
wonders what meaningful gift he can give to the three nice men. He comes
up with the idea of a list of names and addresses -- asylum seekers on the left,
guest workers on the right. "Warum ich soll nichts helfen für wegmachen
Missverständnisse?" ([In broken German:] "Why shouldn't I help to clear up

---

[55]   Asül, *Hämokratie*, track 20.

misunderstandings?") The point is, of course, that racism does not differentiate; in Mölln (1992) and Solingen (1993) it was Turkish women and children
who died in the fires.

Generally, the pillorying of outright racism is not as prominent in Asül's
comedy as it is in Dikmen and Omurca, and it is perhaps significant that it
becomes even less central in his later programmes than it was in *Hämokratie*.
Again, this may reflect his biography, with his origins in a fairly rural part of
Bavaria. Thus the skinhead does not appear here as a principal antagonist. It
is however a cabaretist's job to highlight the failings of politicians, and when
for example Angela Merkel, then leader of the CDU parliamentary party,
shows an ambivalence on immigration and integration questions, the Turkish
voice in *Hardliner* is heard to mock her:[56]

> Frau Merkel ist gegen Alles. Jetzt ist sie gegen Zuwanderung, weil sie sagt, nein, dann
> kommen Fremde. Dann will sie auch nicht Türkei in EU. Ist extra gefahren nach Tür-
> kei und hat gesagt, jo, bleib daheim. Da hat sie gesagt zu Türkei, kannst du haben pi-
> ri-li-vi-li-gierte Partnerschaft. Ja, das ist wie Homoehe. Sagst du mal zu Türke, willst
> du Homoehe? Na jetzt ist sie auch gegen Kopftuch. Frau Merkel sagt, mit Kopftuch
> muslimische Frau in Deutschland macht Parallelgesellschaft. Ja aber jetzt mit neue EU
> kommen Frauen aus Polen und Tschechien und jetzt hast du horizontale Gesellschaft.
> Ja Frau Merkel sagt, Kopftuch ist Sache von Fundamentalist. Im Winter meine Mutter
> auch trägt Kopftuch, und jetzt ist sie Halbjahresfundamentalist oder was? Ja wenn ich
> mal treffe Frau Merkel, dann sag ich, Angela, solange tu selber hast Gesicht wie Bern-
> hardiner mit Kreislaufschwäche, da musst du nicht tragen Kopftuch, musst du tragen
> Schleier. Schon damals Jesus hat gesagt, schau nicht auf Kopftuch von deine Nachbar,
> solange du selber … eh … hast Tür … auf deine … Tisch … oder so ähnlich …

> ([In broken German:] Frau Merkel is against everything. Now she's against immigra-
> tion, because she says, no, then foreigners would come. Then she doesn't want Turkey
> in the EU. She went specially to Turkey and said, oh, stay at home! She said to the
> Turks, they can have a pi-ri-li-vi-leged partnership. But that's like a gay marriage. You
> try asking a Turk if he wants a gay marriage! And now she is against the headscarf.
> Frau Merkel says, with the headscarf Muslim women are building a parallel society.
> But now with the new EU, women are coming from Poland and Czechia and now
> you're getting a horizontal society. Yes, Frau Merkel says, the headscarf is question of
> fundamentalism. In winter my mother wears a headscarf, so now she's a half-year fun-
> damentalist, or what? Yes, if I happen to meet Frau Merkel, I'll say to her, Angela, as
> long as you have a face like a Bernese dog with circulation problems, you don't need a
> headscarf, you need a veil. Jesus said, don't look at the headscarf of your neighbour as
> long as you yourself … eh … have a door .. on your … table … or something.)

The Turkish persona's lack of education and simplistic approach are evident
here at the latest with the inability to pronounce the word "priveleged", and
ultimately results in the collapse of the whole passage into confusion as he

---

[56] Asül, *Hardliner*, track 8.

tries to cite a half-remembered Bible verse. But even in this chaotic form, the verse is unmistakably Matt 7.3ff (removing the plank from one's own eye first) and its message against hypocrisy and intolerance rings out.

In a similar vein, in *Autark* he turns this barbed humour against the Bavarian interior minister Günther Beckstein, who had made a series of pronouncements on immigration which minorities understood as disparaging. Here, however, it is the Bavarian narrator-voice speaking, and therefore the approach is ironic sympathy rather than overt criticism:[57]

> Für Leute, die jetzt ethnisch nicht so bewandert sind, sei erklärt, der bayerische Innenminister Beckstein ist ja gar kein Bayer. Er ist ja Franke. Und die Franken, die haben alle einen Komplex, weil die sind ja in Bayern die Underdogs. Und was macht ein Underdog? Er sucht sich einen anderen Underdog! Und im Falle von Beckstein, ist es der Ausländer. Jetzt gibt es böse Menschen, die sagen, ja der Beckstein, das ist ein Ausländerfeind. Das ist natürlich Blödsinn. Nur weil einer keine Ausländer mag, ist er noch lange kein Ausländerfeind.

> (For those of you who are not so experienced in ethnic questions, I should explain that the Bavarian interior minister Beckstein is not in fact a Bavarian. He's a Frank. And the Franks all have a complex, because they are the underdogs in Bavaria. And what does an underdog do? He looks for another underdog! And in Beckstein's case, that's the foreigner. Now, there are some nasty people who say, Beckstein is a xenophobe. That of course is nonsense. Just because someone doesn't like foreigners doesn't make him a xenophobe.)

The implicit racism of Beckstein's remarks does not need to be exposed; it is enough that his supposed motivation is portrayed as ridiculous. However, despite such occasional forays into the race issues of German foreign and immigration policy, and the rather more frequent bemusement about the German ambivalence towards Turks, Asül never gives the impression of the kind of disillusionment to which Dikmen gave voice. It is his calling as a cabaretist to be critical, but on the whole he seems comfortable in and with Germany.

Consequently, the most frequent focus of Asül's satire is on economic and general social issues, and the intercultural take on these is mostly on the level of fun and nonsense. The problems of German reunification, for example, are discussed repeatedly, and in *Autark* the suggestion is made that the Federal Republic would have done better to unite with Turkey: "Dann kann Türke arbeiten in eigene Land und Deutscher kann Urlaub machen in eigene Land."[58] ([In broken German:] "Then the Turks could work in their own country, and the Germans could go on holiday in *their* own country.") The

---

[57]   Asül, *Autark*, track 3.
[58]   Asül, *Autark*, track 6.

German economic doldrums of the first half-decade of the new millennium have left wide-spread frustrations to which the cabaretist must give voice. Here too, Asül often does this with an inter-cultural aspect, typically connecting the theme to quite different topics, such as the following comment on proposals by Edmund Stoiber (Bavarian Minister President, CSU candidate for Federal Chancellor) relating to the "war on terror":[59]

> Wir kriegen ein Antiterrorgesetz, hat der Stoiber gesagt, wo drin steht, a Ausländer, der sich verdächtig macht, gleich ausse damit, verstehst? Und i sag, a Ausländer, der heut noch nach Deutschland kummt, der *ist* verdächtig.

> ([In light Bavarian:] We're getting an anti-terror law, says Stoiber, which says that a foreigner who makes himself suspicious, throw him out, understand? And I say, a foreigner who comes to Germany these days *is* suspicious.)

The implication: the current state of the German economy would not encourage honest migrants to come.

There is relatively little sense of the exotic in Asül's monologues. Neither the general characterisation of Turkey and the Turkish minority in Germany nor the presentation of Germany through the eyes of the Turkish persona are marked by wide-eyed amazement at the foreign. There is no Ali Baba, no idealising of the East in paradisiacal visions or picturesque scenes, nor anything of the inverted exotic occidentalism which we saw in Dikmen. Individuals, both Turks and Bavarians, are depicted for humorous effect as naïve, chaotic or simple, but these features are not attached to ethnic profiling, nor is the broken German of the first-generation migrants linked to these characteristics as it is in Omurca's cartoons: Asül's father persona is an incisive observer of political affairs.

Asül does of course work with clichés and stereotypes, which are almost unavoidable for a satirist. He does, for example, score points with his audience by blatant ethnic labelling: "Niederbayerische Intellektuelle ... ein Wiederspruch in sich"[60] ("Lower Bavarian intellectuals -- a contradiction in terms"). The Turkish stereotypes have moved on from Dikmen's generation: Asül's diaspora Turks are no longer grocers, they are travel agents: "Das ist das Perfide am Türk -- statt dass er froh ist, dass er hier sein darf, schickt er uns weg."[61] ("That's the perfidious thing about the Turk -- instead of being glad to be here, he sends us away!") Asül encapsulates this shift in the social rôle of the German Turk in the catch-phrase: "früher Türk, jetzt Unternehme-

---

[59]   Asül, *Hardliner*, track 12.
[60]   Asül, *Hämokratie*, track 7.
[61]   Asül, *Hardliner*, track 12.

ner" ("once Turks, now entrepreneurs"),[62] which might remind us of Omurca's *Ex-Türk*, but with a rather different gloss. However, such jibes lack the sense of wonder which might allow us to find anything exotic in them; they might even be taken to be mildly malicious were they not rendered harmless by being dosed out equally in all directions.

In some cases, clichés which traditionally belong to the exotic picture are debunked, such as the erotic-exotic of 19th-century orientalism. Asül assures us, persuasively enough, that if circumcision really did increase the virility of Turkish men, Germans would have been circumcised long ago. And as for the sensuality of the Eastern woman, it only takes the grotesque image of a father hiring a porn video and seeing his daughter in it to bring home to the audience that the tensions between sexual appetite and social restraint run along much the same lines in East and West: "Nicht jeder Türke, der kreativ ist, ist automatisch Pornodarsteller und nicht jeder Pornodarsteller kriegt automatisch auf der Berlinale einen Preis. Deshalb überlegen Sie es sich bitte sehr, sehr gut, falls Sie Türke werden wollen."[63] ("Not every creative Turk acts in porn films, and not every porn actor gets a prize at the Berlin film festival. So please think very, very carefully before you decide to become a Turk.")

Asül's social and political critique of both Turkey and Germany has a general demythologising thrust. In comparison to parallel discussions in Dikmen's texts, the element of cliché is very much reduced, as the immediate point of reference becomes actual current events, which fosters a sense of realism and sobriety despite the humour. When he picks up on actual cultural divergences, it tends to be those which have immediate political relevance -- the headscarf issue is a case in point -- and which are too concrete and controversial to be the stuff of folklore.

Above all, however, the exotic element is diminished because the foreign is brought closer, made to feel familiar, like a minor variant of the homely. Where Omurca's passport experiment failed through an inability to bridge the personal gap, Asül wanders effortlessly back and forth across this bridge and has no need even to attempt the irrelevance of integration on paper.

*   *   *

---

[62] Asül, *Hardliner*, track 12.
[63] Ibid., track 9. The reference is to the Turkish-German Sibel Kekilli, who starred in the film *Gegen die Wand* (English title *Head On*), which won a Golden Bear (best-movie award) at the *Berlinale* in February 2004; in the ensuing publicity she was berated by *Bild* for her earlier involvement in hardcore erotica.

Strategically constructing the "other" was always integral to the European imperial project, and it is therefore easy to dismiss any addiction to the lure of the exotic as complicity in prevailing power-structures, especially when the exoticised object is an ethnic minority which has experienced a history of disempowerment. It is no doubt in this vein that critics of German foreigner literature have seen the self-exoticising trend, when it can be discerned in the works of migrant authors themselves, almost as an unconscious betrayal. It is my contention that, in itself, the exotic is ethically ambivalent, in which case the western addiction to an exotic east, and indeed the instinct for exoticism which appears to reside in all cultures, is a potentially constructive force which migrant writers may legitimately harness. Whether in fact they choose to will ultimately depend on how they wish to locate themselves in relation to the "host" population. Hybrid communities are inevitably torn between a desire to highlight demarcation lines and a need to accentuate the potential for assimilation. Demarcation can be fostered by exoticising, fluidity of identity by rejecting the exotic. Humour, which in any case has a tendency either to underline or to debunk stereotypes, serves as a highly effective tool for working out this dichotomy.

The three satirists discussed in this essay have been seen to have quite different approaches to the exotic. Where Dikmen and Omurca internalise every cliché, Asül either discredits or simply ignores them. It will be no coincidence that this difference falls across the generation gap. The first generation, born in Turkey and painstakingly learning German in adulthood, is primarily aware of differences, and finding integration (let alone assimilation) illusive and possibly threatening, can take refuge behind the exotic, whereas the second generation can wander between its identities, benefiting from both of them, and does not want to place obstacles along the way. The variety of migrant experience is too vast to permit simple generalisations, but these patterns do appear relatively common; at any rate, in the debate about the use or rejection of the exotic in Schami and Şenocak, the same generation difference can be observed.

However, Dikmen and Omurca also differ considerably in their approach. Dikmen plays with the exotic for its own sake. His love affair, as he puts it, with Germany, itself begins with a fascination for the bewitchingly strange world of Europe, and his discovery that Europeans have a rather different yet in a sense parallel construction of the Middle East seems to have inspired him to take these divergent perspectives as obvious sources for his comedy.[64] The domestication of the exotic in simple images of the absolutely other, the idealised, the pure, the paradisiacal, the picturesque, the magical. When the

---

[64] Hasty and Merkes-Frei, p.67.

exotic clichés threaten to get out of hand, he is willing to rein them in a little, but in principle his playful handling of them is not disapproving. The ironic tone and above all the reversibility ensure that the reader will demythologise where appropriate, and in the process will learn to question the hypocrisies and presumptions of both cultures.

In Omurca's satire we see at its clearest how an exotic presentation of the ethnic minority widens the gap between the communities. The basic thesis of the strip, given the ultimate failure of Hüsnü's integration, would seem to be that without dual citizenship the cultural gulf between Turk and German may be insuperable; indeed, we are left with the strong impression that even with the double passport the gap will remain a significant one. Consequently, the accentuation of the alien is unmitigated. This corresponds also to the political message, which is more strident, more unrelenting and certainly more consistently structured than Dikmen's. With Omurca one senses far more strongly that the exotic is being manipulated in the service of a message.

Where Dikmen's and Omurca's exoticisms widen the cultural gap, perhaps in a manner indicative of their experience that it really is wide, Asül's defusing of the exotic narrows the gap, just as it is *de facto* narrow in his own hybrid interaction with diversity. Despite the irreverent humour and sheer sense of nonsense, there is a fundamental sense of realism in Asül's satire. He is clearly not interested in exoticising the orient, let alone simplifying the exotic picture for easy domestic consumption. Sometimes the exotic appears to irritate him, and here he demythologises consciously. For the most part it is simply not part of his picture. Asül offers us Turkey, and Turkish Germany, without the psychedelics -- cold Turkey, so to speak -- and thus reveals the hybridisation of his own identity which brooks no discontinuity. Germanness and Turkishness are no longer opposing poles: they are familiar, natural and unremarkable parts of the artist's world.

Bibliography

Aifan, Uta, 'Staging Exoticism and Demystifying the Exotic: German-Arab *Grenzgängerliteratur*', Trans. by Susan Tebbutt. in *German-Language Literature Today: International and Popular?*, ed. by Arthur Williams et. al. (Oxford: Lang, 2000)

Alles Getürkt, dir. by Yasemin Samdereli, 2002.

Alles Getürkt: Die Buchpiraten vom Bosporus, Zweites Deutsches Fernsehen, March 2004.

Asül, Django, *Autark* (Zampano, 2001)

Asül, Django, *Hämokratie* (Zampano, 1997)

——., *Hardliner* (Zampano, 2004)

——., *Oh Abendland!* (Viechtach: Lichtung Verlag, 1997)

Beil, Ulrich Johannes, 'Wider den Exotismus: Zafer Şenocaks west-östliche Moderne, in *Zafer Şenocak. Contemporary German Writers*, ed by. Tom Cheesman and Karin Yeşilada (Cardiff: University of Wales Press, 2003)

Dikmen, Şinasi, *Hurra ich lebe in Deutschland* (Munich: Piper, 1995)

——., *Wir werden das Knoblauchkind schon schaukeln* (Berlin: EXpress Edition, 1983)

——., *Der andere Türke* (Berlin: EXpress Edition, 1986)

Dunphy, Graeme, 'Zafer Şenocak', *Modern Language Review*, 99 (2004), 1112-1113.

Ein Fressen für Django, dir. by Eduardo Mulargia, 1996.

Engin, Osman, *Alles getürkt* (Hamburg: Rowohlt, 1992)

Hasty, Will, and Christa Merkes-Frei, *Werkheft Literatur: Şinasi Dikmen – Zehra Çirak* (Munich/Atlanta: Goethe Institut, 1996)

Hijiya-Kirschnereit, Irmela, *Das Ende der Exotik: Zur japanischen Kultur und Gesellschaft der Gegenwart* (Frankfurt a.M.: Suhrkamp, 1988)

Hildebrandt, Dieter, Foreword, in Şinasi Dikmen, *Hurra ich lebe in Deutschland* (Munich: Piper, 1995), pp.7-9.

Omurca, Muhsin, *Kanakmän: tags deutscher nachts türke* (Ulm: omu Verlag, 2002)

Ong, Walter J., *Orality and Literacy: The Technologizing of the Word* (London & New York: Methuen, 1984)

Pamuk, Kerim, *Sprich langsam, Türke* (Hamburg: Nautilus, 2002)

Said, Edward W., *Orientalism*, 1978 (New York: Vintage, 2003)

Santaolalla, Isabel, ed., *"New" Exoticisms: Changing Patterns in the Construction of Otherness* (Amsterdam: Rodopi, 2000)

Spohn, Margret, *Alles getürkt: 500 Jahre (Vor)Urteile der Deutschen über die Türken* (Oldenburg: Bibliotheks- und Informationssystem der Univ., 1993)

Terkessidis, Mark, 'Kabarett und Satire deutsch-türkischer Autoren', in *Interkulturelle Literatur in Deutschland: Ein Handbuch*, ed. by Carmine Chiellio (Stuttgart/Weimar: Metzler, 2000), pp.294-301.

Yeşilada, Karin, 'Schreiben mit spitzer Feder: Die Satiren der türkisch-deutschen Migrationsliteratur', in *Spagat mit Kopftuch*, ed. by Jürgen Reulecke (Hamburg: Körber-Stiftung, 1997), pp.529-564.

The Empire Tickles Back: Hybrid Humour (and Its Problems) in Contemporary Asian-British Comedy

Rainer Emig

The limits of hybrid humour can be seen in the appropriation of clichés and stereotypes in and as jokes. When the former butt of the joke becomes the joker, does he therefore cease to be the victim? This question is addressed in relation to successful forms of Asian-British humour in literature, film and radio and television shows. On the one hand, Asian-British comedies correspond closely to Homi Bhabha's model of a third space. They fulfil its criteria of hybridisation and exist in a tension between national and global cultures and in a constant state of interrogation, both by themselves and by their various cultural "outsides". At the same time, the suspicion remains that humour's conciliatory effects also take away much of the potential critical edge of this new space. Films like *My Beautiful Laundrette*, *Bhaji on the Beach*, *East is East*, and *Bend It Like Beckham* show an increasing trend towards "acceptable" and marketable ways of portraying alterity. Successful "ethnic" stories like *The Buddha of Suburbia* and *Anita and Me* use humour to defuse potential tensions. A detailed analysis of selected sketches from *Goodness Gracious Me* shows that subversion and containment are indeed possible within the same humorous format.

"'Have I made the first joke? Will everybody always be told how I made the first joke?' 'No, little friend', said the Lion. 'You have not *made* the first joke, you have only *been* the first joke.'"[1] This charming and seemingly harmless little episode, which concludes the creation of a magical world in a famous English children's book, the first story of C.S. Lewis's *Chronicles of Narnia*, has some relevance for the analysis that the present essay wishes to undertake. The difference between making a joke and being a joke is partly a question of skill, be it linguistic, social and cultural, or all of these. Yet it is also largely a question of one's status and therefore of power. As two scholars of television comedy put it: "funniness is not a property of utterances themselves, but a property of circumstance (social or individual), a property thus subject to negotiation and dispute".[2] In C.S. Lewis's children's tale, the benevolent creator-Lion reminds the forward little jackdaw of this rule when he admonishes it in the above quotation. Yet shortly before, he had encouraged the animals (whom he had just granted speech) to use humour: "Laugh

---

[1]   C.S. Lewis, 'The Magician's Nephew', *The Chronicals of Narnia* (1955; New York: HarperCollins, 2001), 7-106 (p.72).

[2]   Steve Neale and Frank Krutnik, *Popular Film and Television Comedy*, Popular Fiction Series (London and New York: Routledge, 1990), p.65.

and fear not, creatures. Now that you are no longer dumb and witless, you need not always be grave. For jokes as well as justice come in with speech."[3]

This rather philosophical statement on humour shows that it need not be condescending to apply an insight from a children's book to seemingly very different expressions of humour, contemporary Asian-British comedies.[4] On the one hand, Lewis's tale represents in large parts a colonial situation -- with many obvious missionary elements. At the same time it remains noticeably aware of what it is doing and postulating. Its idea of access to speech as a prerequisite to articulation both of jokes and justice also corresponds to various crucial concepts of postcolonial theory that we will encounter below. Furthermore it applies to general theories of power in society, those that emphasise that it rests on articulation. In the case of the media, this articulation requires forms, genres, but also valuable broadcasting time.

Lewis's stance on joking is in fact not very different from that proposed by the most influential twentieth-century theorist on humour, the Russian formalist Mikhail Bakhtin, whose idea of "justice" is a levelling of social hierarchies through humour in his ideal scenario of medieval carnival. There, he suspects "a temporary suspension, both ideal and real, of hierarchical rank [...] permitting no distance between those who came in contact with each other and liberating from norms of etiquette and decency imposed at other times."[5]

Bakhtin's rather utopian view of humour is countered -- in the context of postcolonial situations and texts -- by Gayatri Spivak's cautionary remarks concerning what she terms "subaltern" utterances, that is interventions by those who are relegated to an inferior position of rank and power, namely women and the colonised. Her seminal essay 'Can the Subaltern Speak?' doubts the possibility of creating statements, positions, and texts from a postcolonial position that truly enter into a dialogue with dominant positions.[6] Her point is that a position from which such an utterance can be made and from which it might be comprehensible requires a subscription to the hegemonic power of the coloniser. This power already manifests itself in the structures of the colonising language (English in our case), but also extends

---

[3]   Lewis, p.72.

[4]   This shift also forms the background of Marie Gillespie's essay 'From Comic Asians to Asian Comics: *Goodness Gracious Me*, British Television Comedy and Representations of Ethnicity', in *Group Identities on French and British Television*, ed. by Michael Scriven amd Emily Roberts (New York: Berghahn, 2003), pp.93-107.

[5]   Mikhail M. Bakhtin, *Rabelais and His World*, trans. by Hélène Iswolsky (Bloomington and Indianapolis: Indiana University Press, 1984), p.10.

[6]   Gayatri Chakravorty Spivak, 'Can the Subaltern Speak?', in *Colonial Discourse and Postcolonial Theory: A Reader*, ed. by Patrick Williams and Laura Chrisman (Brighton: Harvester Wheatsheaf, 1994), pp.66-111.

into a multitude of further ideological assumptions of what it means to consider oneself (or be considered) British.

The present essay will therefore ask critically of a range of Asian-British comedies whether they represent an approach to the Bakhtinian ideal of a levelling of hierarchies or even to Lewis's tall order of justice, or whether they rather represent instances of subaltern utterances in Spivak's terminology. In this context it will critically apply the ideas of Homi Bhabha, a prominent postcolonial theorist. He is of relevance moreover because his concept of hybridity and the "third space", which will be elaborated below, owe their formulation to the acknowledged influence of Bakhtinian theory. However, Bhabha's idea of hybridity, a productive, but also destabilising interrogation of positions of self and Other, has its origin rather in Bakhtin's ideas on the dialogicity of literary language than in his thoughts on carnival. Bakhtin developed these ideas in connection with the structures of the novel, which he regards as the dialogic, if not polylogic genre per se, since it almost inevitably incorporates competing perspectives and positions.[7] Whether television comedy can be unproblematically included in this structure requires further structural analysis that exceeds the scope of the present essay. However, it can be postulated that, on the one hand, dialogue and polylogue are indeed essential features of comedy as well, be it traditional theatrical or television comedy. However, the restricted genre conventions of television comedy -- with its usual thirty-minute format, limited number of often cliché characters, and frequent restriction to the white, urban middle classes -- also undercuts any true dialogue, polylogue, or destabilisation of the social, cultural and political status quo. This is all the more poignant in television comedy that makes minority status its theme -- as do the examples of Asian-British comedy explored below. What would undermine established structures of power and knowledge in Bakhtin's view would then indeed work towards their stabilisation -- most prominently in the form of representation that is clichéd and stereotyped.

Nonetheless, even the stereotype (literally a mechanical mould for the production of forever the same) might offer subversive potential, as postcolonial theory suggests. In *The Location of Culture*, Bhabha writes that "the colonial presence is always ambivalent, split between its appearance as original and authoritative and its articulation as repetition and difference".[8] He continues that "Hybridity is a problematic of colonial representation and

---

[7]   Mikhail M. Bakhtin, *The Dialogic Imagination: Four Essays*, trans. by Caryl Emerson and Michael Holquist, ed. by Michael Holquist (Austin: University of Texas Press, 1981).

[8]   Homi K. Bhabha, 'Signs Taken for Wonders: Questions of Ambivalence and Authority under a Tree outside Delhi, May 1817', in *The Location of Culture*, by Homi. K. Bhabha, new edn, Routledge Classics (London and New York: Routledge, 2004), 145-174 (p.153).

individuation that reverses the effects of the colonialist disavowal, so that other 'denied' knowledges enter upon the dominant discourse and estrange the basis of its authority -- its rules of recognition",[9] and concludes, "This partializing process of hybridity is best described as a metonymy of presence".[10] A "metonymy of presence" is a displacement that challenges common perceptions. Entering upon the dominant discourse and estranging the basis of its authority is, of course, also a good structural description of carnival with its joking temporal reversal of rules. Moreover, in an earlier section of his book, which is entitled "The Other Question" (a pun on "question of the Other"), Bhabha, aligns metonymy -- via the Freudian concept of the fetish -- with the structure of stereotypes, important elements of jokes and comedy:

> The stereotype, then, as the primary point of subjectification in colonial discourse, for both colonizer and colonized, is the scene of a similar fantasy and defence [as the fetish] -- the desire for an originality which is again threatened by the differences of race, colour and culture.[11]

According to Bhabha, the ambivalent and self-subverting strategies of repetition and abjection, which are combined in the metonymy and the fetish, create a different reality by their persistent displacements. He calls this the "third space".

> The intervention of the Third Space of enunciation, which makes the structure of meaning and reference an ambivalent process, destroys this mirror of representation in which cultural knowledge is customarily revealed as integrated, open, expanding code. Such an intervention quite properly challenges our sense of the historical identity of culture as homogenizing, unifying force, authenticated by the originary Past, kept alive in the national tradition of the People.[12]

The destruction of the habitual mirror of representation, i.e. essentialist beliefs that are no longer interrogated and a reliance on representation as mimetic and realistic, are, of course, further features of humour. In humorous utterances things are not what they seem. Meaning is inverted or doubled, and identities are challenged, distorted, or even abandoned. In a later essay in

[9]   Bhabha, 'Signs Taken for Wonders', p.162.
[10] Ibid., pp.163-164.
[11] Homi K. Bhabha, 'The Other Question: Stereotype, Discrimination and the Discourse of Colonialism', in *The Location of Culture*, by Homi. K. Bhabha, new edn, Routledge Classics (London and New York: Routledge, 2004), 94-120 (p.107).
[12] Homi K. Bhabha, 'The Commitment to Theory', in *The Location of Culture*, by Homi K. Bhabha, new edn, Routledge Classics (London and New York: Routledge, 2004), 28-56 (p.54).

the same volume Bhabha then explicitly connects this third space with cultural identities in a global environment (and with questions of capital and migration, at least the former of which is also essential to all contemporary media, the latter for the role and depictions of Asian-British people in them):

> The non-synchronous temporality of global and national cultures opens up a cultural space -- a third space -- where the negotiation of incommensurable differences creates a tension peculiar to borderline existences. [...] Hybrid hyphenisations emphasize the incommensurable elements -- the stubborn chunks -- as the basis of cultural identities.[13]

Asian-British comedies indeed correspond closely to Bhabha's model of a third space. They fulfil its criteria of hybridisation and exist in a tension between national and global cultures and in a constant state of interrogation, both by themselves and by their various cultural "outsides". At the same time, an application of Bhabha's concept to Asian-British comedies permits not only a linking of Bhabha's sources in Bakthin's concept of dialogicity with Bakhtin's related ideas on the carnivalesque. It also enables us to fill the somewhat vague metaphoricity of Bhabha's third space with an investigation that includes (unlike Bhabha's formulation, which is saturated with metaphors related to seeing, but leaves them in a mainly psychoanalytic paradigm) both an awareness of the mechanisms of reception that are essential for the confrontation of selfhood and Otherness and of the media that are required to bring about the exchange. The subsequent analysis will therefore ask: What is confronted with what and how? Who are the spectators and who are the objects of the spectacle? What is the role of the medium (here television) and its genre norms in the possible construction (or perhaps prevention) of a third space? But first a short survey of Asian-British comedy is required.

The rise of Asian-British comedy is one of the success stories of contemporary British film and television. Starting slowly with the film *My Beautiful Laundrette* in 1985, the trend gained momentum in the 1990s with the television film *Bhaji on the Beach* (1994), then the international cinema successes *East is East* (1999) and *Bend It Like Beckham* (2002), followed by a further film, *Anita and Me* (2002). On television, the runaway success of the Asian-British comedy show *Goodness Gracious Me* (BBC 1998 ff., first a radio show on BBC Radio 4 from 1996 to 1998, in 1999 even a successful theatre tour) startled even its producers and writers. Its follow-up, *The Kumars at*

---

[13]   Homi K. Bhabha, 'How Newness Enters the World: Postmodern Space, Postcolonial Times and the Trials of Cultural Translation', in *The Location of Culture*, by Homi K. Bhabha, new edn, Routledge Classics (London and New York: Routledge, 2004), 303-337 (pp.312-313).

No. 42 (also on BBC from 2001 onwards) tried out a different format, that of the celebrity interview, and proved less successful.

The phenomenon is, of course, clearly tied in with the increasing prominence of Britons of Asian descent in public functions and in the media themselves. Meera Syal, for example, is a well-known actress in film and television, a scriptwriter for, among other projects, *Bhaji on the Beach*, and an award-winning novelist (for *Anita and Me* -- which was later turned into a film -- and its follow-up, *Life Isn't All Ha Ha Hee Hee*). Syal was also involved in *Tandoori Nights* (Channel 4, 1985 and 1987), the only earlier attempt at an Asian-themed sitcom on British television before *Goodness Gracious Me*. Interestingly, it was held to have failed because apart from Asian characters it did not employ specific Asian plots and themes.[14] *Goodness Gracious Me*, on the other hand, uses these in abundance, but within a firmly established global television format, the sketch show, most successfully employed on British television before in *The Fast Show* (BBC, 1994 ff.). Apart from Syal, co-writers and -actors Sanjeev Bhaskar, Nina Wadia, and Kulvinder Ghir are now also established figures on British television and behind the scenes, as is the show's producer Anil Gupta.[15]

The economic success of many Asian-British entrepreneurs certainly represents a further important factor for the new awareness of an Asian presence in British culture outside the immediate impact zone of the mass media, as is the continuing vogue for Asian food (the replacement of fish and chips by chicken tikka massala as Britain's favourite national dish was noted even by British politicians), fashion, and music -- to the extent that Bollywood films are now a regular feature in British cinemas and on British television and that *Bombay Dreams* succeeded as a West End musical in 2002 (and later on New York's Broadway) -- with a script by Syal, music by Indian composer A.R. Rahman, and produced by Andrew Lloyd Webber.

Nonetheless, the story of the integration of Asians and their cultures in Britain is a many-sided one, with plenty of more sombre aspects. While British-Chinese people and many British-Indian people do well in today's Britain, the story is often different for migrants from Pakistan and Bangladesh, who often feel discriminated against because of their Muslim background. One of the remarkable contrasts of contemporary British culture is indeed the above-mentioned vogue for many things Asian and the simultaneous riots between white locals and Pakistani youths in Northern English towns such as Oldham, Burnley, and Bradford in the Spring and Summer of 2001.[16] Most

---

[14] http://www.screenonline.org.uk/tv/id/529222/.

[15] http://www.bbc.co.uk/comedy/goodnessgraciousme/.

[16] A summary of news items on these riots can be found at http://news.bbc.co.uk/1/hi/in_depth/uk/2001/summer_of_violence/default.stm.

recently, the bomb attacks on London transport in July 2005, despite their background in global terrorism, reminded the British public and the world that all is not well as far as multicultural Britain is concerned. This seeming paradox shows that an investigation into the acceptance of Asian-British culture in the arguably most potent medium of hegemonic cultural power today, television, is by no means an academic pastime, but a serious social concern.

An awareness of the seriousness of the issues can still be discerned in the early films that introduced Asian-British concerns to a British and international audience. *My Beautiful Laundrette* and *Bhaji on the Beach*, although also featuring funny incidents and characters, still have an air of didacticism. This is partly due to their clear orientation towards a white audience that is to be carefully introduced to the mysterious closed world of Asians in Britain. In *My Beautiful Laundrette*, based on a script by the now famous writer Hanif Kureishi, this is achieved by a double focus of the plot on the white punk Johnny and his Asian lover Omar. Problems of disaffected youths, Thatcherism, unemployment, education, and right-wing sympathies within the British skinhead youth culture are as much its concerns as are the family ties and sexual morality among Asian Brits.

Bhaji on the Beach is different, since it is exclusively set in an Asian scenario, and there among women. Their diverse problems, from abusive relationships via marital breakdowns to unwanted pregnancies, are exposed in a way that makes the film look like a cross between an awareness-raising fictional documentary and a tragicomedy. It also hardly features any white British characters. Even the pregnant Asian girl's lover is not white, but Black British, thus avoiding any overt confrontation of majority and minority ideologies. It is not coincidental that *Bhaji on the Beach* was produced and screened by Channel 4 -- for a late-night television audience of enlightened viewers.

This changed with *East is East* and *Bend It Like Beckham*, films that clearly had a mass-cinema audience in view, and succeeded in winning them over, not only in Britain, but throughout Europe. The price to be paid, if one wishes to see it like that, was a depiction of Asian-Britain as essentially quirky. The problems of authority and identity that were raised in both films were framed by a frantic tempo and a groovy 1970s setting in *East is East* and the double exoticism of an Asian girl in a female football team in *Bend It Like Beckham*. Nonetheless, both films also addressed serious issues. *East is East* featured a mixed British-Pakistani couple in a working-class neighbourhood and the multiple problems of adaptation that the family members faced. These by no means only included the adaptation of the migrant perception of life to British standards, but also that of the British mother to Pakistani norms (such as female obedience, circumcision, etc.). It featured rebellion of the family's children both in serious form (the exclusion of a homosexual son from the family after his refusal to marry) and humorous shapes (the clandestine visits by the two remaining sons to white British night clubs and the art college attendance by one of them that is secretly supported by the mother until she realises that, what he understands as art, she considers pornography).

Bend It Like Beckham also negotiated more pressing and general concerns than women's football when it addressed the protagonist's (eventually granted) desire to leave Britain to study in the United States -- on her own, without family supervision and without an engagement to a homosexual cousin that would have covered up for both.

One could argue that the safety of temporal and cultural exoticism within established British culture worked like a double negation on the potentially more threatening ethnic exoticism depicted in the films. (This had already been the case in *My Beautiful Laundrette*, where the tricky issue of Asian culture trying to co-exist with white British middle-class norms was diffused by the equally contentious issue of homosexuality -- and vice versa). The evident humour and comedy of these recent cinematic success stories also facilitated their reception as entertainment rather than problem films. Here we find a first indication that humour and comedy need not always function in a subversive way, but can assist the integration of difference and the problematic homogenisation of culture clashes.

This admittedly sketchy survey will now be complemented by a closer look at the Asian British comedy show that won over mass television audiences in Britain, *Goodness Gracious Me*. Its success even provoked media debates on how it was possible that minorities on television had such a wide appeal and whether this was a good or rather a problematic thing (a similar discussion was generated by the success of the gay comedy *Queer as Folk* on Channel 4 in 1999). As mentioned above, the format of *Goodness Gracious Me* is that of a sketch show. It has recurring scenarios and characters, but also unique sketches. There are musical numbers and scenes enacted before a live studio audience as well as pieces filmed on location or in the studio, such as spoofs of music videos. The multi-genre format of *Goodness Gracious Me* permits an analysis of various types of approaches to the typical postcolonial problem of mimicry. Bhabha defines it as follows:

> Mimicry is, [*sic*] thus the sign of a double articulation; a complex strategy of reform, regulation and discipline, which "appropriates" the Other as it visualizes power. Mimicry is also the sign of the inappropriate, however, a difference or recalcitrance which

coheres the dominant strategic function of colonial power, intensifies surveillance, and poses an immanent threat to both "normalized" knowledges and disciplinary powers.[17]

What Bhabha calls a "double articulation" refers exactly to the disruption within the mimetic norm that humour achieves by taking what is known and expected and then subverting and reversing it. In terms of genres and the media it also applies to the hijacking of established genres, such as tragicomedy, or scenarios, such as the "boy meets girl" scenario, the "embarrassing lecture by one's parents" scenario, etc., in unusual ways that *Goodness Gracious Me* thrives on. On the other hand, mimicry highlights the fact that Otherness is anxiously watched in every culture (this is what Bhabha terms "surveillance"), while it simultaneously turns the tables and shows that those who are watched are aware of the fact -- and stare back! Several typical sketches will enable us to interrogate the mechanisms, effects, and consequences of mimicry and reversals as forms of humour employed in them critically.

In the first sketch of the first series of *Goodness Gracious Me*, a clearly British manager is introduced to his Indian colleagues in what turns out to be a company boardroom in India. Yet there is an unexpected problem. The pronunciation of his first name, "Jonathan", causes his team mates considerable difficulties: "I don't know, you English with your complicated names". After many unsuccessful attempts to negotiate the stress on the first syllable and the "th", they offer him Indian alternatives. At first he rejects these out of hand, but after being called a troublemaker and threatened with negative consequences ("You're not in jolly England any more, sipping tea and doing the Morrison dancing"; "I don't see you progressing very far in this company with a name like that"), he suddenly offers them a highly complex polysyllabic parody of an Indian name, which they gladly accept.

The structure of the sketch is simple. It reverses normal expectations, British expectations that is, by portraying English names as difficult and Indian ones as simple. It is a British expectation, since to non-English speakers "Jonathan" (in its English pronunciation) is indeed far from easy to pronounce. What gives the sketch an additional sombre undertone is that it is ultimately power that decides who agrees to adapt. And, in another reversal, here it is the Indians who hold power over the British person by being his employers. The adaptation happens, for once, by the former coloniser.

Structurally, the sketch displays mimicry and a double articulation. Yet it is doubtful if it opens up a third space inside which a new or hybrid cultural

---

[17] Homi K. Bhabha, 'Of Mimicry and Men: The Ambivalence of Colonial Discourse', in *The Location of Culture*, by Homi K. Bhabha, new edn, Routledge Classics (London and New York: Routledge, 2004), 121-131 (pp.122-123).

form emerges. It rather cements established stereotypes, and, by reversing them, exposes them.

A similar, but more complex reversal takes place in the sketch called "The traditional Bombay Friday Night Out". In a parody of a typical British Friday night and its ritual of getting blind drunk in a pub and then frequenting a curry house, it shows a group of young Indians "getting tanked up on lassis and going for an 'English'".[18] The group then play the typical competitive games played by young Brits in curry houses, i.e. ordering the hottest dish on the menu and harassing the waiters -- only in reverse. Yet the reversal produces a little more than the mere exposure of traditional clichés and power structures, as undertaken in the "Jonathan" sketch. For a start, the binaries are not as firmly in place. There is no such thing as "an English", since British national cuisine lacks the monolithic presence that curries have achieved. Fish and chips would no longer work, since they are neither standard fare nor eaten in restaurants. Roast beef and vegetables would not have the association of a Friday night out, but that of a Sunday lunch.

Another reversal that produces interesting effects is the Indian women in the group harassing the white British waiter, James. They flirtatiously call him by his first name "James", but mispronounce it, then praise his pasty skin, and make insinuations about the size of his penis, since they have heard rumours about certain racial stereotypes in this respect. James's initial embarrassment quickly changes into annoyance. Yet for the audience the scenario is as funny as it is surreal. They are faced with a reversal of binaries, yet the poles that are now exposed in the sketch are blanks for them: there are no particular associations of pale skin and eroticism in contemporary British culture nor of English men with large (or small) penises. There is none of Asians either -- other than the general attribution of a high sex drive to colonised males by the colonisers in general. Thus the opposite of the reversal is also not true.

Here, Bhabha's concept seems to function, at least in an elementary way. What the humorous mimicry of a British Friday night out produces is a double vision, though not of a reversed normality, but rather of something that did not exist before and has not yet been categorised. Bhabha indeed attributes this (perhaps problematically) to all stereotypes: "The stereotype is in that sense an 'impossible' object".[19]

A third example of comic reversals features the Kapoor family, who are so hyper-adapted that they insist on pronouncing their name "Cooper". Father Kapoor generally wears a tweed jacket and a golfing cap. In the sketch "Din-

---

[18]   The title of the sketch as well as the line featuring lassis, non-alcoholic yoghurt drinks, is taken from the cover of the video cassette of series 1 (BBC Worldwide Ltd. 1998).

[19]   Bhabha, 'The Other Question', p.116.

ner with the Coopers" they are treated by their equally adapted friends the Rabindranaths (pronounced "Robinsons") not to a curry dish, but to "roast lamb, roast potatoes, roast vegetables, and roast gravy". Exaggeration and excess are the benchmarks of their adaptation to their British environment. (It goes as far as applauding the message tied to a brick thrown through the window: "Pakis go home!") Yet it is an adaptation that fails because it chooses as is object not a realist idea of Britain, but a cliché. Even the expressions they employ have a quaint and dated air -- exactly like "Goodness Gracious Me", the show's title. This stems from a 1960s film in which Peter Sellers plays a crudely clichéd Indian. The show is therefore a re-appropriation of a racist white and Western cliché -- in a white and Western media format, a good example of the Empire tickling back![20]

During a very British barbecue in another sketch, the hyper-adapted Kapoors/Coopers again get things completely wrong, since they don't even manage to light the grill. The party is thrown in honour of their son Subash (whom they call "Sebastian"), who is about to arrive back from India, where he has travelled in search of his roots. This is something that neither the Kapoors nor their friends the Rabindranaths can understand. And indeed, Subash was born and raised in British suburbia and received his education in an expensive British public school. Subash could, in fact, easily be the equivalent of the protagonist of Hanif Kureishi's hugely successful first novel *The Buddha of Suburbia*. It opens with the narrator's self-characterisation "My name is Karim Amir, and I am an Englishman born and bred, almost."[21] After this joking revision of a well-known English idiom, he continues: "I am often considered a funny kind of Englishman, a new breed as it were, having emerged from two old histories" (p.3). The ambivalent meaning of "funny" as both "strange" and "ludicrous" is exactly what is in the focus of the present essay. The idea of "a new breed" corresponds to the most simplistic conception of cultural hybridity.

The obvious comedy of the Kapoors' and Rabindranaths' grotesque hyper-adaptation is evident. But Subash's is equally noticeable, though more subtle. Despite his "ethnic" shirt, the young man in search of his Indian roots is marked as even more British than his would-be British parents and their friends by his cut-glass RP accent. Who mimics whom in this sketch is ultimately the question. Certainly the Kapoors and Rabindranaths mimic the concept of traditional upper-class imperial Britain in their outdated idea of a

---

[20] My title is in itself of course a pun on a prominent postcolonial textbook, Bill Ashcroft, Gareth Griffiths, and Helen Tiffin, *The Empire Writes Back: Theory and Practice in Post-Colonial Literatures*, New Accents (London and New York: Routledge, 1989).

[21] Hanif Kureishi, *The Buddha of Suburbia* (1990; London: Faber & Faber, 1999), p.3. Further references are given parenthetically in the text.

clichéd Englishness. But the Kapoors' son also mimics supposed enlightened attitudes in his clichéd vision of a search for his roots -- which merely turns him into the equivalent of the thousands of Westerners who travel to India in search of Enlightenment or themselves every year. Neither of the two positions thus mocked is in fact a postcolonial one. Ella Shohat and Robert Stam summarise the crucial features of postcolonial positions as follows:

> Postcolonial theory, in so far as it addresses complex, multilayered identities, has proliferated in terms having to do with cultural mixing: religious (syncretism); biological (hybridity); human-genetic (*mestizaje*); and linguistic (creolization). [...]
>
> The impulses behind the celebration of hybridity are themselves mixed. On one level, the celebration counters the colonialist fetishization of racial "purity". [...] But while reacting against the colonialist mania for purity, contemporary hybridity theory also counterposes itself to the overly rigid lines of identity drawn by Third Worldist discourse.[22]

In their terms, the Kapoors and Rabindranaths represent the traditional colonialist perspective in their absurd claim to be purely British. Subash is a "Third Worldist" by claiming equally erroneously "We're Indian".

In terms of mimicry, something more complex happens here than in the previous examples: what is doubled is already a cliché, something that no British viewer would seriously accept as British reality today. The distorted mirror that Bhabha uses as an illustration of his concept of hybridity here reflects an absence -- or rather a simulation, a copy without original in Baudrillard's terms.[23] The effect, however, is strong, perhaps stronger than in the simple reversal scenarios, since positions of "us" and "them", identification and its denial, become harder to establish. (The same is true for a musical sketch dealing with the marital problems of an Indian couple, who have married for love -- which is enacted in a badly simulated American farmyard scenario to American-style country music complete with a dungaree-clad banjo player and with fake American accents!) *Goodness Gracious Me* does not merely employ stereotypes as "impossible objects" in Bhabha's terminology. It exposes them as such.

This disturbing effect is further strengthened by another difference between the Kapoor/Rabindranath sketch and the previous ones: now the laughter is at the expense of the Indians. This was one of the most quickly noted

---

[22] Ella Shohat and Robert Stam, *Unthinking Eurocentrism: Multiculturalism and the Media*, Sightlines (London and New York: Routledge, 1994), p.41.

[23] "Simulation is no longer that of a territory, a referential being or a substance. It is the generation by models of a real without origin or reality: a hyperreal." Jean Baudrillard, 'Simulacra and Simulations', in *Selected Writings*, trans. and ed. by Mark Poster (Stanford: Stanford University Press, 1988), p.166.

and hotly debated aspects of *Goodness Gracious Me* in the British press and media: Is it acceptable to laugh about ethnic minorities on prime-time television? Does the fact that the scriptwriters are Asian make this acceptable? The conservative *Daily Telegraph* clearly thought so when it wrote in an article on Asian-British pop music entitled 'Coming up from the Underground' on 9 January 1999: "British-Asian comedians have come a long way since the dreadful stereotyping of Seventies sitcoms such as *Mind Your Language*." It did not see, however, that *Goodness Gracious Me* works with stereotypes, too, and not necessarily better or more subtle ones. But will the viewers now laugh for the right reasons (whatever these may be)?

On 7 May 2002, the BBC published an article on its website with the title 'Why Do People Find Racist Jokes Funny?' A write-in yielded, among others, the following response from "Matt, UK" (here reproduced in its original spelling and punctuation): "What about the TV program *Goodness Gracious Me*. That makes fun of white people shouldn't we be talking about that or is this another one sided argument?"[24] The question of making or being a joke was clearly the issue. But the reverse positions can easily be exposed as equally problematic: Why should one not be allowed to laugh about ethnic minorities? Why should ethnicity (and minority status) condemn people to a puritan sobriety (an attitude that still pervades early postcolonial theory of the kind of *The Empire Writes Back*)?

Goodness Gracious Me indeed thrives on scenarios in which jokes are made about prototypical clichéd Asian attitudes. These encompass an "Arranged Shag" sketch, in which concerned parents try to force a modernised version of an arranged marriage on their unwilling son. When he refuses, his mother tearfully collapses and exclaims "You have no respect for the traditional ways!" There is also a detailed spoof of a property commercial called "Bharat Homes" (modelled on the British property developer Barratt). In it an Asian salesgirl praises the Asian-friendly features of a typical modern house: its plastic-covered settees, tupperware in the fridge, concreted backyard, and -- most memorable of all -- the already supplied set of very old suitcases on top of the wardrobe. Clichés of migrant existence and adaptation to a British environment are thus ironically thrown back into the face of Asian viewers. For British viewers, these are highlighted or perhaps made obvious for the first time.

Meera Syal, who also stars in the "Bharat Homes" sketch, in fact started her debut novel *Anita and Me* with a structurally very similar assortment of migration clichés, including the protagonist's parents' arrival "in their dusty Indian village garb" at Heathrow, the "romantic" detail of her father working

---

[24]   http://news.bbc.co.uk/2/hi/uk_news/1972565.stm.

in a sweatshop and her parents sharing a "shabby boarding house room with another immigrant family, Polish, I think",[25] before uncovering the whole story as "the alternative history I trot out in job interview situations or, once or twice, to impress middle-class white boys" (p.9). After this self-effacing lie, the narrator then pretends to tell the truth -- and tells it in such a way that already hints at the importance of humour and of television as the currently most hegemonic mass medium in both adaptation, assimilation, and a critique of these processes:

> My earliest memory, in fact, is of the first time I understood the punchline of a joke. I was watching some kind of Royal Variety television show on ice -- I remember that because it was a balmy summer evening and I wondered how they had managed to keep the floor so cold. A man in a lime green jumpsuit raised a gun and took aim at a fat female ballerina who was gliding towards him like some vast, magnificent galleon, pink tulle emanating in a cloud from around her strong marbled thighs like ectoplasm. The man raised the gun, fired once, twice, and the ballerina fell dramatically to the floor to hilarity and applause.
> "Oh my dearie," said the man. "I think I shot her in the tutu."
> My mother said I laughed so much that I threw up and at one point, called in Mrs Worrall from next door who put her teeth in and solemnly declared that I'd probably "had a turn." But I've always been a sucker for a good double entendre; the gap between what is said and what is thought, what is stated and what is implied, is a place in which I have always found myself. I'm really not a liar, I just learned very early on that those of us deprived of history sometimes need to turn to mythology to feel complete, to belong. (p.10)

The detailed statement is intriguing since it assumes identical positions to those held by Kureishi's protagonist and by Bhabha. The space opened up by a double entendre (an obscene reference to a woman's genitals in this case), a word play or joke, is seen as an alternative space for a self in need of definition.[26] Yet, perhaps paradoxically, it also enables this self "to feel complete, to belong."

Goodness Gracious Me goes as far as making supposed critical postcolonial attitutes the butt of its jokes. In a sketch called "Malkit", a young man whose accent identifies him as Asian, is rudely awakened by a phone-call from his equally Asian employer, who admonishes him for being late for work three times in one week and threatens with consequences. Instead of

---

[25] Meera Syal, *Anita and Me* (1996; London: Flamingo, 1997), p.9. Further references are given parenthetically in the text.

[26] Berthold Schoene-Harwood does Syal's novel an injustice, therefore, when he one-sidedly insists that "In *Anita and Me* hybridity is experienced as an onerous ordeal"; 'Beyond (T)race: *Bildung* and Proprioception in Meera Syal's *Anita and Me*', *Journal of Commonwealth Literature*, 34 (1999), 159-168 (p.161).

apologising, though, the young man, Malkit, starts an extended rant on the racist attitudes that make his employer persecute him:

> Malkit: Oh, I get it. I hear what you're saying. This isn't about work, is it. This is about the colour of my skin. You're picking on me because I'm Asian, you racist bastard! I bet you haven't been calling all your white employees and shouting racist abuse at them, have you?
> Boss: Have you slept in again, Malkit?
> Malkit: No, I've not slept in. I've been up for the last four hours actually [yawns], worrying about my oppressed brothers and sisters. And if it wasn't for people like you, I wouldn't have to do that.
> Boss: This is the third time this week, Malkit. I can't let you keep doing this.
> Malkit: Now what you're gonna do? Sack me? You'd love that, wouldn't you. You'd love to throw me onto the scrap heap, another disillusioned ethnic youth, no job, no hope, marginalised by white society and forced to live in urban squalor.
> Boss: But you live in Hampstead!
> Malkit: Oh, that's not the point. I am Asian youth, torn apart by identity crises, harrassed by the pigs, misunderstood by the older generation. Maybe I need to cry for help. Maybe I need to run in the streets of Hampstead with my Asian brothers, rioting, looting and pillaging. Is that what you want, is it, ey?
> Boss: Alright, alright, alright. I'm sorry. Just take the day off.
> Malkit: Yeah, ok, thanks. [pause] Ah, and Dad, can I borrow the car?
> Boss: Yes, yes, yes. Whatever you want.[27]

The structure of the scene's final gag is simple: it consists of an unexpected role reversal. The supposed racist boss turns out to be Malkit's father. But in fact the reversal is multiple, and it starts earlier. When boss turns into Dad, Malkit turns from rebellious youngster into the cliché of the spoiled Asian son. Yet he has already consciously turned himself and his opposite into clichés before, crude clichés of oppressed ethnic minority and oppressive capitalist. The slogans are indeed well-known. But, similar to the reversed curry house sketch, the reversal only works in parts. The boss is from the start also identified as Asian by his accent. The charge of racism is therefore at least odd, if not paradoxical. It could only work through a complex transfer of oppression from race to capital, a complexity that can hardly be achieved during the brief duration of the sketch. Another interior gag is the absurd linking of affluent Hampstead with urban squalor. Yet the idea of riots, looting, and pillaging in Hampstead (as the epitome of upper-middle-class white English respectability) is not so grotesque, at least as a nightmare scenario (one that became reality, though not in Hampstead, a short while later). In a sketch like "Malkit" *Goodness Gracious Me* shows that it knows the standard mantra of well-intentioned, but simplistic multiculturalism. It knowingly

---

[27] The transcript is based on the BBC radio version. Hampstead is a wealthy area of London. "Pigs" is a slang expression for police.

plays with it and easily reverses it because it is based as much on simple binaries as racism itself. Only now Asians are the good guys and white English society (here represented by the police) are the bad guys.

What is remarkable in *Goodness Gracious Me* is that it hardly shows any instances of traditional racism, and if it does, they are subtle forms that usually consist of attempted overcompensation, as in the series of sketches featuring a sham Indian guru called Charlatan His Serene Calmness the Guru Maharishi Yogi, who distributes dubious improvised pseudo-Buddhist snippets of wisdom to a group of white British disciples. Reversal scenarios, such as "The Rough Guide to the United Kingdom", a spoof television travel programme in which a group of Indian youngsters inform their Indian audience of the perils of travelling in such a backward and underdeveloped country as Britain, where "the pace of life is much slower", or the mimicking of Asian clichés are more common. Yet does this make the show postcolonial? Is colonialisation still an issue -- other than in instances of vague memories (like those of the annoying father who, in a series of sketches, tries to convince his son that everything originates in India)? Do mimicry and a conscious use of stereotypes make it hybrid and an example of the creation of third spaces? Or do they not rather categorise the radio and television programme as an example of completed adaptation and assimilation?

One can ask this question about a sketch of a mixed-sex group of young Asian executives in typical Western business clothes discussing the marriage of one of their friends to a non-Asian wife -- and its "cultural implications". When he presents his British wife Sarah to them, she appears in a Salwar Kameez, a traditional Indian and Pakistani dress, talks with a thick Asian accent (while the group's English is standard with a hint of South London). She greets them with "Namaste" and calls them "my people", insists on sitting on the floor and drinking tap water (not "the alcohol"), and complains about British people staring at her. She even dishes up a tale of her marriage having been arranged by her parents -- to which her husband hurriedly replies: "Met her in a night club in Putney". When he tries to drag her away when the situation becomes too embarrassing, she randomly starts shouting names of Indian dishes, such as Sag Aloo. Who is mimicking whom here -- and for what purpose?

Assimilation is certainly the case with respect to the media format and the genre forms that are employed in *Goodness Gracious Me*. The show follows a format that is not even typical of British television, but ultimately a US-American format popularised by shows such as *Saturday Night Live* and now common all over the world, globalised that is. But which "Asian" media formats would have been the alternative? Which are genuinely "Asian", and why should they be? There are references to Bollywood films in the show, both directly in musical sketches and in those featuring Smita Smitten, the would-be film critic who always manages to miss Bollywood stars or film launches and parties. Perhaps the utilisation of Western or global formats for Asian themes is a much more postcolonial act than the problematic reproduction of (non-existent) authentic media formats in a British media environment. This would also have exempted the show from the controversy it initially caused, since it would have relegated it to a minority niche. It would certainly have prevented it from getting a prime-time slot and from achieving the success it eventually gained.

Goodness Gracious Me also carefully refrains from touching on any controversial subjects connected with Asian-British culture. Physical abuse of married women, perhaps the best publicised controversial issue after the murder of her abusive husband by Tsoora Shah, does not necessarily offer itself to humorous treatment. It is noteworthy that *Goodness Gracious Me* devotes many sketches to relationship problems, but generally represents them as either a case of arranged marriage gone wrong or turned surreal or within the paradigms of Western (and indeed often Hollywood) clichés. Thus a spoof of the famous scene in the Hollywood film *Ghost* (1990), in which Demi Moore as a day-dreaming widow has an erotic encounter with the ghost of her late husband (played by Patrick Swayze) while moulding pots, shows an Indian wife seemingly doing the same -- until it becomes clear that she has been kneading dough for an Indian dinner all the time, and that her husband's libidinous interest has been firmly focused on his stomach.

Religion is another hot subject that is largely sidestepped in *Goodness Gracious Me*. When it is not depicted as sham and obsolete -- as in the above-mentioned guru sketch (or a similar one that has a Muslim door-to-door salesman, identified as such by his beard and skull cap, trading in lectures on Hindu gods) -- it is shown as grotesque and ineffectual, as in a sketch entitled "Buddhist Pest Controller". It features Meera Syal as a modern British-Asian housewife whose kitchen is infested by mice. For reasons of solidarity (mistaken, as it turns out), she has opted for an Asian pest-control company. Yet when she opens her door to its representative, he turns out to be an orange-clad Buddhist monk who promises first to convince the mice of their bad behaviour. When this fails to appease his customer, he suggests that he will instead encourage them to behave even more badly, so that they will be reborn as stones in their next life. Stones are, after all, easier to catch and remove than living mice.

What makes the sketch funny is not merely the outlandish suggestions of the pest controller, but the contrast between his insistence on non-violent means and the increasing demands for violence and savagery made by Syal. Gender expectations are thus reversed more than religious ones. In fact, Buddhism is hardly attacked in the sketch, although some of its ideas are shown as rather unworldly. Moreover, Buddhism is neither a very prominent religion among British Asians, nor is it one that attracts controversy. A similar sketch featuring a Buddhist doctor who has invented a method of killing cancer cells functions along the same lines.

It is therefore interesting when one sketch makes explicit the demands of the religion that has attracted most attention and controversy in Britain (and elsewhere) in recent years: Islam. In a conversion sketch, traditionally-clad Pakistani parents anxiously await the return of their son from work. When he arrives, however, he is neither a traditional-looking Pakistani nor an assimilated Asian-British young man wearing jeans or suit and tie. Instead, Kulvinder Ghir looks like a caricature of Woody Allen, the Jewish-American actor and comedian. He wears the prototypical intellectual's outfit of old and creasy black trousers and a black poloneck and in addition sports a shaggy red wig and glasses. When he opens his mouth, he even talks with a New York accent.

What he has to tell his parents is equally surprising: he has decided to convert -- to Judaism! This causes outrage among his parents, which he tries to quell by rationally outlining to them the similarities of Jewish and Muslim belief -- which he reduces to circumcision and the rejection of pork. Needless to say, his attempts to persuade his parents to accept his decision are unsuccessful, and after much histrionic wailing his mother even threatens suicide by putting her head in the oven. Since it is an electric one, and not gas, the new convert to Judaism is irritated rather than truly concerned. Again, the sketch works not so much by creating a "third space", a new ideological location of an utterance, but by highlighting and partly reversing existing stereotypes and clichés.

What is interesting is that, while the Muslim clichés of strict parents and self-sacrificing mothers are used without inhibitions, the Jewish cliché appears to be a trickier issue. After all, anti-Seminism can get one into serious trouble in the media, anti-Islamism hardly. Asians laughing about themselves is also more acceptable than Asians laughing about other minorities -- rather than their white British counterparts. This, I believe, is the explanation why the (positive) U.S.-American cliché of Woody Allen as the neurotic Jewish New York intellectual is employed in this sketch -- despite the multiple cultural contradictions that this strategy creates. Yet which cliché of British Jewishness would have been available -- and acceptable?

What is ironic (and certainly remained unnoticed by the creators of this sketch) is that the red-haired slightly stooping Jew is in fact among the oldest anti-Semitic clichés in British culture. Already Renaissance actors impersonating Jews (as in Shakespeare's *The Merchant of Venice* or Marlowe's *The*

Jew of Malta) employed red wigs and false noses for their part. Yet *Goodness Gracious Me* clearly aims away from traditional anti-Semitic stereotypes by opting for an adaptation to a U.S.-American, if not indeed global icon of acceptable Jewishness. This hints at the fact that the supposed British focus of its hybrid humour is conveniently transgressed as soon as it starts creating problems. There is a joke at the expense of Jews in this sketch, nonetheless, but it is one tempered by the fact that it is jointly directed against Jews and Muslims. It comments on the similarities between rabbis and Muslim clerics – and states that neither pay their bills!

A similar strategy appears to be at work in the creation of the "Chuddie Boys", two male Asian teenagers whose various attempts at gaining street credibility are constantly frustrated. The term "chuddies" is Gujarati for "underwear". The "Chuddie Boys" proved so popular that the term "chuddies" has now apparently entered the English language -- a telling case of hybridisation![28] Yet it is questionable if the two characters would have appeared as funny and harmless had they been identified as Pakistani, i.e. Muslim, teenagers -- of the type involved in the riots up North and more recently in the first cases of suicide bombing in the United Kingdom. There are clearly limits to Asian-British humour, and there is a price to pay for transgressing cultural norms in the shape of humour. This price is a different form of mimicry. This time it is not the culture of the coloniser that is reproduced (British colonialisation, it has been implied, only forms a remote memory in most of the sketches in *Goodness Gracious Me* and the novels and films discussed above). It is the hegemonic media culture of globalised and largely U.S.-American formats, characters, and clichés.

In terms of this "media mimicry", *Goodness Gracious Me* nonetheless still corresponds very closely to Bhabha's central definition of hybridity quoted above, in which he describes it as "split between its presence as original and authoritative and its articulation as repetition and difference". Only that in the case of present-day Asian British people, their representatives in the media, and the material they produce to negotiate their cultural position, any "original and authoritative" presence is itself highly dubious, especially if this material uses the form of humour and comedy, and Asian-British writers and artists and their works are fully aware of this fact.

To differentiate once again, Asian-British writers (and here it does not matter whether they are writers of fiction or of film and television scripts; in cases like Kureishi or Syal they are all of these things combined anyway)

---

[28]   "'Thanks to British Asian media, the word chuddie (underwear) is now widely known in Britain,' said Mahal, referring to the phrase 'kiss my chuddies' made famous by the Asian television comedy show 'Goodness Gracious Me'"; 'Badmash! English wears chuddie', *The Times of India*, 8 June 2005.

clearly understand that any claim to an authentic "Asian" identity that would be original and authoritative would be dubious. Instead they resort to self-aware cliché and irony. This broken or in itself doubled form -- which thus corresponds to, but also doubles once again the multiple and hybrid position of postcolonial identities -- finds its form in genres like comedy that thrive on the unsettling of identities and authorities. The "impossible object" becomes – very much against the orginal notion of an unbroken stereotype -- the third space for the disruptive articulation of subversion and hybridity.

Humour and comedy grant this hybrid non-identity an articulation, but its creation of a third space between established binary identities is neither automatically guaranteed nor unproblematic. The created space must itself be challenged, subverted, or constructed without unbroken reference to sup-posed certainties. Failure to do so would merely place the complex identities that are meant to be articulated in a slightly different cage, that of reversed stereotypes and clichés. Only when the articulation of the "third space" cre-ates a space that is self-undermining, unsafe, a projection that is a simulation rather than a mimetic mirroring, does it fulfil the demands of identities in transition.

That these identities are not merely located on one side, that of the Asian-British who have to find their place in a British environment or the Asians who have to recover their supposed roots inside an alien environment, but that this British cultural environment, contemporary British identity in short, must understand itself as such a transition, a third space that is no safe place, but perhaps an exciting and productive one, this is the task of contemporary Asian-British comedy. In Bhabha's words: "In place of the polarity of a pre-figurative self-generating nation 'in-itself' and extrinsic other nations, the performative introduces a temporality of the 'in-between'."[29] When it suc-ceeds, the temporality of unsettling laughter produced by the performative of Asian-British comedy of the kind of *Goodness Gracious Me* comes remarka-bly close to fulfilling this mission.

Bibliography

Ashcroft, Bill, Gareth Griffiths, and Helen Tiffin. *The Empire Writes Back: Theory and Practice in Post-Colonial Literatures*, New Accents (London and New York: Routledge, 1989)

---

[29]   Homi K. Bhabha, 'Dissemination: Time, Narrative and the Margins of the Modern Nation', in *The Location of Culture*, by Homi K. Bhabha, new edn, Routledge Classics (London and New York: Routledge, 2004), 199-244 (p.212).

'Badmash! English wears chuddie', *The Times of India*, 8 June 2005.

Bakhtin, Mikhail M., *Rabelais and His World*, trans. by Hélène Iswolsky (Bloomington and Indianapolis: Indiana University Press, 1984)

——., Mikhail M., *The Dialogic Imagination: Four Essays*, trans. by Caryl Emerson and Michael Holquist, ed. by Michael Holquist (Austin: University of Texas Press, 1981)

Baudrillard, Jean, 'Simulacra and Simulations', in *Selected Writings*, trans. and ed. by Mark Poster (Stanford: Stanford University Press, 1988), 166-184.

Bhabha, Homi K., 'Dissemination: Time, Narrative and the Margins of the Modern Nation', in *The Location of Culture*, by Homi K. Bhabha, new edn, Routledge Classics (London and New York: Routledge, 2004), 199-244.

——., 'How Newness Enters the World: Postmodern Space, Postcolonial Times and the Trials of Cultural Translation', in *The Location of Culture*, by Homi K. Bhabha, new edn, Routledge Classics (London and New York: Routledge, 2004), 303-337.

——., 'Of Mimicry and Men: The Ambivalence of Colonial Discourse', in *The Location of Culture*, by Homi K. Bhabha, new edn, Routledge Classics (London and New York: Routledge, 2004), 121-131.

——., 'Signs Taken for Wonders: Questions of Ambivalence and Authority under a Tree outside Delhi, May 1817', in *The Location of Culture*, by Homi K. Bhabha, new edn, Routledge Classics (London and New York: Routledge, 2004), 145-174.

——., 'The Commitment to Theory', in *The Location of Culture*, by Homi K. Bhabha, new edn, Routledge Classics (London and New York: Routledge, 2004), 28-56.

——., 'The Other Question: Stereotype, Discrimination and the Discourse of Colonialism', in *The Location of Culture*, by Homi K. Bhabha, new edn, Routledge Classics (London and New York: Routledge, 2004), 94-120.

Delingpole, James, 'Coming up from the Underground', *Daily Telegraph*, 9 January 1999.

Gillespie, Marie, 'From Comic Asians to Asian Comics: *Goodness Gracious Me*, British Television Comedy and Representations of Ethnicity', in *Group Identities on French and British Television*, ed. by Michael Scriven amd Emily Roberts (New York: Berghahn, 2003), 93-107.

Goodness Gracious Me. BBC. 1998 ff.

http://news.bbc.co.uk/1/hi/in_depth/uk/2001/summer_of_violence/default.stm (accessed 19 May 2009)

http://news.bbc.co.uk/2/hi/uk_news/1972565.stm (accessed 19 May 2009) http://www.bbc.co.uk/comedy/goodnessgraciousme/ (accessed 20 May 2009)

http://www.screenonline.org.uk/tv/id/529222/ (accessed 20 May 2009)

Kureishi, Hanif, *The Buddha of Suburbia*, 1990 (London: Faber & Faber, 1999)

Lewis, C.S., 'The Magician's Nephew', in *The Chronicals of Narnia*, 1955 (New York: Harper Collins, 2001), pp.7-106.

Neale, Steve and Frank Krutnik, *Popular Film and Television Comedy*, Popular Fiction Series (London and New York: Routledge, 1990)

Schoene-Harwood, Berthold, 'Beyond (T)race: *Bildung* and Proprioception in Meera Syal's *Anita and Me*', *Journal of Commonwealth Literature*, 34 (1999), 159-168.

Shohat, Ella and Robert Stam, *Unthinking Eurocentrism: Multiculturalism and the Media*, Sightlines (London and New York: Routledge, 1994)

Spivak, Gayatri Chakravorty, 'Can the Subaltern Speak', in *Colonial Discourse and Postcolonial Theory: A Reader*, ed. by Patrick Williams and Laura Chrisman (Brighton: Harvester Wheatsheaf, 1994), 66-111.

Syal, Meera, *Anita and Me*, 1996 (London: Flamingo, 1997)

Notes on Contributors

Hédi Abdel-Jaouad, a native of Tunisia, is Professor of French at Skidmore College in Saratoga Springs, New York, U.S.A. He is the author of two books: *Fugues de barbarie: les écrivains maghrébins et le surréalisme* (1998) and *Rimbaud et l'Algérie* (2002, reprinted in 2004). In addition to these he has written numerous articles on Francophone literature. He is also the editor of Revue CELAAN Review.

Delia Chiaro holds a chair in English Language and Linguistics at the University of Bologna, Italy. Her research attempts to combine the disciplines of Humour Studies and Translation Studies, and many of her publications have regarded issues involving the translation of Verbally Expressed Humour on screen especially from the point of view of audience perception. Her publications include: *The Language of Jokes: Analyzing Verbal Play* (1992) and the Special Edition of *Humor, International Journal of Humor Research on Humour and Translation* (2005).

Graeme Dunphy studied German and Hebrew/Old Testament at the Universities of Stirling and St Andrews in Scotland, taking a doctorate in mediaeval German literature in 1996. He has taught in the English department at the University of Regensburg since 1993. His main areas of research are mediaeval historiography (he is editing the Brill *Encyclopedia of the Medieval Chronicle*), early modern German philology (monograph on Opitz and the *Annolied*, 2003) and modern intercultural literature (various essays on German and Dutch migrant literature and on British Asian writings).

Rainer Emig is Chair of English Literature and Culture at Leibniz University in Hanover, Germany. He is especially interested in the link between literature and the media and in Literary, Critical, and Cultural Theory, especially theories of identity, power, gender and sexuality. His publications include the monographs *Modernism in Poetry* (1995), *W.H. Auden* (1999), and *Krieg als Metapher im zwanzigsten Jahrhundert* (2001) as well as edited collections on *Stereotypes in Contemporary Anglo-German Relations* (2000), *Ulysses* (2004), and *Gender ↔ Religion* (2008). He has recently completed a monograph entitled *Eccentricity: Culture from the Margins* and a co-edited collection on *Hybrid Humour*. Another, on *Performing Masculinity*, will appear in 2009. He is one of the three editors of the *Journal for the Study of British Cultures*.

Michiel van Kempen studied Dutch literature and history in Nijmegen in the Netherlands and wrote a four-volume history of Surinamese literature as his PhD thesis at the University of Amsterdam (2002). He is the editor of numerous anthologies of Surinamese and Dutch-Antillean literature, among them *Nieuwe Surinaamse verhalen* (1986), *Spiegel van de Surinaamse poëzie* (1995), *Mama Sranan: twee eeuwen Surinaamse verhaalkunst* (1999), and *Noordoostpassanten: 400 jaar Nederlandse verhaalkunst over Suriname, de Nederlandse Antillen en Aruba* (2005, with Wim Rutgers). He is co-editor of two collections of essays: *Tussenfiguren in de literatuur* (1998) and *Wandelaar onder de palmen; Verkenningen in de koloniale en postkoloniale literatuur en cultuur* (2004). He has also written two novels, three collections of short stories and a book on India. He was awarded the 2004 Dutch-Belgian ANV-Visser Neerlandia Prize. Currently he is writing a biography of the first Caribbean-Dutch migrant writer Albert Helman for the Royal Netherlands Institute of Southeast Asian and Caribbean Studies in Leiden.

Alexander Wöll is Professor of Slavonic Studies at the University of Greifswald in Germany. He has previously taught at the University of Regensburg in Germany and at Oxford University. His main areas of interest are Czech, Russian, Polish, Ukrainian; Bosnian, Croatian and Serbian poetry and prose from the turn of the nineteenth into the twenty-first century, Fantastic Literature, Literary Theory, and Comparative Literary Studies. His publications include *Jakub Deml: Leben und Werk* (2006) and *Doppelgänger: Steinmonument, Spiegelschrift und Usurpation in der russischen Literatur* (1999).